NO MORE WAR

NO MORE WAR

How the West Violates International Law by Using 'Humanitarian' Intervention to Advance Economic and Strategic Interests

DAN KOVALIK

FOREWORD BY S. BRIAN WILLSON

Hot Books

Copyright © 2020 by Dan Kovalik

All rights reserved. No part of this book may be reproduced in any manner without the express written consent of the publisher, except in the case of brief excerpts in critical reviews or articles. All inquiries should be addressed to Skyhorse Publishing, 307 West 36th Street, 11th Floor, New York, NY 10018.

Hot Books books may be purchased in bulk at special discounts for sales promotion, corporate gifts, fund-raising, or educational purposes. Special editions can also be created to specifications. For details, contact the Special Sales Department, Skyhorse Publishing, 307 West 36th Street, 11th Floor, New York, NY 10018 or info@skyhorsepublishing.com.

Hot Books® and Skyhorse Publishing® are registered trademarks of Skyhorse Publishing, Inc.®, a Delaware corporation.

Visit our website at www.skyhorsepublishing.com.

10 9 8 7 6 5 4 3 2 1

Library of Congress Cataloging-in-Publication Data is available on file.

ISBN: 978-1-5107-5529-1
Ebook ISBN: 978-1-5107-5530-7

Cover design by Brian Peterson

Printed in the United States of America

DEDICATION

This book is dedicated to the memory of Father Miguel D'Escoto Brockmann, M.M. Father D'Escoto, a Maryknoll priest and Liberation Theologian, served as the first Foreign Minister of the Sandinista government of Nicaragua and later as president of the UN General Assembly. He also served briefly as Libya's UN ambassador in the final days of the Gaddafi government. Amongst his many accomplishments, Father D'Escoto was the moving intellectual force behind Nicaragua's groundbreaking case against the United States before the International Court of Justice—a case dealt with in depth in this book. While Nicaragua won this case, it has yet to receive the justice due under it.

ACKNOWLEDGMENTS

As I write this book, I am reminded often that I stand on the shoulders of giants. My views on the issue of "humanitarian" intervention have been greatly inspired and molded by the works of Noam Chomsky, Edward Herman, Diana Johnstone, and Jean Bricmont, who have been writing on this subject for decades. This book would not have been possible without their prior work. I hope that, by writing this book, I introduce new readers to these great minds and I carry forward their amazing legacy with my own unique insights.

I also wish to thank my son Joe who, using his ample computer skills, helped me put together the Index.

Contents

Foreword   xiii
Introduction   xxi

1 "Humanitarian" Intervention from King Leopold to Samantha Power   1
2 Nuremberg and the Rise of International Law   35
3 Peace Is a Paramount Human Right   54
4 The ICC, the Crime of Aggression, and Western Humanitarians   78
5 The Anticolonial Nature of International Law   97
6 *Nicaragua v. US*, and Lessons about Nonintervention   113
7 The Right of Self-Defense   125
8 The UN and the Responsibility to Protect   137
9 The US Military Is Not a Feminist Organization   163
10 The Genocide Convention and Selective Justice   180
Conclusion: Introspection and Assistance—Not Intervention   207

Appendix A: Charter of the United Nations   221
Appendix B: Statute of the International Court of Justice   261
Endnotes   283
Index   315

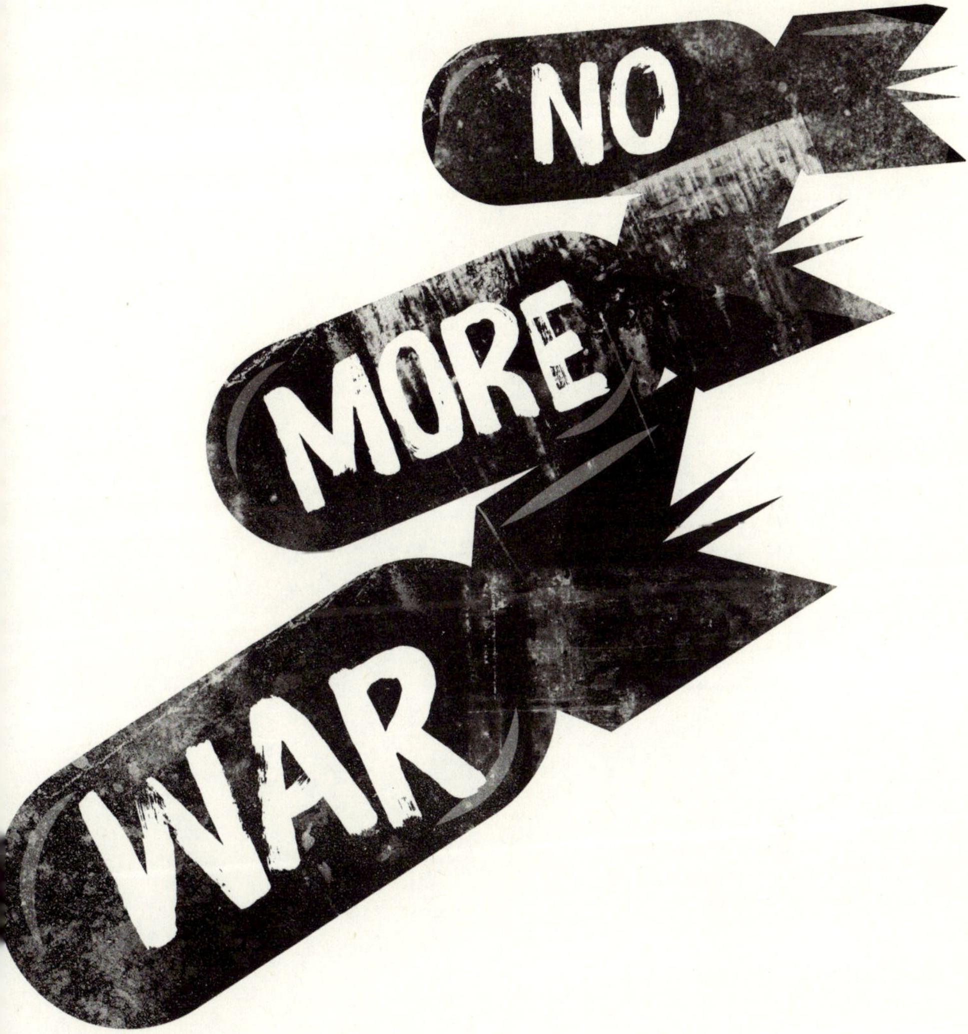
NO
MORE
WAR

"[The US] is the greatest purveyor of violence in the world today."
—Dr. Martin Luther King (1967)

"[The United States] is the most warlike nation in the history of the world."
—Jimmy Carter, 39th President of the United States (2019)

Foreword
BY S. BRIAN WILLSON

"The law locks up the hapless felon who steals the goose from the Common, but lets the real felon loose who steals the Common from the goose."
—Author unknown, from lyrics of an old English labor song critiquing class

CURRENTLY, THE US IS *ILLEGALLY* bombing seven countries, imposing crippling *illegal* sanctions on a number of others, *illegally* dispatching Special Forces units to 70 percent of the world's countries, and overthrowing or attempting to achieve *illegal* "regime change" in others with markedly *selective* "humanitarian intervention." It has 800 military bases positioned in seventy countries. What the hell?

They say peace is priceless. But peace is impossible in a predatory capitalist society. Bipartisan support for military spending and war earnestly continues, with little resistance. The totally rigged political system is not capable of reversing course, because its deep function is to *continue and expand* the obscene oligarchic profit system. It is *part* of it. The government bombs; the people shop. Disappointingly, these days it matters not who is elected president, or to the Congress. To understand this is a precondition for movement toward revolutionary nonviolence.

The Monday, December 12, 2019, *Washington Post* published an explosive report, *The Afghanistan Papers,* disclosing that the Pentagon wasted $1 *trillion* of the US tax dollars in a *deliberate effort to lie* and *mislead* the US American public in a war the military *knew* was unwinnable but kept that knowledge secret. "We were devoid of a fundamental understanding of Afghanistan. We didn't know what we were doing," according to Gen. Douglas Lute, who oversaw the US war under Presidents Bush and Obama. Another *Pentagon Papers*–type revelation, but apparently so what? But this we do know: lots of components of the military-industrial-intelligence-banking-Wall Street-Congressional-corporate media complex made lots of money on the longest war in US history, and it still continues.

Despite this, on Wednesday, December 14, only two days later, 188 House Democrats joined a nearly united Republican caucus to pass a comprehensive $738 billion military spending bill that continues endless wars, including Yemen, as well as funds for Trump's Space Force. Even more insane, Congress rewarded the war bureaucracy with $22 billion *more* than it had asked for. So what if 775,000 troops were dispatched to Afghanistan, killing 2,300, wounding 21,000, while murdering 150,000 Afghans? And now, we may be on the verge of but another war, this time with Iran. Words cannot express my horror at all this.

My own robot-like obedience to patriarchal authority in Viet Nam simply continued a several-millennia pattern. There have been 14,600 reported major wars documented over the past 5,600 years, proving perhaps that war is the original "sin" of humanity.[1] Patriarchy, and hierarchy, both very harmful to a healthy human community, emerged with the advent of "civilization" about 6,000 years ago, producing patterns of systematic violence and war previously unknown.[2] Joseph Conrad, in his 1899 novel *Heart of Darkness*, captured this ugly side of humans, depicting how "civilization" conceals the harsh realities of the cruel exploitation upon which it is built.[3]

Consistent with the nearly 15,000 major wars over the past 5,600 years, there have been 8,400 treaties made since 1500 BCE. This does not count the 400-plus treaties made between the US Government and various indigenous tribes, each violated by the government. Search for being war-free is extremely commendable, though treaties have for the most part proven to be unsuccessful in achieving peace,[4] despite some that temporarily ameliorated tensions.

In analyzing the futile efforts of treaty making, British historian and sociologist F. J. P. Veale cites the highly touted 1928 Kellogg-Briand Pact. A serious effort to restrain wars, it was nonetheless terribly flawed because political leaders continually justified exemptions incorporated into the self-defense provisions of the Treaty. It was violated at least ten times in its first two decades by a number of the 63 nations who had signed it.[5]

Veale noted that the Nuremberg Principles derived from the 1945–46 Nuremberg Trials (where my uncle was a young Army lawyer investigator) were a magnanimous effort to prevent further heinous crimes like those committed by Germany. Yet it, too, was severely flawed because it established the dangerous precedent of *victors'* justice. All restraints on horrific future warfare were removed, because it *exempted* the war crimes of the *US and its allies*, most notably *all the bombings* of civilian targets in England and Germany, but worse, the US atomic bombings of Hiroshima and Nagasaki. The number of civilians murdered by Allied bombings in Germany and Japan far exceeded the bombing casualties of the Axis. Ironically, the signing on August 8 of the London Agreement and Charter authorizing Nuremberg occurred only two days after the August 6, 1945, atomic bombing of Hiroshima, and one day before the August 9 plutonium bombing of Nagasaki. The exception of aerial bombardment as a war crime assured the continuance of global lawlessness.[6]

In trying to understand a way toward a world without war, we can learn from our history and anthropological studies. Cultural historian Lewis Mumford has argued that we may be nearing the end of a long epoch of several thousand years of what we call "civilization." After centuries of forcefully dispossessing others by rule of a small elite class, we ended up with societies gone mad and subsequent nation-states, "democratic" or not, convinced that their continuation is the sole purpose of existence.[7] Certainly in the West, we have been deluded into believing that our "superiority" justified the plundering of "inferiors." Systematic, massive theft and murder have been rationalized under noble rhetoric to assure obscene wealth to a handful of European-based societies, while simultaneously bringing "democracy" (not) and "salvation" (not) to the non-European "savages" of the world. The United States emerged from this "colonizer's model of the world."[8]

This pattern of arrogantly and forcefully dispossessing others enabled the creation of the US, and its "religion" of "exceptionalism." The latter is a totally *fake* story that permits us Americans to avoid feeling the important social emotion of *shame*, making it *seem* unnecessary to address the critical questions about our egregious *genocidal origins* of the indigenous and Africans. The presence of the past in the psyche *never* disappears, as Freud has suggested.[9] Therefore, without acknowledging and addressing its lessons, we fall into a kind of spell or stupor with our sense of being superior, which easily morphs into *stupidity*—thoughtlessness. And the original Grand Lie is preserved with subsequent multiple lies throughout our history.

Our cultural attitudes and politics remind me of a bumper sticker I saw at Ft. Benning, Georgia, a few years ago: "Why do we torture? Because we can!" What or who is able to stop us? Not the law, certainly. Only when people awaken to, or reaccess, their evolutionary *inborn social* emotion of *empathy* will they possess the *visceral* fuel to do that which is necessary to save themselves and other life forms from near extinction or destruction. It will not come through writing a letter to your Congressperson. In the US we now live under a National Security regime that serves as a Fourth Estate, preserved by corporate media that control the neoliberal narrative. The political system is a huge bribery scheme, and our predatory capitalism makes everyone either a predator or prey, destructive to any kind of emotionally secure, justice-based society.

With the advent of *vertical* "civilization" several thousand years ago, a new organizational idea emerged—what Mumford calls a "megamachine"—comprised totally of *human* parts to perform colossal tasks never before imagined.[10] Creation of a bureaucracy directed by a power complex consisting of an authority figure (a king), with scribes and messengers, organized labor machines (masses of workers) to construct pyramids, irrigation systems, huge grain storage systems, among other structures, all enforced by a military. It separated people into classes, required forced labor, created arbitrary inequality of wealth and privilege, and established military power.[11] Mumford makes clear his bias that autonomy in small groups is a human *archetype* that has been repressed in deference to obedience to technology and bureaucracy.[12]

"Civilization" demands massive civil obedience to enable hierarchical authority structures to prevail. Class is an egregious consequence. Autonomous freedoms that people once enjoyed in precivilization tribal groups now defer to belief in authority structures and their controlling ideologies, described as oppressive "domination hierarchies," where private property and male subjugation of women prevail, by force as necessary.[13] Along with forced stratification (class), the separation of people from their intimate connections with the earth has produced deep insecurity, fear, and trauma to the psyche. Ecopyschologist Chellis Glendinning suggests that our disconnection from the intimate earth caused an original, primordial trauma of fragmentation, leading to multiple layers of subsequent traumas. Healing requires us "to reclaim the wisdom of Native peoples and reconnect the psyche to the primal matrix of the Earth.[14]

The weakness of modern *vertical* power structures is that they are totally dependent upon mass cooperation. Simply writing and adopting more peace treaties, or laws, is futile without addressing the inherent corruption and psychological alienation built into a rigged winner-take-all economic-political cabal. Noncooperating with hierarchical power frees us to begin *withdrawing* our complicity, while simultaneously reconstructing locally based cooperative economies living within each bioregion's carrying capacity.[15] *Horizontal* power, in anthropological terms, is often described as tribalism. Though in our mythology we had abandoned tribalism, it turns out that tribalism (various forms and structures of local community) "is not only the preeminently *human* social organization, it's also the only unequivocally *successful* social organization in human history (italics in original).[16] From an evolutionary perspective, sustainable communities are rooted in *innate* human characteristics of empathy, mutual respect, equity, and cooperation.

When the Spanish conquistadors conquered Latin American lands 500 years ago, they forcefully introduced a new concept—ownership of property (fiction of "title"). Land with access to water is the most sacred, indispensable resource enabling sustainable human culture. The indigenous occupants of the land lived and farmed communally. Ownership was a foreign, alienating value. Thus was introduced the idea of protected (via military dictatorships and oligarchic-created Constitutions) private, versus communal, land. The consequential tensions have been played out since: private profit/individualism versus public/social/community; planter (oligarch) versus peasant/indigenous (serf); competition/greed versus cooperation/sharing. By choosing to not directly address this structural "sin" of private versus social good, nothing of substance significantly changes.

The money cabal rules. But this destructive political economy is *human-made*. As US American fiction writer Ursula K. LeGuin (1929–2018) proclaimed: "We live in capitalism. Its power seems inescapable. So did the divine right of kings. Any human power can be resisted and changed by human beings."[17]

In 1936, Australian archaeologist V. Gordon Childe (1892–1957) concluded a masterful archaeological study, *Man Makes Himself*, with these words: "[Behavior] is not fixed and immutable: it is constantly changing as society deals with ever new circumstances. Tradition makes the man *[sic]*, by circumscribing his *[sic]* behavior within certain bounds; but it is equally true that man *[sic]* makes the traditions. And so, we can repeat with deeper insight, 'Man *[sic]* makes himself' *[sic]*."[18]

Will modern humanity recognize the imperative, and promise, of empathic cooperation, locally and internationally? How much do we *really* want to live in mutual respect, absent greed and arrogance, reclaiming authentic humility? Will we *choose* to liberate ourselves from dependence upon traditional institutions that are part of the money-grabbing neoliberal system?

A radical, epistemological, evolutionary shifting of values—from separation from nature to intrinsic integration with nature—cannot be ruled out for the simple reason that our dignified survival is absolutely dependent upon it. Panic leads to the neuro-physiologically-released energy of adrenaline that can change conditions today that seemed impossible yesterday. The choice is ours.

Introduction

AS I WRITE THIS BOOK, the international story *du jour* is that of Turkey invading northern Syria to attack Kurdish forces who had been partnering for the last few years with the United States in ostensibly fighting ISIS—though, of course, the US also aided ISIS and other extremist fighters at times in Syria to try to topple the government of Bashar Assad.[19] The coverage of this event is quite alarmist, much of it focusing on how the US has betrayed its Kurdish allies, as it has done many times before, by leaving northern Syria and thus paving the way for Turkey to move in and assault the Kurds. The thrust of much of the coverage is interventionist—that is, focusing on the need of the US to stay in Syria to protect the Kurds from Turkey.

There indeed seems to be great fear that Trump will be true to his word and pull troops not only from Syria, but the rest of the Middle East. The liberal media is absolutely hysterical in the face of President Trump's tweeting such things as: *"The United States has spent EIGHT TRILLION DOLLARS fighting and policing in the Middle East. Thousands of our Great Soldiers have died or been badly wounded. Millions of people have died on the other side. GOING INTO THE MIDDLE EAST IS THE WORST DECISION EVER MADE. . ."*[20]

Whatever one thinks of Donald Trump, he is, at least in this instance, factually correct and makes a pretty unassailable point. However, the media, always wedded to incessant US interventions, is now latching on to the Kurdish issue to push against the prospect of the US's possible pullout from the Middle East.

A very illuminating editorial in the *New York Times* illustrates the press's true concern with Trump—that he threatens to overturn the post-WWII consensus, enforced by what President Eisenhower termed the "military-industrial complex," that the US must be engaged in permanent war in order to preserve its empire and to feed the voracious defense industry, which depends upon war for its profiteering. An astute article on the alternative news website, *MintPress*, analyzes this article:[21]

> David R. Sanger, writing in the October 7 *New York Times*, represents "liberal" establishment views in support of US imperialism: "Mr. Trump's sudden abandonment of the Kurds was another example of the independent, parallel foreign policy he has run from the White House, which has largely abandoned the elaborate systems created since President Harry Truman's day to think ahead about the potential costs and benefits of presidential decisions."
>
> There you have it. Trump is accused of having an "independent" foreign policy, emanating out of his office of all places, even though he is the elected President of the US and the one charged with executing foreign policy.
>
> Who is Trump "independent" from? It's not the US citizenry according to the *Times*. As the article points out: "Mr. Trump sensed that many Americans share his view—and polls show he is right... Mr. Trump has correctly read the American people who, after Iraq and Afghanistan, also have a deep distaste for forever wars."
>
> So, who might Trump have betrayed? According to the article, it's "circumventing the American generals and diplomats who sing the praises of maintaining the traditional American forward presence around the world." This is who his alleged crime of independence is against. They fear Trump could "abandon" the post-war imperial consensus.

In other words, the true concern about Trump is that he might actually give in to the will of the American people in ending the US's permanent war footing. The crocodile tears shed for the Kurds is simply a fig leaf for this real preoccupation.

Of course, it is true that the Kurds have suffered greatly, including at the hands of Turkey, but the worst of their suffering has largely gone unnoticed and unreported because of the circumstances of their suffering—that is, when the US has been actively participating in their oppression as opposed to just standing aside. As Noam Chomsky explains the situation:

> What's going on in Turkey is pretty bad. On the other hand, it doesn't begin to compare with what was going on in the 1990's. The Turkish state was carrying out a major terrorist war against the Kurdish population: tens of thousands of people killed, thousands of towns and villages destroyed, probably millions of refugees, torture, every kind of atrocity you can think of. The *[New York] Times* barely reported it.
>
> They certainly didn't report—or if they did, it was very marginal—the fact that 80 percent of the weapons were coming from the U.S., and that Clinton was so supportive of the atrocities that in 1997, kind of when they were peaking, that single year Clinton sent more arms to Turkey than in the entire Cold War period combined up until the onset of the counterinsurgency campaign. That's pretty serious. You won't find it in the *New York Times*. Their correspondent in Ankara, Stephen Kinzer, barely reported anything. Not that he didn't know. Everybody knew.[22]

Another terrible case of Kurdish oppression, of course, came at the hands of Iraq's Saddam Hussein at the end of Iraq's war with Iran in 1988—a war that the US supported with large amounts of material support, sometimes to both sides of the conflict. Ultimately, when Hussein was put to death after he was captured in the aftermath of the US invasion in 2003, it was his crimes against the Kurds that sealed his fate. And, as recently explained in *The Intercept*, the US aided and abetted these crimes while the compliant media kept quiet:[23]

> During the 1980s, the Iraqi government moved on to actual genocide against the Kurds, including the use of chemical weapons. The Reagan administration was well aware of Saddam's use of nerve gas, but because they liked the damage Saddam was doing to Iran, it opposed congressional efforts to impose sanctions on Iraq. The US media also faithfully played its role. When a Washington Post reporter tried to get the paper to publish a photograph of a Kurd killed by chemical weapons, his editor responded, "Who will care?"

In truth, *The Intercept* does not quite capture the complicity of the US in this genocide, for it fails to mention that the US, along with Germany and other allies, actually supplied the "dual use" chemical agents that Saddam used to carry out the gassing of the Kurds (and Iranians, as well).[24] The US also provided the helicopters that Saddam used to rain the lethal gas down upon the Kurds, killing around five to eight thousand Kurdish civilians, mostly women, children, and the elderly.[25]

The point is that the worst the US has done to the Kurds has been to actively support their murder at the hands of countries like Turkey and Iraq, but it is those sins of commission, rather than omission, that go largely ignored and unmourned. This is because the prevailing ideology in the United States is that the US military does not commit or aid in the commission of genocide; rather, that it is necessary to the prevention of genocide. The episodes discussed above were swept under the rug by the press because they do not fit this narrative.

Meanwhile, no one seems particularly concerned that Trump is sending in hundreds of troops to prop up the retrograde monarchy of Saudi Arabia and to assist it in its brutal war against Yemen. That sort of maneuver, after all, is quite according to plan.

One of the individuals who has been critical to promulgating the prevailing narrative of the necessity of US intervention is Samantha

Power—an individual who first gained acclaim with her Pulitzer Prize-winning book, titled *A Problem from Hell: America and the Age of Genocide*.[26] The revealing thing about this book is that it decries only other peoples' genocides, and none of those actually committed by the US and Western allies. Rather, the thrust of the book is that the US and the West in general have failed the world not by carrying out genocide, but by failing to act (usually militarily) to prevent it. Power, through this book, became one of the most important intellectual authors of what has come to be known as "humanitarian" interventionism.

Meanwhile, Power would go on to be able to put her views on "humanitarian" interventionism into practice when she was appointed President Obama's UN Ambassador. However, Power's most significant acts in this role were not to promote humanitarianism, but instead to undermine it. One of Power's greatest acts of treachery was to run interference at the Security Council to make sure that the US-backed war in Yemen, still ongoing, be permitted to continue without pause and without any pesky war crimes investigations getting in the way.[27] This was no small failing on Power's part, for it helped pave the way for what quickly became the very worst humanitarian crisis on Earth.

As *Foreign Policy* noted back in October 2015,[28] the fact that the United States was supporting the Saudi coalition military offensive against Yemen—in the form of intelligence, logistics (including midair refueling of Saudi jets), and even cluster bombs—and "inflicting extreme hardship on civilians in one of the Mideast's poorest countries provides an awkward counterpoint to the Obama administration's stated commitment to stand up for the region's oppressed people." The same article noted that even some US lawmakers were concerned about the legal implications for the United States: "The humanitarian crisis in Yemen has received too little attention, and it directly, or indirectly, implicates us," said Sen. Patrick Leahy (D-Vt.), who noted that the airstrikes may violate legislation he authored barring the United States from providing security assistance to countries responsible for gross human rights abuses. "The reports of civilian casualties from Saudi air attacks in densely populated areas compel us to ask if these operations, supported by the United States, violate" that law, Leahy told *Foreign Policy* in an emailed statement.[29]

In addition to the military support for the Saudi coalition operations, this same piece mentions that the United States also provided diplomatic cover to these operations at the United Nations. Thus, the US Mission to the UN Security Council, including Samantha Power herself, scuttled a proposal that merely would have asked all the key actors to cooperate with human rights investigations in Yemen and would have reminded them to abide by international humanitarian law norms and human rights law in the prosecution of the conflict. Even this was too much for the United States, which has been hell-bent on seeing that this war goes on without limit.

Moreover, even after such serious criticism was being leveled against his actions, Obama decided to double down support for the Saudi coalition offensive, approving the sale of $1.29 billion in smart bombs to Saudi Arabia—a sale that among other things, was intended to replenish Saudi Arabia's arsenal in attacking Yemen.[30]

For his part, President Trump entered into a historically massive arms deal with Saudi Arabia near the beginning of his term in the spring of 2017, and as the war continued unabated. As *The Independent* explained,[31] Donald Trump has signed the largest arms deal in history with Saudi Arabia despite warnings he could be accused of being complicit in war crimes and after blaming Saudi Arabia himself for producing the terrorists behind 9/11. The President confirmed he had signed a weapons deal with the Saudis worth $109.7 billion, predicted to grow to a $380 billion Saudi investment within ten years, during his first trip abroad since his Inauguration.

And, of course, Trump has been very open about the fact that the Saudi war on Yemen is great for US arms manufacturers, who are making a killing on sales to Saudi Arabia as a result. And, indeed, they are. As an article in *In These Times* explains, "US arms merchants . . . have grown rich" on the war on Yemen.[32] These merchants of death include General Dynamics, Raytheon, Boeing, Lockheed Martin, and General Electric, who have all made billions on this war.[33] Indeed, the CEO of Lockheed Martin, Marillyn Hewson, publicly stated, "I love the war in Yemen! It's great for business!"[34] That pretty much sums it up.

Meanwhile, the human toll of the Yemen conflict is simply staggering. Indeed, the war on Yemen could in fact be the worst humanitarian disaster since WWII. In early 2018 *Al Jazeera* quoted UN humanitarian chief Mark Lowcock as saying that what we are witnessing in Yemen "looks like an apocalypse" and predicting that Yemen could become the worst humanitarian disaster in half a century, with millions on the verge of starvation; the largest cholera outbreak in modern history, with a million people afflicted so far; and with an epidemic of diphtheria that will "spread like wildfire."[35]

In terms of Yemenis starving as a result of the combination of the war and US/Saudi blockade, the numbers are monumental. As the UN Office for the Coordination of Human Affairs (OCHA) relates:

> After more than three years of escalating conflict, Yemeni people continue to bear the brunt of ongoing hostilities and severe economic decline. An alarming 22.2 million people in Yemen need some kind of humanitarian or protection assistance, an estimated 17.8 million are food insecure—8.4 million people are severely food insecure and at risk of starvation—16 million lack access to safe water and sanitation, and 16.4 million lack access to adequate healthcare. Needs across the country have increased steadily, with 11.3 million who are in acute need—an increase of more than one million people in acute need of humanitarian assistance to survive.[36]

Yemeni health officials have predicted that six million children could starve if the war on Yemen continues.[37]

Millions will certainly die in Yemen as a result of the US-backed campaign of the Saudis, as even Power recognized at the time, but neither she nor our nation's press corps will ever view this as a "problem from hell," or even as a matter to be much concerned about at all.

And quite tellingly, Power does not even mention the Yemen conflict once in her new memoir, ironically titled *The Education of an Idealist*, nor does she even once mention the nation of Saudi Arabia. Apparently, a holocaustal number of dead children does not even deserve an honorable mention, recalling to mind a similar indifference shown by Power's mentor, Madeleine Albright, another "humanitarian" interventionist, when asked whether 500,000 dead Iraqi children due to US sanctions was worth it. Albright famously said, "Yes."

Quite curiously, though, Power did recently sign on to a letter urging Trump to stop aiding the Saudi war effort in Yemen. Discussing this letter, an article by CNN first explains that "[a] report from the Armed Conflict Location & Event Data Project in June found that more than 91,000 people have been killed in the conflict since 2015. It also found that the Saudi-led coalition and its allies had been responsible for more than 8,000 of the approximately 11,700 deaths connected to the direct targeting of civilians in the conflict."[38] CNN goes on to relate that Power, along with her former partner in crime, Susan Rice—another proponent of "humanitarian" intervention and another official in the Obama Administration who was complicit in the Administration's criminal Yemen policy—both signed on to this letter even though it amounted to their opposing the very "policy they were instrumental in implementing." Sadly, when these two "humanitarians" had the chance to prevent this genocidal policy, they did not do so.

Meanwhile, for her part, Susan Rice was just carted out by *National Public Radio* to decry Trump's Syria pullout as a great betrayal of human rights.[39] Rice is a quite interesting figure herself, for while she is always quick to claim to support US intervention in support of human rights, she has, like Power, aided and abetted yet another of the worst human rights catastrophes in modern history.

As an expose in *The Atlantic* explains, Rice, while serving in Bill Clinton's diplomatic corps, played a key role in providing diplomatic coverage for Rwanda and Uganda as they, with military support from the US, invaded and plundered the Democratic Republic of the Congo, leading to the deaths of at least six million, and quite possibly as many as eight million, Congolese.[40] This was but another example of a notable human rights advocate, blind to the evils of US intervention, becoming a major war criminal.

Quite tellingly, in her NPR interview, Rice decried the decision to pull out of Syria as "Trump's Saigon"—referring of course, to the 1975 fall of the capital of the US's puppet government in South Vietnam that followed the US military's withdrawal. As an interventionist, the problem for Rice was not the US's invasion and brutal war on Vietnam that killed anywhere between two and four million, mostly civilian Vietnamese, but the US's inevitable pullout from the country that ultimately left the country in peace. We are actually seeing such a development toward a permanent peace in Syria now, with the Kurds agreeing with the sovereign government of Syria to accept Syrian protection against the Turkish incursion—the only realistic and permanent solution to the problem of the Kurds in Syria.

As an initial matter, when considering the situation in Syria, it is important to first acknowledge that what is taking place there is a civil war with, quite predictably, extreme violence on all sides. While the West is quick to condemn the Assad government for acts of brutality—real, imagined, and made-up—and to justify intervening in Syria's civil war based on these acts, this ignores the fact that all civil wars are marked by brutality, even the US Civil War. As one historian reminds us:[41]

The most dramatic forgotten atrocity in the Civil War occurred 155 years ago when Union General Philip Sheridan unleashed a hundred-mile swath of flames in the Shenandoah Valley that left vast numbers of women and children tottering toward starvation . . .

> In August 1864, supreme Union commander Ulysses S. Grant ordered Sheridan to "do all the damage to railroads and crops you

can . . . If the war is to last another year, we want the Shenandoah Valley to remain a barren waste." Sheridan set to the task with vehemence, declaring that "the people must be left nothing but their eyes to weep with over the war" and promised that, when he was finished, the valley "from Winchester to Staunton will have but little in it for man or beast." . . .

After one of Sheridan's favorite aides was shot by Confederate soldiers, Sheridan ordered his troops to burn all houses within a five mile radius. After many outlying houses had been torched, the small town at the center, Dayton, was spared after a federal officer disobeyed Sheridan's order. The homes and barns of Mennonites—a peaceful sect who opposed slavery and secession—were especially hard hit by that crackdown, according to a 1909 history of Mennonites in America.

By the end of Sheridan's campaign, the former "breadbasket of the Confederacy" could no longer even feed the women and children remaining there. . . .

Some defenders of the Union military tactics insist that there was no intent to harshly punish civilians. But, after three years of a bloody stalemate, the Lincoln administration had adapted a total war mindset to scourge the South into submission.

Of course, Syria has now been involved in a civil war for almost nine years, and with a number of other nations and armed militias, such as ISIS, intervening to fan the flames of this conflict, something that was not a factor in the US Civil War.

This is not to justify such internecine violence, but such violence also should not be seen as some type of carte blanche for nations to get involved in other's civil conflicts, especially, when, as in the case of Syria, other nations, most notably the US, were greatly responsible for starting the civil conflict there in the first place. Thus, the dirty little secret is that the US was the prime mover in destabilizing Syria to begin with and creating the conditions for the civil war that ultimately has taken place. And the US has done so by supporting terrorists in Syria at times and fighting these same terrorists as it suited its purposes.

An opinion piece in the London *Guardian* concisely explains:[42]

> A revealing light on how we got here has now been shone by a recently declassified secret US intelligence report, written in August 2012, which uncannily predicts—and effectively welcomes—the prospect of a "Salafist principality" in eastern Syria and an al-Qaida-controlled Islamic state in Syria and Iraq. In stark contrast to western claims at the time, the Defense Intelligence Agency document identifies al-Qaida in Iraq (which became Isis) and fellow Salafists as the "major forces driving the insurgency in Syria"—and states that "western countries, the Gulf states and Turkey" were supporting the opposition's efforts to take control of eastern Syria.
>
> Raising the "possibility of establishing a declared or undeclared Salafist principality," the Pentagon report goes on, "this is exactly what the supporting powers to the opposition want, in order to isolate the Syrian regime, which is considered the strategic depth of the Shia expansion (Iraq and Iran).
>
> . . . A year into the Syrian rebellion, the US and its allies weren't only supporting and arming an opposition they knew to be dominated by extreme sectarian groups; they were prepared to countenance the creation of some sort of "Islamic state"—despite the "grave danger" to Iraq's unity—as a Sunni buffer to weaken Syria.

As the *Guardian* piece concludes, "US and western policy in the conflagration that is now the Middle East is in the classic mould of imperial divide-and-rule. American forces bomb one set of rebels while backing another in Syria. . . . However confused US policy may often be, a weak, partitioned Iraq and Syria fit such an approach perfectly."

> For his part, the great journalist Stephen Kinzer, who has spent decades criticizing US intervention, explains the roots of the current

crisis confronting the Kurds in Syria which few will discuss, and it is a crisis borne of many years of disastrous US foreign policy. As Kinzer explains, "[t]he deeper history of our Middle East tragedy begins in 1980, when President Carter declared that any challenge to American power in the Persian Gulf region would be repelled "by any means necessary, including military force."[43] One of the first manifestations of the "Carter Doctrine", of course, was the US support of the brutal Mujahadeen in Afghanistan, a portion of which, led by Osama bin Laden, would later become Al Qaeda. Then, as Kinzer notes, President George W. Bush's invasion of Iraq would lead to the formation of ISIS. Not to be outdone, Obama would himself foster terrorism in the region.

Kinzer explains:

The more recent set of causes for our Kurdish misadventure began in 2011, when President Obama ordered President Bashar al-Assad of Syria to "step aside." Beyond the arrogance that leads American presidents to think they can and should decide who may rule other countries lay the utter impossibility of achieving that goal.

Following the example his predecessor set when invading Afghanistan, Obama looked for "partners" who would fight the anti-Assad war for us. Many of the militias we hired and armed were connected to jihadist terror gangs. That made sense, because the Assad government is resolutely secular and those fanatics hate secularism.

While Kinzer properly mentions the invasion of Iraq as the first blow against stability in neighboring Syria as the consequence of the rise of ISIS, he does not mention one other huge result of the disastrous intervention. Thus, the US invasion of Iraq created a refugee crisis (as wars often will) that ultimately sent over one million Iraqis fleeing into Syria, a small country of about twenty million at the time.[44]

Amnesty International explained in a 2008 report, "it is costing

Syria billions of dollars to host so many refugees from Iraq and ... the cost is continuing to rise. In addition to the strain placed on education and health infrastructures, the number of refugees is said also to have had a large impact on water resources, garbage disposal and other aspects. The Syrian government subsidizes key items such as petrol, flour, gas and electricity, which both Syrians and refugees then buy at reduced cost. Despite the large number of Iraqi refugees in Syria and despite pledges made by the international community at the Geneva conference in April 2007 to support Iraqi refugees, Syria has received little bilateral financial assistance."[45] And the US was not one of the countries that provided such assistance, despite its responsibility for the refugee crisis.

Quite relevant to the issue right now of Turkish forces attacking the Kurds in Syria, *The Gray Zone* just did an exposé on how the US has been funding and arming nearly all of these Turkish forces for years. Thus, *The Gray Zone*, noting the fierce attack on Trump's current Syria withdrawal by liberal politicians and pundits, explains that

> the fighters involved in the atrocities in northern Syria were not just random tribesmen assembled into an ad hoc army. In fact, many were former members of the Free Syrian Army, the force once armed by the CIA and Pentagon and branded as "moderate rebels." This disturbing context was conveniently omitted from the breathless denunciations of US officials and Western pundits.
>
> According to a research paper published this October by the pro-government Turkish think tank, SETA, "Out of the 28 factions [in the Turkish mercenary force], 21 were previously supported by the United States, three of them via the Pentagon's program to combat DAESH. Eighteen of these factions were supplied by the CIA via the MOM Operations Room in Turkey, a joint intelligence operation room of the 'Friends of Syria' to support the armed opposition. Fourteen factions of the 28 were also recipients of the US-supplied TOW anti-tank guided missiles." ...

In other words, virtually the entire apparatus of anti-Assad insurgents armed and equipped under the Obama administration has been repurposed by the Turkish military to serve as the spearhead of its brutal invasion of northern Syria.[46]

In addition, as the UN, Amnesty International, and Human Rights Watch have all reported, US forces have been directly involved in war crimes in Syria through, amongst other things, massive aerial bombing campaigns that have killed untold numbers of Syrian civilians—most likely many more than the US and its allies are willing to admit.[47]

Intellectuals such as Power and Rice, with the help of the press, which gives them a ready megaphone for their views, purposefully obscure such facts and, along with them, the lesson we should have learned from such cruel interventions in Iraq, Syria, Yemen, the DRC, and Vietnam—that human rights are best protected by not intervening in the first place.

Or, as Noam Chomsky has been advising for many years, these countries would have been better off if the US had abided by the first precept of the Hippocratic Oath: "Do No Harm," which, as Chomsky, as well as many physicians who believe in taking the least invasive approach to medicine, interpret as meaning, "Do Nothing."

And this is in fact the lesson that international law teaches us, as well—that taking the least invasive approach to foreign policy is not only best, it is required.

* * *

Meanwhile, as I write this book, President Trump has announced that the US has no intention to leave Syria any time soon after all; that it indeed intends to keep troops there to continue occupying about one-third of Syria's land mass and to exploit the oil and gas reserves found therein. Indeed, Russian satellite imagery shows that the US has been smuggling oil out of Syria for some time.[48] As *Yahoo Finance* explains, "[a]ccording to the [Russian Defense] ministry, the photos confirm that 'Syrian oil, both before and after the routing defeat of the Islamic State terrorists in land beyond the Euphrates River, under the reliable protection by US military servicemen, oil was actively being extracted and then the fuel trucks were massively being sent for processing outside of Syria.'"[49]

This, by the way, constitutes a war crime, violating the Fourth Geneva Convention prohibitions against pillaging.[50] Indeed, law professor James Graham Stewart, who was interviewed about this, pointed "to a chilling precedent. 'One defendant at Nuremberg called Walther Funk, who was the chairperson of the Continental Oil Company, was convicted of pillaging oil from throughout occupied Europe . . . precisely because the German army expropriated it for the purposes of the Nazi apparatus.'"[51]

For his part, Trump has stated, "We're keeping the oil—remember that. . . . We want to keep the oil. Forty-five million dollars a month? Keep the oil. We've secured the oil."[52] Trump further explained, "What I intend to do, perhaps, is make a deal with an ExxonMobil or one of our great companies to go in there and do it properly . . . and spread out the wealth."[53]

The above reveals the dirty little truth about Western intervention—somehow, it always comes back to being about controlling other peoples' resources, regardless of the lofty reasons invariably given for the intervention. Indeed, Trump received well-deserved props for his candor from Syrian President Bashar Assad, who opined that "Trump is 'the best American president.' . . . Why? Not because his policies are good. . . . But because he's the most transparent president."[54] As Assad explained, and quite correctly, I might add:

> All American presidents commit crimes and end up taking the Nobel Peace Prize and appear as a defender of human rights, and the "unique" and "brilliant" American or Western principles. . . .
> But all they are is a group of criminals who only represent the

interests of the American lobbies of large corporations in weapons, oil and others.

This recalls to mind the following remarks of philosopher Bertrand Russell regarding British claims about its war aims. As Belgian physicist and philosopher Jean Bricmont relates, "[d]uring the Boer War, the British prime minister, Lord Salisbury, declared that it was 'a war for democracy,' and 'we seek no goldfields, we seek no territory.' Bertrand Russell, citing these remarks, commented that 'cynical foreigners noted that we nevertheless got both goldfields and territory.'"[55] Bricmont also notes, by the way, how "Hitler, for his part, waged his wars to protect (German) minorities and defend Europe from Bolshevism." That is, even Hitler claimed to be a "humanitarian" interventionist of sorts, which should give anyone pause about such self-serving claims.

Meanwhile, US troops are already killing hundreds of Syrians, and possibly Russians too, in the pursuit of the goal to exploit Syrian oil.[56] However, given that this is quite according to the US's imperial plan, one can expect to see little hand-wringing from the liberal humanitarians.

ONE

"Humanitarian" Intervention from King Leopold to Samantha Power

"The domination of the West is the worst in human history, in its duration and in its planetary extension."
—Edgar Morin, *Vers l'abîme?* (Paris 2007)

WHEN THINKING OF "HUMANITARIAN" INTERVENTIONISM, we must first face the fact that such interventions, as Jean Bricmont has noted, invariably run, like the Mississippi River, from North to South.[57] And this is because the countries of the Global North—and in this book I am focusing on those northern countries most commonly referred to as the West, which includes the US, Canada, and Western Europe—have the superior military might to invade the poorer of nations of the South and, believing themselves to be morally superior as well, have almost always justified such invasions as serving the lofty goals of advancing civilization, democracy, and human rights.

But of course, the West's claim of moral superiority is at best a dubious one, and, almost invariably, the wars it has waged on the world, while usually having some type of humanitarian goal as a pretext, are about theft, pillage, and domination.

A classic case of the West's moral decrepitude, and of the lie of "humanitarian" intervention, was the foray of Belgium's King Leopold in Congo in the early part of the 20th century. Leopold's incursion into Congo coincided with other Western countries' forays into Africa, including the US's substantial intervention in South Africa, as these countries would seek to exploit African labor in their homelands after the trans-Atlantic slave trade had ended.[58] Historian Gerald Horne relates that "the imminent decline of enslavement of Africans as the basis for society signaled by 1865 led to a renewed scramble for Africa as what then ensued was exploiting Africans shamelessly on their home turf."[59]

As so well explained in Adam Hochschild's *King Leopold's Ghost*,[60] Leopold took over Congo in order to plunder this vast nation of its rich resources, most notably ivory and rubber. But, for a very long time, Leopold convinced the gullible liberal do-gooders of the West (it seems we have always been plagued by such fools) that he was in Congo on a humanitarian mission.

It is credibly estimated that King Leopold's reign in Congo killed 10 million Congolese, or half of Congo's population,[61] making this one of the greatest known mass killings in world history.

Current Western interventionists understand all too well that King Leopold himself "recognized that a colonial push of his own would require a strong humanitarian veneer. Curbing the [very real Arab] slave trade [in Congo], moral uplift, and the advancement of science were the aims he would talk about, not profits. In 1876, he began planning a step to establish his image as a philanthropist and advance his African ambitions: he would host a conference of explorers and geographers" to whom he would put his alleged humanitarian concerns on display.[62] Leopold even set up a magnanimous-sounding International African Association as a front for his imperialist schemes. As

Hochschild explains, "[t]he new body was welcomed throughout Europe. Prominent citizens, from the Rothschilds to Viscount Ferdinand de Lesseps, the builder of the Suez Canal, hastened to send contributions. . . . Viscount de Lesseps, for one, declared Leopold's plans 'the greatest humanitarian work of this time.'"[63]

And what did this great "humanitarian" work look like in reality? Like something out of a horror film. Thus, Hochschild details Leopold's rule over the Congolese, which was enforced systematically by whippings with "the *chicotte*—a whip of raw, sun-dried hippopotamus hide, cut into a long sharp-edged cork-screw strip."[64] Such whippings were meted out liberally by sadistic overseers, to adults and children alike. Hochschild describes one scene in which a recent arrival to Congo, Stanislav Leflanc, is disturbed by the sound of screaming:

> On tracing the howls to their source, Lefranc found "some thirty urchins, of whom several were seven or eight years old, line up and waiting their turn, watching terrified, their companions being flogged. Most of the urchins, in a paroxysm of grief . . . kicked so frightfully that the soldiers ordered to hold them by the hands and feet had to lift them off the ground . . . 25 times the whip slashed down on each of the children." The evening before, Lefranc learned, several children had laughed in the presence of a white man, who then ordered that all the servant boys in town be given fifty lashes.[65]

The cruelty of Leopold's reign over Congo knew no bounds. Thus, this reign was famously marked by the enslavement of millions of Congolese who were forced to harvest ivory and rubber, and to build the massive infrastructure necessary for the international trade in these items; the mass cutting off of hands and penises of Congolese men; the kidnapping and rape of girls and women; the maintenance of "child colonies" in which children were forcibly raised to be soldiers to oppress their fellow countrymen; and forced starvation.[66]

As Hochschild tells us, the US was the first nation in the world to recognize Leopold's dominion over Congo, with then-Secretary of State Frelinghuysen announcing in 1884:

> The Government of the United States announces its sympathy with and approval of the humane and benevolent purposes of the International Association of the Congo, administering, as it does, the interests of the Free States there established, and will order the officers of the United States, both on land and sea, to recognize the flag of the International African Association as the flag of the Government.[67]

This recognition, wrote explorer and mapper Henry Morton Stanley, the Welsh-American of "Stanley and Livingstone" fame who aided King Leopold in his takeover of Congo and who curiously was a veteran of both sides of the US Civil War, "'was the birth unto new life of the Association,' . . . and he was right."[68] This was also the birth of "humanitarian" interventionism, as it is known today—the fantastic doctrine pursuant to which the West, and especially the US, forcibly spreads disaster and chaos throughout the world in the name of human rights and freedom.

It must be pointed out that this US recognition of Leopold's giant slave plantation in the heart of Africa made perfect sense, for the US—even at the time, decades after the Civil War—continued to maintain a huge slave economy.

As Douglas A. Blackmon, then-Atlanta bureau chief of the radical left-wing newspaper, the *Wall Street Journal*, explains in his groundbreaking book, *Slavery by Another Name*,[69] possibly hundreds of thousands of African Americans were enslaved in the South after the end of the Civil War until "the dawn of WWII." This mass enslavement was accomplished, he tells us, through the systematic manipulation of vagrancy and loitering laws that allowed African Americans to be arrested for the "offense" of standing or waiting around, including, for example, in a suit waiting for a train, while black. Then, the courts would intentionally impose debt upon these innocents they could not pay. And so, they were forced to work off this debt, many times till premature death, through back-breaking work in the burgeoning industry of the South, including the coal mines of such "reputable" companies as Pittsburgh's US Steel.

Blackmon explains:

> Altogether, millions of mostly obscure entries in the public record offer details of a forced labor system of monotonous enormity.
>
> Instead of thousands of true thieves and thus drawn into the system over decades, the records demonstrate the capture and imprisonment of thousands of random indigent citizens, almost always under the thinnest chimera of probable cause or judicial process. The total number of workers caught in this net had to have totaled more than a hundred thousand and perhaps more than twice that figure.
> ... Hundreds of forced labor camps came to exist, scattered throughout the South—operated by state and county governments, large corporations, small-time entrepreneurs, and provincial farmers. Where mob violence or the Ku Klux Klan terrorized black citizens periodically, the return of forced labor as a fixture in black life ground pervasively into the daily lives of far more African Americans.
> ... Revenue from the neo-slavery poured the equivalent of tens of millions of dollars into the treasuries of Alabama, Mississippi, Louisiana, Georgia, Florida, Texas, North Carolina, and South Carolina—where more than 75 percent of the black population in the United States then lived.[70]

Quite tellingly, Hochschild fails to even mention the US's parallel slave system during this time even in the context of the US's ready acceptance of Leopold's enslavement of Congo. Instead, he incessantly tries to draw comparisons between Leopold and Joseph Stalin, in what I view as an apparent, and quite typical, attempt to avoid the painful realization that what Leopold was doing in Congo was not so different from what the US and other Western nations have done, and indeed continue to do, around the world. For Hochschild, and so many other Western thinkers, the Leopolds of the world must be seen as an aberration, not as the norm that they in fact are.

Not too surprisingly, then, Hochschild ends up drawing the wrong conclusion from his otherwise excellent description of Leopold and Congo—that is, that, in his view, the current Western human rights movement is a direct descendant of the anti-imperialist movement that brought Leopold down, and that "there is no tradition more honorable."[71]

The problem is that Hochschild, as so many others under the spell of Western hubris, fails to see that the current human rights movement tends to enforce empire, and that is what distinguishes it from the explicitly anti-imperialist movement that ultimately ended Leopold's hold over Congo. Indeed, the current human rights movement is an enabler of the King Leopolds of our time, not an impediment. And, while Hochschild believes that the human rights movement remains "a profound threat to the established order of most countries on earth,"[72] the truth is that it is only a real threat to the countries of the Global South and is used against them by the countries of the North.

For example, one of the chief examples he gives of his thesis is "the half-century of resistance that brought Nelson Mandela to power in South Africa."[73] But where did this resistance, or at least the most effective part of it by far, come from? It certainly did not come from Western governments that, led by the US, Britain, and Israel, supported Apartheid until the bitter end. Moreover, Western human rights groups were not particularly helpful.

And indeed, Amnesty International (AI)—the quintessential Western human rights NGO and the organization Hochschild claims to be the successor to the groups that successfully challenged King Leopold's hold over Congo—would not even back the Free Mandela Campaign because of Mandela's advocacy of armed struggle, or at least, that was the ostensible reason.[74] I suspect that AI's anticommunism had as much to do with its refusal to support Mandela. Indeed, there is strong evidence of this, with Amnesty International cofounder Peter Benenson, a man with close ties to the pro-Apartheid British Foreign Office and Colonial Office, stating in 1963, "Communist influence should not be allowed to spread in this part of Africa, and in the present delicate situation, Amnesty International would wish to support Her Majesty's Government in any such policy. . . ."[75] Of course, the British and US policy of fighting what they saw as Communist influence in South Africa made them active allies in propping up the Apartheid government.

Whatever the reasons, Amnesty International was, in the end, not even able to condemn the Apartheid system in South Africa. As Professor Francis A. Boyle explained,

> Amnesty International refused adamantly to condemn Apartheid in South Africa. Despite my best efforts while I was on the board, and other board members, they would not do it. They are the only human rights organization in the world to have refused to condemn Apartheid in South Africa. Now they can give you some cock-and-bull theory about why they wouldn't do this. But the bottom line was that the biggest supporter, economic and political supporter of the criminal Apartheid regime in South Africa was the British government, followed by the United States government. And so no matter how hard we tried, no matter what we did, they would not condemn Apartheid in South Africa.[76]

Similarly, Amnesty International has been quiet in opposing the US's armed interventions in countries like Iraq and Libya, if not even tacitly supporting such violent intervention in the name of humanitarianism.

Meanwhile, the main resistance to Apartheid came of course from the South African people themselves, led by the ANC, the allied South African Communist Party, and by the significant military assistance of Cuba and the USSR—two countries of the Global South and East, respectively, which were deemed morally deficient by Western human rights groups, but which actually supported the anticolonial struggles of the Global South against the imperialist United States.

As Mandela would say, "I appreciate the Soviet Union because it was the one country that long ago condemned racialism . . ."[77] But even more so, Mandela appreciated Cuba, who, with the force of arms, legally assisted the sovereign nation of Angola with its self-defense against the CIA-backed counterrevolutionary groups in Angola as well as the South African military itself, which was occupying the nation of Namibia just to the south of Angola. The South African military, "urged by Washington," was violently trying to roll back the anticolonial uprisings taking place throughout what was known as the Southern African front-line states, including Angola.[78]

All told, the intervention of both South Africa and the US under Ronald Reagan in the war against the front-line states—a war we were told was for democracy and freedom when it was anything but—cost the lives of at least 1.5 million Africans. As Noam Chomsky explains, "I recall it during the 1980s, by then there was enormous pressure to end all support for the Apartheid government. Congress passed legislation barring trade and aid. The Reagan administration found ways to evade the congressional legislation, and in fact trade with South Africa increased in the latter part of the decade. This is incidentally the period when Collin Powell moved to the position of national security adviser. The US was strongly supporting the Apartheid regime directly and then indirectly through allies. Israel was helping get around the embargo. . . . In Angola and Mozambique, the neighboring countries, in those countries alone, the South African depredations killed about million-and-a-half people and led to some $60 billion in damage during the period of constructive engagement with the US support. It was a horror story."[79]

In case readers have forgotten, or maybe never knew, which side the US was on during this time, a retrospective in McClatchy newspapers explained:[80]

> Concerned that communism could triumph as post-colonial conflicts
> raged in a region abounding in strategic minerals and Western

corporate investments, President Ronald Reagan swung US policy from opposition to support of South Africa's white rulers soon after his 1980 election.

"Can we abandon a country that has stood by us in every war we've fought, a country that is strategically essential to the free world?" Reagan asked in a 1981 CBS News interview.

The Reagan administration invited senior South African security officials to the United States, violating a UN arms embargo, and the United States vetoed a UN Security Council resolution that would have imposed economic sanctions on Pretoria.

Reagan also had Mandela placed on the US international terrorist list, where the anti-Apartheid leader remained until 2008.

Again, it bears repeating that Amnesty International did nothing to counter the designation of Mandela as a terrorist.

Meanwhile, Cuba voluntarily entered the fray in Angola at a critical moment and, with help from the USSR, beat back this counterrevolutionary effort.[81] The turning point of this effort came with the 1988 defeat of the South African military in the legendary battle of Cuito Cuanavale—a battle, sadly, that few Americans have ever heard of.

Here is how Nelson Mandela himself explained the impact of all of this:

> I was still in prison when I first heard of the massive help which the Cuban international forces were giving to the people of Angola. The help was of such a scale that it was difficult for us to believe it, when the Angolans were under attack by the combined forces of South Africa, the FALA [Armed Forces for the Liberation of Angola] who were financed by the CIA, mercenaries, UNITA [National Union for the Total Independence of Angola], and Zaire in 1975.
>
> In Africa we are used to being victims of countries that want to take from us our territory or overthrow our sovereignty. In African history there is not another instance where another people has stood

up for one of ours. We also acknowledge that the action was carried out by the masses in Cuba and that those who fought and died in Angola are only a small portion of those who volunteered to go. To the Cuban people internationalism is not only a word but something which they have put into practice for the benefit of large sectors of mankind. We know that the Cuban forces were ready to retreat after driving back the invasion in 1975 but the continued aggressions of Pretoria did not allow them to do so. Your presence there and the reinforcements sent for the battle of Cuito Cuanavale has a historical meaning. The decisive defeat of the racist army in Cuito Cuanavale was a victory for all Africa. This victory in Cuito Cuanavale is what made it possible for Angola to enjoy peace and establish its own sovereignty. The defeat of the racist army made it possible for the people of Namibia to achieve their independence.

The decisive defeat of the aggressive Apartheid forces destroyed the myth of the invincibility of the white oppressor. The defeat of the Apartheid army served as an inspiration to the struggling people of South Africa. Without the defeat of Cuito Cuanavale our organizations would not have been legalized. The defeat of the racist army in Cuito Cuanavale made it possible for me to be here with you today. Cuito Cuanavale marks the divide in the struggle for the liberation of southern Africa. Cuito Cuanavale marked an important step in the struggle to free the continent and our country of the scourge of Apartheid.[82]

The legendary Soweto uprising in 1976—an uprising that marked the beginning of the end of the Apartheid system—took place after and in direct response to the Cuban victory over the South African army.[83]

All of this may come as a surprise to many readers who, under the sway of our Orwellian propaganda system, believe that the US was always friends with Nelson Mandela and who know nothing about the anti-Apartheid contributions of the oft-vilified Cuba and the USSR. Equally surprising may be the revelation that the US did not aid in the dismantling of Apartheid, but that it in fact helped create the Apartheid system to begin with, patterning it after its own Jim Crow system of racial segregation, and then defended Apartheid until its end.[84] But of course, those of us who do know of such things know that the US has always been on the wrong side of the anticolonial struggle. Or, more to the point, as Daniel Ellsberg has remarked, it's not really that the US is on the wrong side; "it *is* the wrong side."

Moreover, it must be emphasized that while it was not Western intervention in South Africa that ended Apartheid, it was in fact Western intervention (Dutch, British, American, and Israeli) that created and sustained it. And Cuba's intervention was never claimed to be a "humanitarian" one, but rather one of anti-imperialist solidarity and, more important, of collective self-defense of Angola *against Western intervention*. Because Angola requested and assented to this Cuban assistance, assistance that even the CIA acknowledged was "the guarantee for the independence of Angola,"[85] this intervention was lawful under the UN Charter (see UN Charter at Appendix A). And ultimately, the case of South Africa's liberation lends no support to the Western "humanitarian" interventionists, but instead greatly undermines it.

Finally, one more important factor in the overthrow of Apartheid in South Africa was, of course, the international divestment and disinvestment campaign pursuant to which universities and other institutions and corporations were pressured by solidarity groups to withdraw economic investment in and support for the South African Apartheid government. This campaign was organized in response to the explicit calls of the African National Congress and was, at its heart, an anti-imperialist and anti-interventionist movement. I would submit that this movement constitutes a much better model for responding to international human rights/humanitarian issues than the standard Western human rights NGO model.

Going back to the issue of Congo, it should also be recalled that the US has played a key role in the persecution of Congo, dating back centuries and continuing to the present time. Thus, from the early

1500s to 1860, millions of Congolese were forcibly taken from their land and sold as slaves, first in Europe and then in the "New World." Even by 1526, the country, then a kingdom, was becoming devastated by the slave trade. As Congo's king, Nzinga Mbemba Alffonso wrote at this time, "'[e]ach day the traders are kidnapping our people—children of this country, sons of our nobles and vassals, even people of our own family. . . . This corruption and depravity are so widespread that our land is entirely depopulated.'"[86] At the time, Congo's children were being shipped to Europe.

Then, from 1650 to 1860, approximately three million slaves were carried across the "dreaded passage" from Congo (along with what is now Angola) to the Americas.[87] Indeed, "[r]oughly one of every four slaves imported to work the cotton and tobacco plantations of the American South began his or her journey across the Atlantic from equatorial Africa, including the Kongo Kingdom."[88]

As noted above, it was US recognition of King Leopold's takeover of Congo that helped to give cover to and to solidify that takeover. Ultimately, however, Leopold's scheme was outed by the Congo Reform Association, and most notably by one of the leaders of its US branch, Mark Twain—a cofounder of the Anti-Imperialist League—whose honest and revelatory writings about Leopold in Congo shocked the world, and especially Leopold's benevolent benefactors.[89] This ultimately led to Belgium taking Congo out of Leopold's hands and to Belgium's administering it as a traditional European colony. As Hochschild laments, however, while the worst excesses of Leopold ended at this point, the Congolese continued to be forced into labor and chewed up in the rubber plantation system that Leopold created.[90] And their exploitation only increased after WWI with the discovery of rich copper, gold, tin, and uranium deposits that the Congolese were then forced to mine in terrible, back-breaking conditions.

Relief at least appeared in sight in 1960, when the people of Congo won their independence from Belgium and elected their first president, Joseph Kasavubu, and their first prime minister, Patrice

Lumumba. However, the hope for an independent Congo was short-lived, thanks to continued intervention by Belgium and, even more so, by the United States.

As an initial matter, despite its formal independence from Belgium, white Belgians continued to command the Congolese armed forces. These armed forces, understandably upset by this incongruent state of affairs as well as their poor pay and treatment, quickly mutinied against their Belgian commanders and then turned their wrath against Belgian settlers. In response, Belgium military forces unilaterally intervened to protect their interests. UN mission forces were then sent in ostensibly to keep peace. However, these forces were fully under the control of the US, which was "the[ir] major financier and political supporter . . ."[91] Moreover, while they were to replace the Belgian forces, the latter refused to leave.[92] It was in this situation of uncertainty that the US saw an opportunity at regime change.

Georges Nzongola-Ntalaja, writing for *The Guardian* of London, called it "the most important assassination of the 20th century."[93] He was referring to the murder of the first legally elected prime minister of the Democratic Republic of the Congo ("DRC" or "Congo"), Patrice Lumumba, on January 17, 1961, through the combined efforts of the United States and Belgium. The assassination took place less than seven months after Congolese independence from Belgium. Congo has yet to recover from this tragic event.

In his *Guardian* article, Nzongola-Ntalaja explains that Lumumba's murder—"the country's original sin"—was motivated by the US desire to control the Congo's resources. Indeed, as he relates, the US had begun to intervene in Congo even before independence:

> When the atrocities related to brutal economic exploitation in Leopold's Congo Free State resulted in millions of fatalities, the US joined other world powers to force Belgium to take over the country as a regular colony. And it was during the colonial period that the US acquired a strategic stake in the enormous natural wealth of the

Congo, following its use of the uranium from Congolese mines to manufacture the first atomic weapons, the Hiroshima and Nagasaki bombs.

With the outbreak of the Cold War, it was inevitable that the US and its western allies would not be prepared to let Africans have effective control over strategic raw materials, lest these fall in the hands of their enemies in the Soviet camp. It is in this regard that Patrice Lumumba's determination to achieve genuine independence and to have full control over Congo's resources in order to utilize them to improve the living conditions of our people was perceived as a threat to western interests.

The US State Department has also admitted that the US intervened before independence to try to prevent Lumumba from being elected in the first place. As its Office of the Historian explains, "Even before Congolese independence, the US Government attempted to ensure election of a pro-Western government by identifying and supporting individual pro-US leaders."[94]

The desire to keep Lumumba out of power was based on assessments of the Eisenhower Administration that he was a Communist under undue influence of the Soviets—assessments that former US officials who knew Lumumba at the time later admitted were mistaken.[95] Based upon this mistaken assessment, the CIA would embark on its largest covert operation in its history to that time.[96]

Thus, when US machinations failed to prevent Lumumba's election, the US quickly turned to other means. According to the Office of the Historian of the US State Department,

> In August 1960, the US Government launched a covert political program in the Congo lasting almost seven years, initially aimed at eliminating Lumumba from power and replacing him with a more moderate, pro-Western leader. The US Government provided advice and financial subsidies.[97]

This covert program included "organizing mass demonstrations, distributing anti-Communist pamphlets, and providing propaganda material for broadcasts."[98] But this was just the tip of the iceberg. Again, according to the State Department's Office of the Historian:

> based on authorization from President Eisenhower's statements at an NSC meeting on August 18, 1960, discussions began to develop highly sensitive, tightly-held plans to assassinate Lumumba. After Lumumba's death at the hands of Congolese rivals in January 1961, the US Government authorized the provision of paramilitary and air support to the new Congolese Government.[99]

As for the assassination efforts, there is no question that the CIA initially made plans to poison Lumumba, with the CIA's top scientist transporting the poison to Congo, where it was to be placed in Lumumba's food or toothpaste.[100] This plot was made pursuant the orders of "Director of Central Intelligence Allen Dulles [who] cabled the Leopoldville Station Chief that there was agreement in 'high quarters' that Lumumba's removal must be an urgent and prime objective."[101] While the plan to poison Lumumba ended up being abandoned, the assassination plot did not end there. Thus, the US was able to carry out its plans to eliminate Lumumba through its chief asset in Congo, Joseph Mobutu, as well as through the US's Belgian allies.

As Stephen R. Weissman, who has written extensively on the CIA operation against Lumumba, explains,

> Covert CIA actions against the Lumumba government, often dovetailing with Belgian ones, culminated in Colonel Joseph Mobutu's military coup, which was "arranged and supported and indeed managed" by the CIA alone, according to [CIA Station Chief Larry] Devlin's private interview with the [Senator Frank] Church Committee staff.
>
> The CIA station and US embassy provided their inexperienced

and politically weak Congolese protégés with a steady stream of political and military recommendations. . . . Devlin's counsel was largely heeded on critical matters, especially when it came to Lumumba. Thus Mobutu and former President Joseph Kasavubu were persuaded to resist political pressures to reconcile with Lumumba, and Mobutu reluctantly acceded to Devlin's request to arrest him.[102]

And then Devlin assented to Lumumba's being moved from the capital, Kinshasa, by Mobutu to his "sworn enemy" in Katanga, where, Mobutu made it clear, he "might be executed."[103] Devlin not only assented to this move, but he held off telling the US State Department for three days lest the State Department try to intervene to stop the execution.[104] Lumumba was, within those three days, murdered by Congolese secessionists who were being backed by Belgian forces. For their part, the Belgians, for good measure, "attempted to erase all memory of Lumumba by chopping up his corpse and dissolving the butchered pieces in acid."[105]

The Congo would never be the same. As Weissman explains, "Fifty years ago, the former Belgian Congo received its independence under the democratically elected government of former Prime Minister Patrice Lumumba. Less than seven months later, Lumumba and two colleagues were, in the contemporary idiom, 'rendered' to their Belgian-backed secessionist enemies, who tortured them before putting them before a firing squad. The Congo would not hold another democratic election for 46 years."

And indeed, the US would see to it that no such elections would be held, making sure that their man in Zaire, as it came to be known under his rule, Joseph Mobutu (later self-named Mobutu Sese Seko), remain in power with an iron hand. Recall from above that Zaire, in turn, aided the US and South Africa in their joint efforts to subdue the front-line states during their independence struggles.

All told, the US gave Mobutu "well over a billion dollars in civilian and military aid during the three decades of his rule," helping him to "repel several attempts to overthrow him."[106] The State Department, in quite sober but revealing terms, puts it this way:

> Despite periodic uprisings and unrest, Mobutu ruled the Congo (renamed Zaire in 1971) until the mid-1990s. Viewed as mercurial and occasionally irrational, Mobutu nonetheless proved to be a staunch ally against Communist encroachment in Africa. As such, he received extensive US financial, matériel, and political support, which increased his stature in much of Sub-Saharan Africa where he often served the interests of administrations from Johnson through Reagan.[107]

Sadly, as we find throughout the rest of the world, the end of the Cold War has not slowed the US in its aggressive pursuit of other peoples' wealth. Indeed, in large part because of the demise of the Soviet Union, which had been a check on US intervention, the US aggression has only increased.

And so, as the Soviet Union was collapsing, US President Bill Clinton began to pave the way for a giant resource grab in the Congo—the most resource-rich country on Earth, and also the poorest, with the very lowest Human Development Indicator of the 187 countries ranked by the United Nations. And Clinton, just as King Leopold before him, would pull off this feat by claiming to usher in a new era of human rights and "humanitarian" interventionism.

Thus, in 1996, President Clinton, with not a peep from Western human rights groups, backed the invasion of Congo by Uganda and Rwanda. Rwanda's invasion of the Congo was expressly carried out under the "humanitarian" pretext of chasing after alleged Hutu genocidaires who fled there. As Armin Rosen summarizes (in a bit of understatement) in *The Atlantic*, "Clinton's policy enabled both Rwandan and Ugandan adventurism in Eastern Congo, prolonging a conflict that still reverberates."[108] The result has been the greatest mass killing since WWII, with around eight million killed in the Congo, half under the age of five, and still counting.[109]

And, while UN forces were sent in long ago to intervene in Congo to halt this blood-letting, it has done little to do so. Ann Garrison, writing in the *Black Agenda Report*, explains, "[w]ith 18,000 troops, the UN Peacekeeping Mission in Congo is the largest in the world, and it has been in Congo for 20 years without protecting the people or peace." She cites Congolese-Swiss historian Benedicte Kumbi Njoko for the proposition that

> If we think about the UN and its presence, we need to go back to almost 59 years that the UN has been working in the Congo because there were problems in the country. And I think that if we take that into perspective, we can of course question the utility of this organization, because what we have seen the last 20 years now is that people are still dying and this war that is happening in the Congo has caused already more than eight million deaths, so maybe the response that the UN is giving to that situation is not an appropriate one.

South African mining researcher and community organizer David van Wyk agreed. "Sadly," he said, "it's one more failed intervention. The UN has failed the Congolese people from the very first day of the Congo's independence 59 years ago."[110]

The failure of the UN troop intervention in Congo at least compares favorably to the intervention in the neighboring Central African Republic (CAR), where there were scores of complaints of French troops, working as peacekeepers both directly for France as well as the UN, raping children as young as six years old—many times forcing starving children to have sex in return for food—and forcing still other children to have sex with animals.[111] Similar allegations have been made against peacekeepers in Haiti who are being accused of fathering, and then abandoning, hundreds of children with Haitian women and girls, some as young as 11 years old.[112]

As France's UN Ambassador, speaking of the allegations arising out of CAR, put it well, "[p]eople who were sent to protect the civilians are in fact becoming perpetrators . . . We must face the fact that a number of troops sent to protect people instead acted with hearts of darkness . . ."[113] The problem is that this can be said all too often of troops sent to far-flung nations, even for the ostensible purpose of preserving the peace or protecting human rights.

Meanwhile, the war in Congo, now known as the Democratic Republic of the Congo (DRC), has been marked by particular cruelty, including the use of child soldiers and the mass rape of girls and women. Indeed, Hillary Clinton, as Secretary of State under Obama, shamelessly condemned the sexual violence in the DRC while refusing to ever acknowledge Bill Clinton's very real role in it. Thus, as the UN High Commissioner for Refugees explained: "US Secretary of State Hillary Clinton called widespread sexual violence against women in eastern Congo 'a crime against humanity' during a visit to the region Tuesday where she met with displaced civilians at a UNHCR-run camp. . . . More than half of the two million people displaced in the Democratic Republic of the Congo (DRC) are women and in an area where the use of rape and sexual violence are endemic, many of those forced from their homes have been victimized."[114]

In an interview with me, Kambale Musavuli of Friends of the Congo explained that US economic and geopolitical interests have motivated its continuing support for the bloodbath in the Congo, which continues to this day. As Kambale explains,[115]

> Economic interests in Congo are that which we need in our daily life. The coltan which comes out the Congo can be found in your cell phone, the cobalt of the Congo can be found in the battery of the broker of Congo's minerals, and they loot Congo's mineral resources while they commit atrocities. . . . Chaos allows resources to leave from the Congo at a cheap price, and of course it's not actually just leaving, it's actually being stolen from the Congolese people.

The companies benefiting from the modern-day conquest of Congo, many of which have close ties to Bill Clinton and other US and Canadian politicos, are too numerous to mention but include the following, which "have rarely if ever been mentioned in any human rights report. One is Barrick Gold, who operates in the town of Watsa, northwest of the town of Bunia, located in the most violent corner of the Congo. . . . George H.W. Bush served as a paid advisor for Barrick Gold. Barrick directors include: Brian Mulroney, former PM of Canada; Edward Neys, former US ambassador to Canada. . .; former US Senator Howard Baker; . . . and Vernon Jordan, one of Bill Clinton's lawyers."[116]

Of note, Barrick Gold's mining partners have included "Adastra Mining, formerly named America Mineral Fields (AMFI, AMX, other names), formerly based in Hope, Arkansas, Bill Clinton's hometown."[117] In April of 1997, shortly after the US-backed invasion of Congo that would ultimately bring Laurent Kabila to power in Congo, "Jean-Ramon Boulle, a cofounder of Adastra (then AMFI), received a $1 billion dollar deal for mines in the Congo at Kolwezi (cobalt) and Kipushi (zinc) from Laurent Kabila's Alliance of Democratic Forces for the Liberation of Zaire (ADFL) before they were even officially in power. . . . Meanwhile, directors of Adastra are also former directors of Anglo-American. Other Clinton-connected founders of Adastra include Michael McMurrough and Robert Friedland, both involved in shady, criminal, offshore businesses in Indonesia, Africa, Burma and the Americas."[118]

The list goes on, but at least one gets a good taste of just how downright lucrative "humanitarian" interventions can be.

Meanwhile, another "humanitarian" intervention in Africa was carried out by NATO in 2011. This was the intervention in Libya. And, just as the intervention in Congo, the result would be slavery.

Thus, on March 19, 2011, NATO began its "humanitarian bombing" of Libya. While "humanitarian bombing" is an oxymoron, many believe that the US is not truly advancing human rights if it's not bombing another back to the Stone Age. Indeed, NPR's Scott Simon, a quintessential liberal pundit and a Quaker, referred to the US "shock and awe" attack against Baghdad in 2003 as a "humanitarian bombing."[119] Orwell would be proud.

As an initial matter, it must be said that while the UN had authorized a NATO fly-zone over Libya to protect civilians—all civilians, by the way—there was never authorization for the full-scale invasion that was carried out and that quickly became aimed at regime change. Therefore, the NATO operation quickly became an illegal one.

What's more, the Libyan invasion did more to undermine human rights than it did to protect them. According to a recent report of Amnesty International on Libya,[120] there are now three rival governments vying for power in the country along with various militias, smugglers, and other sundry armed groups. As Amnesty International explains, all participants in the armed conflict in Libya "carried out indiscriminate attacks in heavily populated areas leading to deaths of civilians and unlawful killings. Armed groups arrested and indefinitely detained thousands of people. Torture and other ill-treatment was widespread in prisons under the control of armed groups, militias and state officials."[121] And, to top it all off, slaves are being sold in public markets in Libya for $400 a piece—something not seen in the world for over a century.[122]

And this is the aftermath of an intervention that, we were told, was supposed to improve human rights in Libya. Indeed, the intervention was spearheaded by Hillary Clinton, Samantha Power, and Susan Rice[123]—three self-described warriors for human and women's rights. As Maureen Dowd wrote at the time, "[t]hey are called the Amazon Warriors, the Lady Hawks, the Valkyries, the Durgas."[124] Of course, quite appropriately, these terms of endearment place all emphasis on these individuals' war-like qualities rather than their desire to protect human rights. And this excited Maureen Dowd, for she lauded all of this as a breakthrough for feminism. As she wrote,

> There is something positively mythological about a group of strong

women swooping down to shake the president out of his delicate sensibilities and show him the way to war. And there is something positively predictable about guys in the White House pushing back against that story line for fear it makes the president look henpecked.

It is not yet clear if the Valkyries will get the credit or the blame on Libya. But everyone is fascinated with the gender flip: the reluctant men—the generals, the secretary of defense, top male White House national security advisers—outmuscled by the fierce women around President Obama urging him to man up against the crazy Qaddafi.

Sadly, the results of the intervention, which hurt women and men alike in Libya and elsewhere, cannot be seen as some victory for feminism. Indeed, war rarely if ever is.

While Gaddafi certainly was no saint, he was a much better leader for his country than many of those the West supports, such as the monarchy of Saudi Arabia, the death squad state of Colombia, or the coup government in Honduras. Indeed, Muammar Gaddafi, at the urging of his son, Saif, was attempting to democratize Libya at the time of the invasion, and the pair were willingly accepting the help of the US's National Democratic Institute to do so.[125]

In addition, Gaddafi had taken Libya from being the least prosperous country in Africa to the being the most prosperous by the time of the NATO operation.[126] Thus, as one commentator explains, before the intervention, "Libya had the highest GDP per capita and life expectancy on the continent. Less people lived below the poverty line than in the Netherlands."[127]

Moreover, one of the main reasons, we were told, that NATO needed to intervene in 2011 was to save Benghazi from imminent harm from the government forces of Gaddafi. However, Hillary Clinton's own internal emails show that her team recognized that any humanitarian problems confronting Benghazi had passed by the time of the NATO bombing. For example, Clinton's assistant, Huma Abedin, in an email dated February 21, 2011—that is, just a mere four days after the initial antigovernment protests broke out in Libya—explains that the Gaddafi forces no longer controlled Benghazi and that the mood in the city was indeed "celebratory" by that time.[128] Then, on March 2, just over two weeks before the bombing began, Harriet Spanos of USAID sent an email describing "[s]ecurity reports" that "confirm that Benghazi has been calm over the past couple of days."[129]

As these emails demonstrate, while Clinton was able to obtain passage of UN Security Council Resolution 1973—a resolution that authorized a no-fly zone to protect civilians—on March 17, 2011, those civilians that Clinton claimed needed most urgent protection (the civilians in the town of Benghazi) were relatively safe by this time.

Meanwhile, other internal emails of the Hillary Clinton team from this time demonstrate that, very shortly after the NATO bombing started, there was no need to continue the bombing.

Probably the most revealing email is dated March 30, 2011, just 11 days into the NATO bombing campaign that would go on until October, 20, when Qaddafi was finally murdered (after being sodomized). In this email titled "Win War,"[130] Clinton's closest adviser, Sidney Blumenthal, makes it clear that, in terms of the continuing reasons for the war, any **"humanitarian motive offered is limited, conditional and refers to a specific past situation."** (emphasis added) In other words, while NATO would go on bombing for another 7 months, Blumenthal is already admitting that there is really no humanitarian basis for continuing the conflict, and that further bombing did not meet with the Geneva Conventions' requirements of proportionality and necessity.

Still, Blumenthal insists on the importance for pressing on until final victory (i.e., the overthrow of Qaddafi, whom he calls "Q"). And he explains that the reasons for doing so include, first and foremost, boosting Obama's then-anemic approval ratings, an issue Blumenthal seems obsessed with. The other reasons he outlines are "establishing security in North Africa, securing democracy in Egypt and Tunisia, economic development, effect throughout Arab world and Africa, extending US influence, counter-balancing Iran, etc." Again, humanitarianism is notably absent from this list.[131]

The emails actually demonstrate a complete lack of concern for humanitarian violations by the pro-NATO rebels. Thus, in but another email to Hillary, dated March 27, 2011, Blumenthal explains, "[s]peaking in strict confidence, one rebel commander stated that his troops continue to summarily execute all foreign mercenaries in the fighting."[132] Now, summarily executing even armed combatants is a clear violation of the Geneva Conventions, but neither Blumenthal nor Hillary demonstrates much concern about such trifles.

Even more concerning, it became known during the course of the NATO invasion that the claims the troika of human rights intervention had made of foreign "black mercenaries" fighting for Qaddafi in order to justify military invasion were false; that, in fact, the alleged foreign mercenaries were really African guest workers or the descendants of slaves who had been living in Libya for many years.[133] The claim about "black mercenaries" was an obviously racist appeal to rally Western support against Qaddafi—just as Americans had been rallied in the early 20th century against the British for siding with black South Africans in their fight against the Dutch for control of South Africa[134]—but few liberals seemed bothered by this.

The truth is that Amnesty International, always happy to lend a hand in support of Western intervention, also perpetrated the "black mercenary" lie, issuing a press release in February of 2011, stating, "Amnesty International . . . criticized the response of the African Union to the unfolding crisis, which has seen hundreds killed and persistent reports of mercenaries being brought in from African countries by the Libyan leader to violently suppress the protests against him."[135] Amnesty International only corrected the record later, once the NATO invasion had actually begun.[136] And it was this lie that actually spurred on a very real genocide against black Africans living in Libya.

As it turned out, NATO sided with antiblack racists in Libya to topple Gaddafi, and, with the lies of "black mercenaries" inciting racial hatred, NATO's allies in Libya carried out pogroms as they began to take power in Libya with the help of NATO air power. As an article in the *Guardian* explained:[137]

> Lurking behind this is racism. Libya is an African nation—however, the term "Africans" is used in Libya to reference the country's black minority. The Amnesty International researcher Diana Eltahawy says that the rebels taking control of Libya have tapped into "existing xenophobia." The *New York Times* refers to "racist overtones", but sometimes the racism is explicit. A rebel slogan painted in Misrata during the fighting salutes "the brigade for purging slaves, black skin". A consequence of this racism has been mass arrests of black men, and gruesome killings – just some of the various atrocities that human rights organizations blame rebels for. The racialization of this conflict does not end with hatred of "Africans". Graffiti by rebels frequently depicted Gaddafi as a demonic Jew.

Another example of the crimes against black people in Libya as a result of the NATO operation and its lie about "black mercenaries" was the ethnic cleansing of the town of Tawergha. As the *BBC* explained in December of 2011, shortly after the killing of Gaddafi:

> In the middle of August 2011, between the end of the siege and the killing of Gaddafi, Misratan forces drove out everyone living in Tawergha, a town of 30,000 people. Human rights groups have described this as an act of revenge and collective punishment possibly amounting to a crime against humanity.
>
> Tawerghans are mostly descendants of black slaves. They are generally poor, were patronized by the Gaddafi regime and were broadly supporters of his regime.[138]

Not surprisingly, NATO, which had been given a mandate by the UN

Security Council to protect all Libyan civilians, did not move in to protect these descendants of black slaves, nor did any Western "humanitarians" ask it to.

NATO also did not move to assist the town of Bani Walid when it was being sacked by NATO's Libyan partners at the end of the intervention. Amnesty International details the brutal assault upon this town:

> Bani Walid was among the last cities to fall under the control of anti-Gaddafi forces during Libya's internal [sic] conflict last year. Hundreds of residents from Bani Walid have been arrested by armed militias. Many continue to be detained without charge or trial across Libyan prisons and detention centres, including Misratah. Many have been tortured or otherwise ill-treated. The entrance of anti-Gaddafi forces into Bani Walid in October 2011 was accompanied by widespread looting and other abuses.
>
> Thousands of individuals suspected of having fought for or supported the government of Mu'ammar al-Gaddafi continue to be detained across Libya. The vast majority have yet to be officially charged or brought to trial. Since the fall of Tripoli and the vast majority of the country under the control of anti-Gaddafi forces in August 2011, human rights abuses by armed militias such as arbitrary arrest and detention; torture or other ill-treatment—including death; extrajudicial executions and forced displacement continued to take place in a climate of impunity. To date, armed militia seize people outside the framework of the law and hold them incommunicado in secret detention facilities, where they are vulnerable to torture of other ill-treatment.

Not only did NATO fail to assist the people of Bani Walid, but the Obama Administration, through UN envoy Susan Rice, blocked a draft UN resolution proposed by Russia that would have called for a peaceful resolution of the conflict in that town.[139]

Meanwhile, Benghazi itself became the site of a grave humanitarian crisis and a hotbed for terrorists postintervention. Again, Amnesty

International writes that "[a] number of mass graves were uncovered in Benghazi between February and October [2017]. On at least four occasions, groups of bodies were found in different parts of the city with their hands bound behind their backs, and in some cases blindfolded with signs of torture and execution-style killing."[140]

In addition, during the early part of 2017, one armed faction laid siege to an apartment complex in the Ganfouda area of Benghazi, "cutting off all supplies to the area, including food and water, and had trapped civilians and wounded fighters [of another faction] without access to medical care and other basic services."[141] And when the same faction broke the siege by launching an armed assault on this area, it engaged in "indiscriminate" killings, with fighters from the faction posing for photos with the dead bodies.

And yet, where are the self-proclaimed defenders of human rights for all Libyans and Benghazi now? Where are their cries for humanitarian intervention? Of course, all of those responsible for this absolute disaster have moved on and remain silent about the tragedy they have wrought in that country.

What about the conduct of NATO itself during its "humanitarian" intervention ostensibly to save Libyan lives? Again, NATO was quite selective in this effort at best, attacking civilians and civilian infrastructure when it suited its purposes.

Maximilian Forte details this very well in his book, *Slouching Towards Sirte*. As the title of the book suggests, Sirte, a target of NATO bombing, is the symbol of NATO's other-than-humanitarian aims in Libya. As Forte explains, Sirte, in addition to being the hometown of Muammar Gaddafi and the second capital of Libya under his government, has been the gateway of would-be invaders of Africa for centuries. On this point, Forte quotes Gaddafi himself, who welcomed African leaders to Sirte at the Fifth Ordinary Summit of the African Union in 2005 by describing it as "'the frontline city because it confronted the colonial onslaughts and resisted several colonial campaigns aimed at the heart of African since Roman, Byzantine, Turkish and colonial eras, alongside other incursions by the Vandals who were seeking to penetrate deep in to the African continent. . . . Sirte was always the first line of defense against those campaigns.'" Forte further relates that Sirte, the city in which the African Union was founded in 1999 largely due to Gaddafi's own urging, remained a key frontline city—and indeed the envisioned capital for a new United States of Africa—until the time of the NATO invasion.

According to Forte, Sirte, as the frontline city, was an important symbolic prize and target for NATO, which, to make its message loud and clear to Libya and all of Africa that it too was preparing a new round of vandalizing and plundering Africa, worked in conjunction with the antigovernment rebels to level the city to the ground. Quoting David Randall, a reporter from the *Independent* of London on this subject, Sirte after the NATO intervention "was found 'without an intact building,' with 'nearly every house . . . pulverized by a rocket or mortar, burned out or riddled with bullets'—'the infrastructure of a city upon which the Libyan leader lavished millions has simply ceased to exist.'"

Moreover, though NATO, along with its chorus of cheerleaders amongst the Western human rights organizations, claimed that it was invading Libya to protect civilians, the civilian population of Sirte was decimated with the city itself. As Forte describes:

> Sirte suffered a catastrophe according to . . . many eyewitness descriptions of endless rows of buildings on fire, corpses of the executed lying on hospital lawns, mass graves, homes looted and burned by insurgents, apartment blocks flattened by NATO bombs. This is what "protecting civilians" actually looks like, and it looks like crimes against humanity. Far from the romantic image of all of Libya having risen up against the "evil tyrant," this was one side of Libya destroying the other with the aid (to say the least) of foreign forces.

And, while Amnesty International ended up applauding NATO for allegedly making "significant efforts to minimize the risk of causing civilian casualties," Forte demonstrates that NATO and its rebel allies targeted civilians and civilian infrastructure in Sirte, with the result being many more civilians killed than the mere "scores of [dead] Libyan civilians" that AI attributes to NATO over the course of the entire conflict. Indeed, there is good evidence that there were individual NATO bombing raids—raids entailing the typical US policy of "double tapping" in which an area is bombed once and then again to kill the civilians who come to the scene to retrieve the injured and dead after the first bombing—which killed scores of civilians in Sirte and other locations in one fell swoop. But again, groups such as Amnesty International were unmoved.

As all of this demonstrates, the intervention in Libya was not truly about human rights, just as other similar Western interventions in countries like Iraq, Afghanistan, and Syria have not been about either human rights or even fighting terror. And indeed, these interventions have only undermined human rights and further spread terror. In the case of Libya, the predictable havoc unleashed there has spread to neighboring states such as Niger, Tunisia, Mali, Chad, and Cameroon.[142] In addition, the refugee crisis created by the chaos unleashed by the NATO intervention in Libya is undermining the stability of all of Europe.

If the intervention was not about protecting human rights, however, what was it about? In short, it was about profit, power, and imperial domination.

First of all, Italy and France, which also helped lead the charge for invasion, had some of their own peculiar reasons for intervening in Libya. For his part, French President Nicolas Sarkozy appeared to be singularly focused on killing Libyan leader Muammar Gaddafi, who allegedly gave him €50 million for his presidential campaign—a claim that was just coming to light and to which Gaddafi was the chief witness.[143]

This concern is touched upon in an email by Sidney Blumenthal to Hillary Clinton in which he lists a number of Sarkozy's goals in attacking Libya, one being his desire to "[i]mprove his internal political situation in France."[144] Other interests of Sarkozy that Blumenthal lists: Sarkozy's desire to get his hands upon Libya's $7 billion of gold reserves; "to gain a greater share of Libya oil production"; to "[i]ncrease French influence in North Africa"; "[p]rovide the French military with an opportunity to reassert its position in the world"; and "[a]ddress the concern of his advisors over Qaddafi's long term plans to supplant France as the dominant power in Francophone Africa)."[145] Again, no humanitarian concerns here.

As for Italy, the former colonial power that once held dominion over Libya, it had agreed with Gaddafi to pay $5 billion in reparations to Libya for its brutal treatment of its former colony. Italy's goal in toppling Gaddafi was to get out of this agreement, and this gambit worked. As *The Times* of London explains, "[t]he agreement was forged by Silvio Berlusconi and Colonel Gaddafi, but lapsed when the Libyan dictator was overthrown and killed in 2011."[146]

In short, the lineup of Western leaders who wanted Gaddafi dead to protect their own pecuniary interests, as well as their own hides, was like something out of an Agatha Christie novel. Incredibly, however, it was Gaddafi who was portrayed as the "rogue" madman.

Beyond these more idiosyncratic goals, all NATO countries shared the goal of profiteering from the destruction of Libya itself. For example, the main instigator and leader of the NATO intervention, the US, wasted no time in moving into Libya after the fall of the Gaddafi government to collect its spoils of war. Thus, in September of 2011, even before Gaddafi's violent murder in October, US Ambassador Gene Cretz "participated in a State Department conference call with about 150 American companies hoping to do business in Libya." As Maximilian Forte emphasizes in his book, US access to infrastructure investment was an even bigger motive for the intervention than access to oil, the business opportunities discussed in this meeting indeed being infrastructure projects.

Other NATO countries had very similar plans. Thus, as the *New*

York Times explained[147] in an article just after the NATO operation ended with the brutal killing of Gaddafi—an article accompanied by a photo of an oil terminal in Misurata, Libya, on fire and with black smoke billowing out—"Western security, construction and infrastructure companies that see profit-making opportunities receding in Iraq and Afghanistan have turned their sights on Libya. . . . Entrepreneurs are abuzz about the business potential of a country with huge needs and the oil to pay for them, plus the competitive advantage of Libyan gratitude toward the United States and its NATO partners." The article continues: "A week before Colonel Qaddafi's death on Oct. 20, a delegation from 80 French companies arrived in Tripoli to meet officials of the Transitional National Council, the interim government. Last week, the new British defense minister, Philip Hammond, urged British companies to 'pack their suitcases' and head to Tripoli."

Forte makes a strong case that the US and other NATO countries—despite some warming of relations with Gaddafi before the February 2011 uprising—had continued to be frustrated with Gaddafi's blocking of infrastructure projects for such US companies as Bechtel and Caterpillar, instead granting these projects to Russian, Chinese, and German concerns. The invasion solved this problem in two big ways. First, of course, the US ensured by its intervention in Libya that a substantial portion of future infrastructure projects would be awarded to US companies. However, the more important, and more diabolical, part of the plan is that the violent intervention itself created the very need for infrastructure projects—what better way to create such a need, after all, than by leveling entire cities to the ground? And, while the US certainly has a great need for infrastructure investment here at home (e.g., to keep cities such as New York from sinking into the sea), such investment has the distinct drawback of having to be paid out of US coffers.

In the case of Libya, as was the case of Iraq, the US devastated the country, thereby creating a great demand for infrastructure projects, and then required the country to pay for the projects out of its own oil revenues. "Vulture capitalism" is indeed too kind a term for this type of creative destruction, for vultures feed off carrion that is already dead; in this case, on the other hand, the US creates the carrion for its corporations to feed on, and at someone else's expense. Brilliant!

As just one example, a quick Google search I ran pulled up a May 31, 2012, article from a business publication called *Venture*,[148] which explained that General Electric alone "expects to generate as much as $10bn in revenue from Libya, as the North African country aims to rebuild its economy, infrastructure, and institutions in the post-Gaddafi era." The same article explains that"[i]n 2011, UK Department of Trade and Investment estimated the value of contracts to rebuild Libya, in areas ranging from electricity and water supplies to healthcare and education, to be upwards of $300 billion over the next 10 years." The article goes on to quote the GE spokesman as rejoicing in the fact that, after the NATO invasion, "'[t]he country needs everything, development of oil and gas, which will create the wealth to improve the life of people, clean water, reliable power, a good healthcare system, building the transportation system both rail as well as the aviation system so that you can get the economy going—all of these things are areas of focus for us in Libya, like we did in Iraq.'"

One can only conclude from this that the West, and especially the United States, is hell-bent on spreading instability throughout the world, despite its pretending to accomplish the very opposite. Indeed, the US continues to bomb Libya periodically in an effort to at least contain the very forces of chaos it helped unleash there.[149]

In chaos, Western countries and their transnational corporations see opportunity for more domination and more profits. As with Little Finger in *Game of Thrones*, they see chaos not as a pit, but as a ladder. In the case of countries like Libya, the West goes in and bombs it to oblivion and then brings in companies that charge that country to rebuild it. And the West is not shy about this grisly strategy for moneymaking.

In addition to short-term moneymaking, moreover, the other goal of the intervention was to pave the way for the greater penetration and domination of Africa. Indeed, with Libya's Pan-Africanist leader Gaddafi out of the way, the US eagle and its newly formed African Central Command (AFRICOM) swooped in to other parts of Africa to begin further penetration of the continent.

Quoting British journalist Dan Glazebrook, Forte explains:

> in taking out Muammar Gaddafi, AFRICOM had actually eliminated the project's fiercest adversary.... Gaddafi ended his political life as a dedicated pan-Africanist and, whatever one thought of the man, it is clear that his vision for Africa was very different from that of the subordinate supplier of cheap labour and raw materials that AFRICOM was created to maintain.
>
> Furthermore, "barely a month after the fall of Tripoli—and in the same month Gaddafi was murdered (October 2011)—the US announced it was sending troops to no less than four more African countries: the Central African Republic, Uganda, South Sudan and the Democratic Republic of Congo." AFRICOM further announced 14 major joint military exercises planned with African states for 2012, an unprecedented number of such exercises.

In short, as King Leopold II before them, the Western "humanitarians" such as Hillary Clinton, Samantha Power, and Susan Rice are not about spreading human rights, but about making the world amenable to maximum exploitation by the West. In the case of Libya, the West was brazen in its outright theft of Libya's riches in the aftermath of the NATO operations, with the Wall Street firm Goldman Sachs "losing" $1.2 billion in Libyan assets[150] and Belgium also "losing" over $5 billion of the $67 billion in Libyan government assets frozen at the outset of the NATO operation.[151]

Sadly, Western human rights groups will not raise a hand to stop such imperial violence and plunder. A perfect example of this is the fact that, after the NATO destruction of Libya, Amnesty International USA hired on Suzanne Nossel as its Executive Director. Suzanne

Nossel, just before being hired by AI, played a direct role while at the US State Department in ginning up the pretexts for the NATO intervention in Libya. As journalist Diana Johnstone explains, "[a]s Deputy Assistant Secretary of State for International Organizations, Ms. Nossel played a role in drafting the United Nations Human Rights Council resolution on Libya. That resolution, based on exaggeratedly alarmist reports, served to justify the UN resolution which led to the NATO bombing campaign that overthrew the Gaddafi regime."[152] Obviously, the NATO war for dominance in Libya fits quite well into the mission of Amnesty International, though it had absolutely no justification in international law.

TWO

Nuremberg and the Rise of International Law

THE DAWN OF THE 20TH century witnessed the first "total war," World War I, in which nations used advanced technological weaponry, including poison gas, machine guns, aerial bombers, tanks, and submarines to inflict huge casualties upon enemy troops and civilians alike.[153] Around 16 million died as a consequence.

Famed historian Eric Hobsbawm describes the carnage on the Western Front, which, in his words, "became a machine for massacre such as had probably never before been seen in the history of warfare." As Hobsbawm explains:

> Millions of men faced each other across the sandbagged parapets of the trenches under which they lived like, and with, rats and lice. From time to time their generals would seek to break out of the deadlock. Days, even weeks of unceasing artillery bombardment—what a German writer later called "hurricanes of steel" (Ernst Junger, 1921)—were to "soften up" the enemy and drive him underground, until at the right moment webs of barbed wire, into "no-man's land," a chaos of waterlogged shell-craters, ruined tree-stumps, mud and

abandoned corpses, to advance into the machine-guns that mowed them down. As they knew they would. The attempt of the Germans to break through at Verdun in 1916 (February–July) was a battle of two millions, with one million casualties. It failed. The British offensive on the Somme, designed to force the Germans to break off the Verdun offensive cost Britain 420,000 dead—60,000 on the first day of the attack. It is not surprising that in the memory of the British and French . . . it remained the "Great War," more terrible and traumatic in memory than the Second World War.[154]

This war, which "ruined both victors and vanquished," was truly a global war on a scale never seen before. As Hobsbawm explains, "The First World War involved *all* major powers and indeed all European states, except Spain, the Netherlands, the three Scandinavian countries and Switzerland.[155] What is more, troops from the world overseas were, often for the first time, sent to fight and work outside their regions." Such foreign troops and "labor battalions" who came to Europe to join the conflict included those from Canada, Australia, New Zealand, India, Africa, China, and of course the United States.[156] And the naval war was fought worldwide.

While World War I was to be, in the words of President Woodrow Wilson, the "war to end all wars," like most promises we are told about war, World War I, and the flawed peace treaty at Versailles that ended it, in fact inevitably led to a much worse conflagration—World War II. World War II had an even greater global reach than its predecessor. As Hobsbawm relates, "[t]hat the Second World War was literally global hardly needs to be demonstrated. Virtually all independent states of the world were involved, willingly or unwillingly," including even Latin American nations to a limited extent, and battles were fought throughout Europe, Russia, China, Japan, Burma, the Philippines, and Northern Africa.[157]

And it goes without saying that the world had never seen carnage and brutality on such a scale ever before, nor has it seen such since. It is estimated that between 70 and 85 million people died in World War II, including around six million Jews who were systematically killed by the Nazis in the Holocaust along with untold numbers of Gypsies, homosexuals, communists, and socialists. And World War II ended, of course, with the only use of nuclear weapons ever—those used by the United States to incinerate Nagasaki and Hiroshima, Japan. In addition, cities like Dresden, Germany, and Tokyo, Japan, were leveled to the ground with conventional aerial weapons by Allied Forces.

However, out of the ashes of these staggering conflicts arose an unprecedented effort to bring those responsible for war crimes to justice. That effort took the form of the acclaimed Nuremberg Trials and Judgment. While most people know about Nuremberg and the trial of German and Japanese leaders for their vast atrocities during the course of the war, what few know or remember is that the prime crime these leaders were tried for and ultimately convicted of was the planning and initiation of the war to begin with—that is, for the "crime against peace" itself.

As the Nuremberg Justices explained in their Judgment of October 1, 1946, they carried out their trials and rendered their judgment pursuant to the Nuremberg Charter, which was initially entered into by the main Allied Powers—the US, UK, France, and the USSR—and then agreed to by nineteen other countries of the newly formed United Nations. As the Justices wrote,

The individual defendants are indicted under Article 6 of the Charter, which is as follows:

> Article 6. The Tribunal established by the Agreement referred to in Article 1 hereof for the trial and punishment of the major war criminals of the European Axis countries shall have the power to try and punish persons who, acting in the interests of the European Axis countries, whether as individuals or as members of organizations, committed any of the following crimes:
>
> The following acts, or any of them, are crimes coming within

the jurisdiction of the Tribunal for which there shall be individual responsibility:

(a) **Crimes Against Peace**: namely, planning, preparation, initiation or waging of a war of aggression, or a war in violation of international treaties, agreements or assurances, or participation in a common plan or conspiracy for the accomplishment of any of the foregoing:

(b) **War Crimes**: namely, violations of the laws or customs of war. Such violations shall include, but not be limited to, murder, ill-treatment or deportation to slave labour or for any other purpose of civilian population of or in occupied territory, murder or ill-treatment of prisoners of war or persons on the seas, killing of hostages, plunder of public or private property, wanton destruction of cities, towns or villages, or devastation not justified by military necessity:

(c) **Crimes Against Humanity**: namely, murder, extermination, enslavement, deportation, and other inhumane acts committed against any civilian population, before or during the war, or persecutions on political, racial or religious grounds in execution of or in connection with any crime within the jurisdiction of the Tribunal, whether or not in violation of the domestic law of the country where perpetrated.

These provisions are binding upon the Tribunal as the law to be applied to the case.

The Nuremberg Justices explained that the Crime Against Peace was the most serious of all the charges against the Defendants. In words oft-quoted, the Justices wrote, "[t]he charges in the Indictment that the defendants planned and waged aggressive wars are charges of the utmost gravity. War is essentially an evil thing. Its consequences are not confined to the belligerent States alone, but affect the whole world. To initiate a war of aggression, therefore, is not only an international crime; it is the supreme international crime differing only from other crimes in that it contains within itself the accumulated evil of the whole."

As "[r]enowned scholar Benjamin Ferencz observed '[t]he most important accomplishment of the Nuremberg trials was the condemnation of illegal war-making as the supreme international crime. . . . Nuremberg was a triumph of Reason over Power. Allowing aggression to remain unpunishable would be a triumph of Power over Reason.'"[158]

Of course, what the Justices said about aggressive war stands to reason. The terrible crimes of the Nazis throughout Europe, including the Holocaust itself, could not have been possible and would never have taken place without the war of aggression Germany commenced and waged against other nations. Indeed, many of the infamous Nazi death camps were not in Germany itself, but in the countries that Germany invaded and vanquished—Auschwitz, Belzec, Chelmno, Majdanek, Sobibor and Treblinka in Poland; Maly Trostenets in Belarus; Janowska and Syrets in Ukraine; and Sajmiste in Serbia.

It is important to note here that the US—the nation we are so often told by the Western "humanitarians" is the bulwark against genocide in the world and that we are to believe saved the day during World War II—did nothing to prevent or stop the genocide of six million Jews by the Nazis. It did not even do the minimum of allowing Jews to find safe haven in the US even when it is was common knowledge that they were being horribly persecuted. And it did nothing because of its own deep-seated racism.

As James Grossman, executive director of the American Historical Association, explained in an op-ed in the *LA Times*,[159] a stroll through the exhibition entitled "Americans and the Holocaust" illustrated the racist policies of the US during WWII:

> It is a sobering journey. Americans knew that something was dreadfully wrong in Germany. As early as 1932, and even more in 1933, popular magazines including *Cosmopolitan, Time,* and *Newsweek*

included major stories on the persecution of Jews in Germany and on Nazi governance. . . .

In 1933, the US ambassador to Germany recorded in his diary Roosevelt's instructions: "The German authorities are treating the Jews shamefully and the Jews in this country are greatly excited. But this is also not a governmental affair." It comes across as cold-hearted in retrospect, but Roosevelt understood his fellow Americans; they would not march to war—or even expend substantial public resources—to save Jews.

. . . Even when 94 percent of polled Americans claimed to "disapprove of the Nazi treatment of Jews in Germany," 71 percent of them opposed permitting any more than a trickle of German Jews to enter the United States—two weeks after Kristallnacht. Two-thirds of Americans opposed admitting refugee children in 1939.

America kept its doors closed to the people for whom they professed sympathy. This sentiment, shaped by racism, was nothing new, nor was it confined to immigrants. One need only cross the Mall to the National Museum of African American History and Culture to be reminded that in the 1850s white Northerners were as repulsed by the suggestion that emancipation would result in black migration northward as they were by the cruelty of slavery.

In addition, the Allies famously did not bomb the Auschwitz death camp even when it knew of its existence, its whereabouts, and the horrible crimes taking place there. As Pope Francis recently decried, "The great powers had photographs of the railway routes that the trains took to the concentration camps, like Auschwitz, to kill the Jews, and also the Christians, and also the Roma, also the homosexuals. . . . Tell me, why didn't they bomb those railroad routes?"[160] One answer to this question should be obvious to all concerned about such matters—that nations and their military forces are not human rights organizations and generally do not operate altruistically or to advance humanitarian concerns.

Indeed, George Kennan, the intellectual author of the US's

post-war foreign policy, in his famous policy statement to the US State Department in 1948, stated with much candor what US warfare is all about: "we have about 50 percent of the world's wealth but only 6.3 percent of its population. This disparity is particularly great as between ourselves and the peoples of Asia. In this situation, we cannot fail to be the object of envy and resentment. Our real task in the coming period is to devise a pattern of relationships which will permit us to maintain this position of disparity without positive detriment to our national security. To do so, we will have to dispense with all sentimentality and day-dreaming; and our attention will have to be concentrated everywhere on our immediate national objectives. We need not deceive ourselves that we can afford today the luxury of altruism and world-benefaction."[161]

And the US has remained true to this realist, self-interested, and nonaltruistic foreign policy to this day. Thus, with less than 5 percent of the world's population, the US consumes "one-third of the world's paper, a quarter of the world's oil, 23 percent of the coal, 27 percent of the aluminum, and 19 percent of the copper. . . . Our per capita use of energy, metals, minerals, forest products, fish, grains, meat, and even fresh water dwarfs that of people living in the developing world."[162] And the US has only been able to maintain this disproportionate share of the world's wealth by constantly waging war upon it, and in particular upon the Global South. Of course, all of this undermines the very idea that there can be a truly "humanitarian" military intervention, and certainly that the US would ever lead one.

The other fact that should be kept in mind when thinking about the lessons to be derived from WWII is that, while it was a nation of the West—namely, Germany—which began the war in the European theater, it was not, as we have been led to believe, the nations of the West that ended it. In fact, any honest historian must recognize that it was the Soviet Union that won the war against Germany, albeit with important help from the UK and US. But even that help came relatively late, with the Soviet Union fighting Germany alone from 1941 until the US and UK finally opened up the Western front with the invasion of

Normandy, France in 1944. An opinion piece in the *Washington Post*, titled, "Don't Forget How the Soviet Union Saved the World from Hitler" explains: "[t]he Red Army was 'the main engine of Nazism's destruction,' . . . The Soviet Union paid the harshest price . . . an estimated 26 million Soviet citizens died during World War II, . . . At the same time, the Germans suffered three-quarters of their wartime losses fighting the Red Army."[163]

In addition, while the Western Allies largely failed to save Jews from the Nazi genocide, the USSR, which famously liberated Auschwitz 75 years ago, actually went out of its way to save tens of thousands of Jews from certain death. Thus, according to James N. Rosenberg, citing figures gathered by the Carnegie Endowment for International Peace, "Russia has saved over ten times as many Jews from Nazi extermination as all the rest of the world put together."[164] As Rosenberg detailed in 1943, "of some 1,750,000 Jews who succeeded in escaping the Axis since the outbreak of hostilities, about 1,600,000 were evacuated by the Soviet government from Eastern Poland and subsequently occupied Soviet territory and transported far into the Russian interior and beyond the Urals."

Acknowledging this reality is important to the current subject of "humanitarian" interventionism, for a critical underpinning of this doctrine is the belief that it was the US and UK that stopped the Nazis and their genocidal crusade, and that it is they who are thereby tasked by history to stop the next genocide. But this doctrine is constructed with a myth stacked upon a myth and collapses quickly upon the most cursory scrutiny.

Meanwhile, the terrible crimes of the Japanese during WWII, including the enslavement of laborers and systematic rape and sexual abuse of Chinese and Korean women, could not have been possible and would never have taken place without the wars of aggression upon China and Korea.

For that matter, the crimes of the Allies also, including the saturation bombing of Dresden, Germany; the cruel firebombing of Tokyo,

Japan; and the nuclear bombing of Nagasaki and Hiroshima would never have taken place either in the absence of the war. Nor would terrible crimes back in the US homeland have taken place, such as the mass internment of the Japanese.

War also was an excuse for the crackdown on free speech in the US, done in the infamous name of preventing "clear and present danger"—that is, the danger of people such as Eugene V. Debs speaking out against the evils of war during WWI, a "crime" for which he received a ten-year jail term before his sentence was commuted after his serving three years in jail. However, he did not leave jail before contracting a cardiovascular illness that would ultimately kill him. Curiously, I had an argument with my Columbia Law Professor—Louis Henkin, who is considered the "father of human rights law"—about this episode, with Henkin arguing with me as I followed him down the hall after class that the case against Debs was rightly decided.

Such horrors, which engulfed the world, happened because of the scourge of aggressive war, and the world wanted to prevent such horrors from taking place again by ensuring future peace and preventing future armed conflict. Therefore, when the nations of the world, in the form of the United Nations, created the UN Charter—the main instrument of international law and relations—they prioritized the prevention of war and the concomitant "maintenance of international peace and security" as their main goals.

As an initial matter, it is important to emphasize the supreme importance of the UN Charter both to international as well as US domestic law. Thus, it is universally recognized that "[t]he UN Charter is the highest treaty in the world, the embodiment of international law that codifies and supersedes all existing international laws and customs. . . . The Charter's legal authority rests with its status as a treaty to which nations have agreed to abide. Violations of a treaty are violations of law no less than are violations of domestic law. In the United States, no legal bright line separates international law from domestic law. Once the US Senate has ratified a treaty, it becomes the 'supreme law of the land' under

Article VI, Clause 2 of the US Constitution. Thus, a violation of the UN Charter is also a violation of domestic law in the United States."[165]

And: "[a]t the heart of the UN Charter is the prohibition against war."[166] Thus, in the Preamble of the UN Charter, the very first stated goal is "to save succeeding generations from the scourge of war, which twice in our lifetime has brought untold sorrow to mankind ."[167]

Then, when they state, still in the Preamble, the ends they wish to achieve, the United Nations sets forth these as the very first goals:

- to practice tolerance and live together in peace with one another as good neighbours, and
- to unite our strength to maintain international peace and security, and
- to ensure, by the acceptance of principles and the institution of methods, that armed force shall not be used, save in the common interest

In Chapter I of the Charter, the UN then sets forth its primary purposes and rules that are to guide and govern nations. Again, the promotion of peace and prevention of war are at the top of this list. Thus, in Article 1, the Charter states:

The Purposes of the United Nations are:

1. To maintain international peace and security, and to that end: to take effective collective measures for the prevention and removal of threats to the peace, and for the suppression of acts of aggression or other breaches of the peace, and to bring about by peaceful means, and in conformity with the principles of justice and international law, adjustment or settlement of international disputes or situations which might lead to a breach of the peace;
2. To develop friendly relations among nations based on respect for the principle of equal rights and self-determination of peoples, and to take other appropriate measures to strengthen universal peace;
3. To achieve international co-operation in solving international

problems of an economic, social, cultural, or humanitarian character, and in promoting and encouraging respect for human rights and for fundamental freedoms for all without distinction as to race, sex, language, or religion; and

4. To be a centre for harmonizing the actions of nations in the attainment of these common ends.

In Article 2, the UN states that all of its Members "shall act in accordance with the following Principles":

1. The Organization is based on the principle of the sovereign equality of all its Members.
2. All Members, in order to ensure to all of them the rights and benefits resulting from membership, shall fulfill in good faith the obligations assumed by them in accordance with the present Charter.
3. All Members shall settle their international disputes by peaceful means in such a manner that international peace and security, and justice, are not endangered.
4. All Members shall refrain in their international relations from the threat or use of force against the territorial integrity or political independence of any state, or in any other manner inconsistent with the Purposes of the United Nations.
5. All Members shall give the United Nations every assistance in any action it takes in accordance with the present Charter, and shall refrain from giving assistance to any state against which the United Nations is taking preventive or enforcement action.
6. The Organization shall ensure that states which are not Members of the United Nations act in accordance with these Principles so far as may be necessary for the maintenance of international peace and security.
7. Nothing contained in the present Charter shall authorize the United Nations to intervene in matters which are essentially within the domestic jurisdiction of any state or shall require the

> Members to submit such matters to settlement under the present Charter; but this principle shall not prejudice the application of enforcement measures under Chapter VII.

Breaking this down a bit, several key international law principles emerge. First, note what should be obvious to all, but which seems to be lost in the daily practice of international relations: that all nations of the world have "sovereign equality"—that is, no nation is more important or privileged under international law than any other. Of course, the only way any rule of law can truly operate is by binding and governing all parties alike, the weak and the strong and the poor and the rich. No one must be above the law, we are so often told.

In keeping with the principle of "sovereign equality," and in the interest of "the maintenance of international peace and security," each nation must respect each other nation's sovereignty and must not use force, or even threaten the use of force, against another nation. Rather, the UN Charter requires that member states "shall settle their international disputes by peaceful means." The foregoing are prime dictates of the UN Charter, though again, one would be forgiven for not knowing this as we witness our own president, Donald Trump, for example, threatening to invade and even annihilate other nations (e.g., North Korea, Iran, Venezuela) on a regular basis.

Lest there be any doubts on the matter, Article 2(7) of the UN Charter makes it clear that the UN shall not "intervene in matters which are essentially within the domestic jurisdiction of any state. . . ." The origins of Article 2(7) highlight that it is a legal prohibition directed against intervention initiated by the developed nations of the North in the affairs of the developing nations of the Global South.

Thus, as the official introductory note in the UN archives explains, "[i]t should be recalled that, already at the founding conference of the United Nations at San Francisco in 1945, as a result of their common historical experiences, Latin American delegates presented a common front which became the driving force leading up to the adoption of

Article 2, paragraph 7, of the Charter, prohibiting interventions by the United Nations in matters essentially within the domestic jurisdiction of any State. Article 2, paragraph 7, of the Charter of the United Nations thus became the master-clause, in legal terms, on non-intervention as imperative legal principle of contemporary international law."[168]

The "historical experiences" referenced here, of course, were centuries of colonial domination and exploitation of the Latin American nations by Spain and then by the United States. As for US interference in Latin America, it must be pointed out that the US had been quite active in intervening in that region with great frequency beginning with the Spanish-American war of 1898—a war in which the US would appropriate Puerto Rico, effectively annex Cuba, and step into Spain's shoes as the colonial power in Latin America and The Philippines.

Thus, between 1898 and 1945, when Article 2(7) was adopted, the US engaged in the following interventions in Latin America and the Caribbean:

- 1901 Platt Amendment to Cuba's new constitution gives the US the unilateral right to intervene in the island's political affairs.
- 1901–11/1903 Repeated interventions in Colombia's Panama Province, capped by Theodore Roosevelt intervene[ing] to assist Panamanian independence from Colombia. The resulting Hay-Bunau-Varilla Treaty makes the US sovereign "in perpetuity" in the ten-mile wide Panama Canal Zone.
- 1904 (Theodore) Roosevelt's Corollary to the Monroe Doctrine declares the US to be the policeman of the Caribbean. US forces place the Dominican Republic under a customs receivership.
- 1905 US Marines land in Honduras.
- 1906–09 Under the Platt Amendment, US forces occupy Cuba and direct its political and economic development.

- 1912 * United Fruit Company begins operations in Honduras and later becomes a major force throughout Central America.
- 1912-25 US Marines intervene in Nicaragua.
- 1914 Panama Canal opens [under US control].
- 1914 US forces shell and then occupy Vera Cruz, Mexico.
- 1915–34 US Marines stationed in Haiti.
- 1916–24 US Marines occupy the Dominican Republic.
- 1917–22 US troops in Cuba.
- 1918 US army lands in Panama to protect United Fruit plantations.
- 1920–21 US troops support a coup in Guatemala.
- 1926–33 US Marines occupy Nicaragua and fight against the nationalistic forces led by Augusto Cesar Sandino.
- 1936–79 US supports three different Somozas as dictators of Nicaragua.[169]

Any interpretation of the UN Charter must take into account this history, which motivated the Latin American nations to insist on the legal principle of nonintervention in the domestic affairs of sovereign states—a principle that would be repeated and reaffirmed by the UN on numerous occasions.

Significantly, Chapter VI of the UN Charter is titled "Pacific Settlement of Disputes," and Article 33(1) expressly requires that "the parties to any dispute, the continuance of which is likely to endanger the maintenance of international peace and security, shall, first of all, seek a solution by negotiation, enquiry, mediation, conciliation, arbitration, judicial settlement, resort to regional agencies or arrangements, or other peaceful means of their own choice."

The UN Charter then goes on to set up two main avenues for helping states settle their differences peacefully, for preventing war, and for ensuring that member states live up to their international law commitments. First and foremost, the Charter makes it clear, in Chapter VII, titled "Action with Respect to Threats to the Peace, Breaches of the Peace, and Acts of Aggression," that member states must bring their concerns with other states to the UN Security Council rather than taking matters into their own hands. It is the Security Council that has a monopoly on the authority to order "enforcement measures," including both military action and economic sanction, in the interest of maintaining international peace and security and enforcing the Charter. Individual states are not to make the decision on their own to carry out such "enforcement measures."

The only exception to this, and it is a quite narrow one, lay in Article 51 of the UN Charter, which provides that "[n]othing in the present Charter shall impair the inherent right of individual or collective self-defense if an armed attack occurs against a Member of the United Nations, until the Security Council has taken measures necessary to maintain international peace and security. Measures taken by Members in the exercise of this right of self-defense shall be immediately reported to the Security Council and shall not in any way affect the authority and responsibility of the Security Council under the present Charter to take at any time such action as it deems necessary in order to maintain or restore international peace and security."

Thus, nations may take necessary action against another state, including military action, if and only if they are the victim of "an armed attack," and even then, the state engaging in self-defense must report its actions to the Security Council, which then must then decide how to resolve the situation.

Moreover, even the Security Council has limits on its authority to use force as world-renowned human rights scholar, Professor Francis A. Boyle, has explained.[170] First and foremost, Article 24(2) requires that "[i]n discharging these duties [to promote international peace and security] the Security Council shall act in accordance with the Purposes and Principles of the United Nations." That is, the Security Council does not have boundless authority. Rather, it must act in accordance with the UN Charter and its requirements, for example, that national sovereignty be respected; that all efforts be made to resolve disputes peacefully; that all state parties are equal; and that force be used only as a last resort.

As Boyle notes, Article 39 of the UN Charter requires that, as a prerequisite to resorting to force, the Security Council "shall determine the existence of any threat to the peace, breach of the peace, or act of aggression. . . ." And, even once it makes this determination, Article 40 requires that the Security Council order the parties in dispute to abide by "provisional measures" of the Security Council's choosing to try to ward off war.

In addition to the Security Council, Chapter VIII of the UN Charter allows for the creation of "regional arrangements or agencies for dealing with such matters relating to the maintenance of international peace and security as are appropriate for regional action provided that such arrangements or agencies and their activities are consistent with the Purposes and Principles of the United Nations." Such regional arrangements that have been created pursuant to Chapter VIII are the Organization of American States, the European Union, and the African Union.

And, as usual, Chapter VIII, Article 52 requires that

1. The Members of the United Nations entering into such arrangements or constituting such agencies shall make every effort to achieve pacific settlement of local disputes through such regional arrangements or by such regional agencies before referring them to the Security Council.
2. The Security Council shall encourage the development of pacific settlement of local disputes through such regional arrangements or by such regional agencies either on the initiative of the states concerned or by reference from the Security Council.

Again, the peaceful resolution of disputes by these regional arrangements is required.

The other mechanism created by the Charter (in Chapter XIV) for peacefully resolving issues between nations is the International Court of Justice (ICJ or World Court) to which states may submit disputes for binding resolution. The ICJ is empowered by the Charter to interpret and apply international law—including the UN Charter, covenants, treaties, and customary international law—to resolve such disputes, and the state parties to ICJ cases are obligated to follow the decision of the World Court. As Article 94 provides, "[e]ach Member of the United Nations undertakes to comply with the decision of the International Court of Justice in any case to which it is a party."

In short, the paramount instrument of international law, the UN Charter, is clear: it prohibits aggressive war and the use of force and requires that nations instead attempt to resolve their differences through peaceful means such as negotiation and mediation. Sadly, these clear legal precepts have, as legal scholars unanimously agree, "fallen into disuse."[171] Indeed, as far back of 1971, Noam Chomsky, a strong proponent of the need for the US to abide by Articles 2(4) and (2) of the UN Charter and their prohibition of the use of force, lamented in a *Yale Law Journal* article even then that these Articles had practically been written out of the Charter.[172]

However, these principles have not simply "fallen" or disappeared through magic; they have been intentionally undermined and destroyed by the US and its Western allies so that they could pursue their policy of eternal war on the world in pursuit of profit and domination. And the tool for systematically chipping away at these legal precepts has been the doctrine of "humanitarian" intervention—a tool that is wielded selectively as a sword against the West's ostensible enemies and as a shield for the West and its own misdeeds.

Indeed, even at Nuremberg and soon thereafter, we see the Allies beginning to selectively create and apply rules of law and administer justice. For example, as Noam Chomsky also noted in his 1971 *Yale Law Journal* article, the Allies exempted their own crimes—and in particular their carpet bombing of cities like Dresden, Germany, and Tokyo, Japan, and their obliteration of Nagasaki and Hiroshima with nuclear weapons—from prosecution. This was, indeed, a classic case of "victor's justice"—a form of justice the world would witness time and again in the years to come.

In addition, while it should be obvious to honest observers, the Allies made a key, fateful decision in how to mete out justice and remedy for the Holocaust—a supreme crime carried out, of course, by Germany, a Western nation that would quickly be forgiven and welcomed back into the fold as a "Great Power." That is, they made the Palestinian people, and not the Germans, pay for this crime by helping to create Israel as a refuge for Jews in the form of a Jewish state, with little to no regard for the hundreds of thousands of Palestinians already living there. What quickly followed was the violent ethnic cleansing of over 700,000 Palestinians in what is now known as the Nakba, meaning, "catastrophe."

And, in truth, the Palestinians, whose land, property, resources, and rights continue to be whittled away at by Israel, to the point where the UN now predicts that the Palestinian territory of Gaza will be unlivable by 2020—that is, dear reader, by the time you are reading this book—continue to pay for this crime they had nothing to do with. As the UN announced in 2018:[173]

> MICHAEL LYNK, Special Rapporteur on the Situation of Human Rights in the Palestinian Territories Occupied Since 1967, drew attention to Israel's persistent non-cooperation with the Special Rapporteur's mandate. As with his two predecessors, Israel has not granted him entry to visit the country, nor the Occupied Palestinian territory. He recalled that cooperation is a fundamental obligation of the Charter of the United Nations. The World Bank described Gaza's economy in free fall, contracting by 6 per cent during the first quarter of 2018. In fact, the United Nations has stated that Gaza may well be unlivable by 2020: safe drinking water has almost disappeared, the economy is cratering and "the state of unlive-ability is upon us," he said, urging the international community to insist that all parties bring an immediate end to this disaster.

In response to this inflicted misery, Gazans organized the "Great March of Return," he recalled. To date, in the context of these demonstrations, more than 200 Palestinians have been killed, including 40 children. Almost 23,000 Palestinians have been injured, with half of them requiring hospitalization. In addition, the West Bank village of Khan al-Ahmar is being threatened with complete demolition by Israel, which plans to build new settlements and annex the area. The settlements are a grave breach of international law. Israel's Knesset has adopted a number of laws that are a flashing green light for more formal annexation steps. For the past 50 years, "the international community has been playing checkers while Israel plays chess," he said, stressing that a deep-rooted problem at the heart of this conflict is the lack of clarity of international law.

The situation has deteriorated so badly that UN Secretary-General António Guterres has recently proposed sending a military or police force to Gaza and the West Bank to protect the Palestinians from Israel's intensifying predations, especially "[t]he targeting of civilians, particularly children" by Israeli security forces.[174]

In other words, Guterres is calling for a "humanitarian" intervention in the Palestinian Territories. But such an intervention to protect the Palestinian people will never happen, and the US, with support from the Western "humanitarians," will ensure that it will not happen. This is because, in practice, "humanitarian" intervention is carried out to protect the West's economic and strategic interests against those in the Global South struggling to take control of their own resources and their very fate—not the other way around. And so, the Palestinian people will keep fitting the bill for Germany's WWII crimes down to the very last Palestinian.

THREE

Peace Is a Paramount Human Right

MEANWHILE, ONCE THE CHARTER WAS agreed to, the UN General Assembly got busy drafting what would become the most important and most cited human rights instrument in the world—the Universal Declaration of Human Rights (UDHR). While the UDHR is not a binding, international covenant, it is nonetheless the most influential human rights document and would give rise to binding human rights covenants.

As the introductory note to the UDHR on the UN website, written by Antônio Augusto Cançado Trindade, former president of the Inter-American Court of Human Rights, explains:

> When the General Assembly of the United Nations adopted, on 10 December 1948, the Universal Declaration of Human Rights, in one of the brief spells of enlightenment in the twentieth century, one could hardly anticipate that a historical process of generalization of the international protection of human rights was being launched, on a truly universal scale. Throughout the last six decades, of remarkable historical projection, the Declaration has gradually acquired an authority which its draftsmen could not have foreseen.[175]

The introductory note relates that this "happened mainly because successive generations of human beings, from distinct cultures and all over the world, recognized in it a 'common standard of achievement' (as originally proclaimed), which corresponded to their deepest and most legitimate aspirations."

Underscoring the importance of the UDHR, the note continues:

> The 1948 Universal Declaration of Human Rights is widely recognized as having inspired, and paved the way for, the adoption of more than seventy human rights treaties, applied today on a permanent basis at global and regional levels (all containing references to it in their preambles). In addition, the Universal Declaration served as a model for the enactment of numerous human rights norms in national constitutions and legislations, and helped to ground decisions of national and international courts. The Universal Declaration, moreover, is today widely recognized as an authoritative interpretation of human rights provisions of the Charter of the United Nations itself, heralding the transformation of the social and international order to secure the enjoyment of the proclaimed rights.

And incredibly, the UDHR has been translated into 520 different languages!

What is notable about the UDHR, moreover, is that it fully recognizes that peace, national sovereignty, and human rights are inextricably linked. Indeed, the very first paragraph of the Preamble states that "recognition of the inherent dignity and of the equal and inalienable rights of all members of the human family is the foundation of freedom, justice and peace in the world." The Preamble further states that "it is essential to promote the development of friendly relations between nations."[176]

Article 2 provides, furthermore, that in regard to the exercise of human rights, "no distinction shall be made on the basis of the political, jurisdictional or international status of the country or territory to which a person belongs, whether it be independent, trust, non-self-governing or under any other limitation of sovereignty." That is to say that all state and other national entities are equal under international law, and all peoples within those states and entities are equal, as well.

Article 28 further provides that "[e]veryone is entitled to a social and international order in which the rights and freedoms set forth in this Declaration can be fully realized." And, in Article 29, it is emphasized that "[t]hese rights and freedoms [of the UDHR] may in no case be exercised contrary to the purposes and principles of the United Nations." Given the clear purpose of the UN to eliminate war and promote international peace, it is clear that the "international order" all human beings have a right to is a peaceful one, free from aggressive war.

Lest there be any doubt about the meaning of the UDHR in these respects, the introductory note to the UDHR relates that, with "the first International Conference on Human Rights (Teheran, April to May, 1968), two decades after the adoption of the Universal Declaration, . . . the reassertion of the holistic view and interrelatedness of all human rights (nowadays universally acknowledged) took place. . . ." The Proclamation of Teheran[177] is unambiguous as to how freedom from war and aggression is crucial to the exercise of human rights.

The Proclamation of Teheran, which laments the fact that we live "in an age when conflict and violence prevail in many parts of the world," states unequivocally that "peace is the universal aspiration of mankind and that peace and justice are indispensable to the full realization of human rights and fundamental freedoms. . . ." The Proclamation further states that "[m]assive denials of human rights, **arising out of aggression or any armed conflict** with their tragic consequences, and resulting in untold human misery, engender reactions which could engulf the world in ever growing hostilities. It is the obligation of the international community to co-operate in eradicating such scourges." (emphasis added)

The Proclamation also sets forth as a key goal disarmament, explaining that "[d]isarmament would release immense human and material resources now devoted to military purposes. These resources should be used for the promotion of human rights and fundamental freedoms. General and complete disarmament is one of the highest aspirations of all people."

As the introductory note to the UDHR also explains, the details of how the goals and principles of the UDHR were to be implemented were later set forth in the Vienna Declaration and Programme of Action, as adopted by the World Conference on Human Rights on 25 June 1993.[178] And again, the Vienna Declaration is explicitly antiwar, anticolonialist, and anti-interventionist.

Thus, the Preamble of the Vienna Declaration emphasizes "the determination expressed in the Preamble of the Charter of the United Nations to save succeeding generations from the scourge of war,"

Paragraph 2 of the Vienna Declaration makes it clear that "[a]ll peoples have the right of self-determination. By virtue of that right they freely determine their political status, and freely pursue their economic, social and cultural development." The Vienna Declaration makes it clear that, in pursuing this right of self-determination, the peoples of the world have the right to engage in anticolonialist struggle. Thus, the Declaration states:

> Taking into account the particular situation of peoples under colonial or other forms of alien domination or foreign occupation, the World Conference on Human Rights recognizes the right of peoples to take any legitimate action, in accordance with the Charter of the United Nations, to realize their inalienable right of self-determination. The World Conference on Human Rights considers the denial of the right of self-determination as a violation of human rights and underlines the importance of the effective realization of this right. In accordance with the Declaration on Principles of International Law concerning Friendly Relations and Cooperation Among States in accordance with the Charter of the United Nations, this shall not be construed as authorizing or encouraging any action which would dismember or

impair, totally or in part, the territorial integrity or political unity of sovereign and independent States conducting themselves in compliance with the principle of equal rights and self-determination of peoples and thus possessed of a Government representing the whole people belonging to the territory without distinction of any kind.

These words should ring in one's ears as we witness the current attempt of the US to dismember and control Syria, and as the "humanitarian" interventionists push for more intervention in Syria rather than less. The Vienna Declaration draws the direct link between war and human rights abuses as well as humanitarian crises in the world, stating, for example, "that gross violations of human rights, **including in armed conflicts**, are among the multiple and complex factors leading to displacement of people." (emphasis added). The drafters of the Declaration further express their "dismay at massive violations of human rights especially in the form of genocide, 'ethnic cleansing' and systematic rape of women **in war situations**, creating mass exodus of refugees and displaced persons. While strongly condemning such abhorrent practices it reiterates the call that perpetrators of such crimes be punished and such practices immediately stopped." (emphasis added). And similarly, the Vienna Declaration laments the "violations of human rights **during armed conflicts**, affecting the civilian population, especially women, children, the elderly and the disabled." (emphasis added).

The Vienna Declaration reflects what the drafters of the UN Charter and its progeny have recognized for many years—that armed conflict and war is destructive to the rights of people in ways predictable and not, intended and unintended. An example of a huge unintended consequence of US military buildup and war-making is the devastating toll this is taking upon the environment and the world's climate. As a report from the Watson Institute at Brown University explains:[179]

In its quest for security, the United States spends more on the military than any other country in the world, certainly much more than the combined military spending of its major rivals, Russia and China. Authorized at over $700 billion in Fiscal Year 2019, and again over $700 billion requested for FY2020, the Department of Defense (DOD) budget comprises more than half of all federal discretionary spending each year. With an armed force of more than two million people, eleven nuclear aircraft carriers, and the most advanced military aircraft, the US is more than capable of projecting power anywhere in the globe, and with "Space Command," into outer space. Further, the US has been continuously at war since late 2001, with the US military and State Department currently engaged in more than 80 countries in counterterror operations.

All this capacity for and use of military force requires a great deal of energy, most of it in the form of fossil fuel. . . . Indeed, the DOD is the world's largest institutional user of petroleum and correspondingly, the single largest producer of greenhouse gases (GHG) in the world. . . . The best estimate of US military greenhouse gas emissions from 2001, when the wars began with the US invasion of Afghanistan, through 2017, is that the US military has emitted 1,212 million metric tons of greenhouse gases (measured in CO2equivalent, or CO2e). In 2017, for example, the Pentagon's greenhouse gas emissions were greater than the greenhouse gas emissions of entire industrialized countries as Sweden or Denmark. DOD emissions for all military operations from 2001 to 2017 are estimated to be about 766 million metric tons of CO2e. And of these military operations, it is estimated that total war-related emissions including for the "overseas contingency operations" in the major war zones of Afghanistan, Pakistan, Iraq and Syria, five are more than 400 Million Metric Tons of CO2e.

Any discussion of the US use of force to allegedly advance the interests of humanity must include the discussion of how the US's military is destroying the environment, which sustains humanity. Sadly, this rarely, if ever, figures into the talking points of the West's "humanitarian" warriors.

Meanwhile, the Vienna Declaration "calls upon States to refrain from any unilateral measure not in accordance with international law and the Charter of the United Nations that creates obstacles to trade relations among States and impedes the full realization of the human rights set forth in the Universal Declaration of Human Rights and international human rights instruments, in particular the rights of everyone to a standard of living adequate for their health and well-being, including food and medical care, housing and the necessary social services. The World Conference on Human Rights affirms that food should not be used as a tool for political pressure."

This is an important provision, for it makes clear that unilateral economic sanctions imposed by powerful countries such as the US upon the Global South (most notably upon Iran, Venezuela, Cuba, Nicaragua, and North Korea) are not permitted. This is a fact lost upon many human rights groups that are either silent or even supportive of such unilateral measures as somehow representing a nonviolent form of coercion.

But such measures are, in reality, far from nonviolent. For example, the US sanctions against Venezuela alone were, according to economists Jeffrey Sachs and Mark Weisbrot, responsible for the deaths of 40,000 Venezuelans in one year alone due to the sanctions' resulting denial of Venezuela's ability to obtain food and life-saving medicines[180] —a clear violation of the Vienna Declaration. Sachs and Weisbrot also argue persuasively that such sanctions constitute collective punishment in contravention of the Geneva Conventions. At the same time, the Red Cross has condemned the failure to fund the Red Cross's and other humanitarian aid programs to Venezuela, clearly laying blame on the US and others interested in regime change. As *Telesur* reported,

> The president of the International Federation of the Red Cross (IFRC) has criticized the "unacceptable" politicization of humanitarian aid to Venezuela.
>
> Speaking in a press conference in Geneva on Monday, Francesco

Rocca denounced a lack of funding for the organization's programs in Venezuela.

"This is not about resources, this is about political will," he told reporters, adding that less than ten percent of the IFRC's September US $50 million emergency appeal had been met.

Rocca went on to state that aid programs run by United Nations agencies and other international actors in Venezuela were being likewise underfunded, slamming the privation of aid "as a tool to destabilize the country."[181]

How one could argue, as nearly all US politicians as well the compliant press do, that the US is advancing humanitarian efforts in Venezuela by destabilizing the nation and denying it humanitarian aid is simply baffling. But this shows just how powerful, and powerfully distorting, the religion of "humanitarian" interventionism is.

The next leap forward in the development of international human rights was the International Covenant on Civil and Political Rights (ICCPR) of 1966.[182] This is a binding international human rights document that even the US has ratified and is one of the premier instrument requiring states to guarantee enforceable human rights to their citizens. While the ICCPR focuses on key human rights such as the right to life, liberty, physical integrity, free speech, assembly, religion, due process, voting, etc., it also highlights the importance of nonintervention and anticolonialism to the maintenance of such rights.

Thus, right up front, in Article 1, the ICCPR provides the following:

1. All peoples have the right of self-determination. By virtue of that right they freely determine their political status and freely pursue their economic, social and cultural development.
2. All peoples may, for their own ends, freely dispose of their natural wealth and resources without prejudice to any obligations arising out of international economic co-operation, based upon

the principle of mutual benefit, and international law. In no case may a people be deprived of its own means of subsistence.

3. The States Parties to the present Covenant, including those having responsibility for the administration of Non-Self-Governing and Trust Territories, shall promote the realization of the right of self-determination, and shall respect that right, in conformity with the provisions of the Charter of the United Nations.

Again, this core human rights document recognizes what should be self-evident—that international human rights standards are worthless if the stronger countries can intervene in the weaker ones with the purpose of interfering with and/or dictating their economic, social, and cultural development, or to exploit these countries' natural resources for their own purposes. That is why, first and foremost, all peoples have the right to self-determination—that is, the right to determine their own destiny without outside interference. This right, moreover, is simply antithetical to the self-proclaimed license of the Great Powers to intervene in other states because they judge the poorer states to have inferior political or economic systems.

This right of countries to "freely dispose of their natural wealth and resources," moreover, is often trampled upon, quite ironically, in the name of democracy and human rights. For example, as I write these words, there has just been a coup in Bolivia that has toppled the government of President Evo Morales. This coup was preceded, and indeed largely precipitated, by US government and media claims, echoed loudly by the Organization of American States (OAS), that Morales is a dictator and that his recent reelection was marked by irregularities that warranted a rerun election.[183] Though a statistical analysis of the vote count by the Center for Economic Policy Research (CEPR) showed that there really were no election irregularities,[184] and despite the fact that Morales agreed to a new election, the coup proceeded nonetheless to great applause by the US press, which declared that democracy in Bolivia had been restored. For his part, Trump promised more coups in Latin America, particularly in Nicaragua and Venezuela.[185]

But of course, the real story of the coup is much more nuanced. As a few commentators in the alternative press have noted:

> . . . the Bolivia coup may be linked to a decision by Morales on November 4 to cancel a "December 2018 agreement with Germany's ACI Systems Alemania (ACISA) [which] came after weeks of protests from residents of the Potosí area. The region has 50 percent to 70 percent of the world's lithium reserves in the Salar de Uyuni salt flats."
>
> Morales canceled the contract while Western press spread allegations that election fraud occurred in Bolivia. Industry players that rely on Bolivia's lithium were apparently confident that "political calmness" would be restored soon enough, and they would return to business as usual.[186]

Afghanistan's huge lithium reserves, as revealed in a 2007 Pentagon memo, are also a big motivating reason for the US's continued occupation of that country. As the *New York Times* reported in 2010, "[t]he United States has discovered nearly $1 trillion in untapped mineral deposits in Afghanistan, far beyond any previously known reserves. . . . The previously unknown deposits—including huge veins of iron, copper, cobalt, gold and critical industrial metals like lithium—are so big and include so many minerals that are essential to modern industry that Afghanistan could eventually be transformed into one of the most important mining centers in the world, the United States officials believe. An internal Pentagon memo, for example, states that Afghanistan could become the 'Saudi Arabia of lithium,' a key raw material in the manufacture of batteries for laptops and BlackBerrys."[187]

Meanwhile, calm has not been restored in Bolivia, with the police and military attacking pro-Morales demonstrators, most of whom are indigenous as Morales himself is, with brutal violence.[188] Condemning both the US and the OAS for their role in the Bolivian coup, former

Uruguayan President Jose "Pepe" Mujica—known as the world's poorest president—stated quite correctly, "The vision of Latin America from Washington is not the vision of Latin America of our Indigenous, broke, forgotten, subdued, trampled people."[189]

But this, of course, is business as usual, and the predictable consequence of outside intervention into another country's internal affairs. And that is precisely why such intervention is prohibited by international law. But again, the Western "humanitarians" are unconcerned about this aspect of international law.

Thus, for example, Human Rights Watch and its director, Kenneth Roth, have applauded the military coup in Bolivia as a restoration of democracy. Thus, Roth gleefully tweeted, "Bolivia's Evo Morales was 'the casualty of a counter-revolution aimed at defending democracy against electoral fraud & his own illegal candidacy,'"[190] ignoring the fact that the claims of "electoral fraud" have now been debunked by at least two independent studies.[191]

Roth continued his tweet, claiming that "[t]he army w/drew its support because it was not prepared to fire on people in order to sustain him in power." However, it is now incontrovertible that the army is willing to fire on its own people to keep Morales out of power and to keep the indigenous people down, but this, apparently, is of no moment. Moreover, it is simply incredible that Roth could find a restoration of democracy in the self-declaration of Jeanine Añez as Bolivian president though her party had received only 4 percent of the vote share in the October elections, and though she has openly called for the ethnic cleansing of Bolivian indigenous from the cities and for "taking all measures necessary to 'pacify' the population."[192] This should not be all too surprising, of course, given the prior positions of Human Rights Watch, for example its remaining "relatively silent on the [2009] Honduran coup d'état that deposed leftist President Manuel Zelaya, and the repression that came after."[193]

The next significant international covenant to be drafted and ratified by most of the world's nations (a total of 170 thus far), but of course not by the United States, is the International Covenant on Economic, Social & Cultural Rights (ICESCR).[194] The ICESCR, along with the UDHR and the ICCPR, are the three pillars of the international human rights system and are known collectively as "The International Bill of Rights."[195]

As the name suggests, the ICESCR focuses on individuals' access to certain economic and social rights, including the right to work with decent wages and working conditions; the right to leisure and rest; the right to form trade unions and to strike; the right to social security and social insurance; paid maternity leave; adequate food, clothing, and housing; the right to education; the right to proper medical care; etc.

But again, the nations of the world recognized that these rights too depend upon peace, the protection of national sovereignty, and the prevention of intervention to be fully realized. For example, the ICESCR, just as the ICCPR, expressly provides right up front in Article I that:

1. All peoples have the right of self-determination. By virtue of that right they freely determine their political status and freely pursue their economic, social and cultural development.
2. All peoples may, for their own ends, freely dispose of their natural wealth and resources without prejudice to any obligations arising out of international economic co-operation, based upon the principle of mutual benefit, and international law. In no case may a people be deprived of its own means of subsistence.

The ICSECR also requires all state parties to realize the rights provided in the Covenant "to the maximum of its available resources." Implicit in this, of course, is that states should focus their resources on obtaining these goals rather than, for example, putting their resources into its military and war-making capabilities. President Dwight D. Eisenhower—a former general of course and the individual who coined the term "military-industrial complex" and warned of its dangers—famously recognized the connection between military spending and a nation's ability to take care of its people's needs, stating that "[e]very gun that is made, every warship launched, every rocket fired signifies, in the final sense, a theft from those who hunger and are not fed, those who are cold and are not clothed. This world in arms is not spending money alone. It is spending the sweat of its laborers, the genius of its scientists, the hopes of its children."

And of course, this stands to reason. But on this score, the US is famously lacking, spending more on its military than nearly all the other countries in the world *combined* and consequently falling further and further behind in its duty to provide for its people. As the National Priorities Project, an advocacy group that tracks US military spending, explains, "[t]he US outpaces all other nations in military expenditures. World military spending totaled more than $1.6 trillion in 2015. The US accounted for 37 percent of the total. US military expenditures are roughly the size of the next seven largest military budgets around the world, combined."[196]

The results of this binge spending on the military has been, as President Eisenhower predicted, mass deprivation in the land of plenty. The Human Rights Council, a UN Charter organization and the highest human rights body in the world, recently detailed this misery in a comprehensive document titled "Report of the Special Rapporteur on extreme poverty and human rights on his mission to the United States of America." As the Human Rights Council, from which the US actually withdrew around the same time as the publication of this report, explains:

> The United States is a land of stark contrasts. It is one of the world's wealthiest societies, a global leader in many areas, and a land of unsurpassed technological and other forms of innovation. Its corporations are global trendsetters, its civil society is vibrant and sophisticated and its higher education system leads the world. But its immense wealth and expertise stand in shocking contrast with the conditions

in which vast numbers of its citizens live. About 40 million live in poverty, 18.5 million in extreme poverty, and 5.3 million live in Third World conditions of absolute poverty. It has the highest youth poverty rate in the Organization for Economic Cooperation and Development (OECD), and the highest infant mortality rates among comparable OECD States. Its citizens live shorter and sicker lives compared to those living in all other rich democracies, eradicable tropical diseases are increasingly prevalent, and it has the world's highest incarceration rate, one of the lowest levels of voter registrations in among OECD countries and the highest obesity levels in the developed world.[197]

As the Human Rights Council, citing an IMF report, explains, the high poverty rates in the US, moreover, are "creating disparities in the education system, hampering human capital formation and eating into future productivity." The Human Rights Council declares the American Dream dead, writing, "[d]efenders of the status quo point to the United States as the land of opportunity and the place where the American dream can come true because the poorest can aspire to the ranks of the richest. But today's reality is very different. The United States now has one of the lowest rates of intergenerational social mobility of any of the rich countries."

In addition, the Human Rights Council complains about how the homeless are criminalized and grossly neglected in the US. In one quite telling line, the HRC writes, "The criminalization of homeless individuals in cities that provide almost zero public toilets seems particularly callous. In June 2017, it was reported that the approximately 1,800 homeless individuals on Skid Row in Los Angeles had access to only nine public toilets. . . . **Los Angeles failed to meet even the minimum standards the United Nations High Commissioner for Refugees sets for refugee camps in the Syrian Arab Republic and other emergency situations.**" (emphasis added)

The HRC also points out how the US is a virtual Dickensian nightmare, with poor people being thrown in jail because they are poor and in court-imposed debt; that is, into old-fashioned debtors' prisons. As the HRC explains:

> In many cities and counties, the criminal justice system is effectively a system for keeping the poor in poverty while generating revenue to fund not only the justice system but many other programs. The use of the legal system to raise revenue, not to promote justice, as was documented so powerfully in a 2015 report on Ferguson, Missouri by the Department of Justice, is pervasive around the country.
>
> So-called fines and fees are piled up so that low level infractions become immensely burdensome, a process that affects only the poorest members of society, who pay the vast majority of such penalties. Driving licences are also commonly suspended for a wide range of non-driving related offences, such as a failure to pay fines. This is a perfect way to ensure that the poor, living in communities that have steadfastly refused to invest in serious public transport systems, are unable to earn a living that might have helped to pay the outstanding debt. Two paths are open: penury, or driving illegally, thus risking even more serious and counterproductive criminalization.
>
> Another practice that affects the poor almost exclusively is that of setting large bail bonds for a defendant who seeks to go free pending trial. Some 11 million people are admitted to local jails annually, and on any given day more than 730,000 people are being held, of whom almost two thirds are awaiting trial, and thus presumed to be innocent. Yet judges have increasingly set large bail amounts, which means that wealthy defendants can secure their freedom, while poor defendants are likely to stay in jail, with all of the consequences in terms of loss of their jobs, disruption of their childcare, inability to pay rent, and a dive into deeper destitution.

As the HRC concludes, "[p]unishing and imprisoning the poor is the distinctively American response to poverty in the twenty-first century."

A quite shocking example of the Dickensian nature of the US's very real debtors' prison system was recently reported in Utah. As the *Salt Lake Tribune* notes, in spite of debtors' prisons being ruled banned by the US Congress in 1833, they continue to thrive for the benefit of predatory loan companies that lend money to needy and desperate individuals at usury interest rates:

> Across Utah, high-interest lenders filed 66 percent of all small claims cases heard between September 2017 and September 2018, according to a new analysis of court records conducted by a team led by Christopher Peterson, a law professor at the University of Utah. . . .
>
> Companies can sue for up to $11,000 in Utah's small claims courts, which are stripped of certain formalities: There are rarely lawyers, judges are not always legally trained and the rules of evidence don't apply.
>
> Lenders file thousands of cases every year. When defendants don't show up—and they often don't—the lenders win by default. Once a judgment is entered, companies can garnish borrowers' paychecks and seize their property. If borrowers fail to attend a supplemental hearing to answer questions about their income and assets, companies can ask the court to issue a bench warrant for their arrest.[198]

The *Salt Lake Tribune* makes it clear that this is happening throughout the country, for example in Kansas, where people are suffering the same fate as the result of crushing medical debt.

Similarly, as a fourteen-month study in Mississippi demonstrated, the state is running "restitution centers" that are nothing more than modern debtors' prisons where people convicted of the pettiest of crimes are forced to work off debts, including at employers like McDonald's, many not knowing if or when they have actually paid enough to be free. The result is that many actually overpay their debts, after first paying the courts, of course. As *Mississippi Today* explains:[199]

> The Mississippi Department of Corrections runs the modern-day debtors prisons it calls restitution centers. But not very well.

The agency doesn't keep close track of how much people sentenced to the program earn and owe, according to dozens of current and former inmates interviewed by *Mississippi Today*. That makes it hard for them to figure out how long they need to work at mostly low-wage jobs to make enough money to earn their freedom.

Mississippi prohibits the workers from handling their own earnings and gives them little documentation of their debts. Where their money goes and whether it reaches the victims of their crimes remains a mystery to most inmates we talked to.

The state doesn't even keep accurate records on who is in the program at any given time, how many people judges send there each year or how long they stay, according to data analyzed by *Mississippi Today* and The Marshall Project.

Oversight is so lax that a guard at one restitution center was able to steal more than $1,000 of inmates' paychecks over four months.

If some of this sounds familiar, by the way, it should, for this process of locking people up for simply being too poor to pay fines and fees the courts know are too exorbitant for them to pay is exactly how, as described in the book *Slavery by Another Name*, African Americans continued to be enslaved even decades after the Civil War.

And such enslavement continues to this day, with prisoners being forced to engage in all sorts of labor for next to no compensation. The most famous case of this, of course, involves the devastating fires in California, which are now being largely fought by poorly paid prisoners who are being paid $2 a day to risk their lives to do so.[200] In addition, billionaire Michael Bloomberg, now running for president as a Democrat, has admitted that he used female prison labor to make calls for his presidential election campaign.[201] As *The Intercept* noted, "[t]he workers were required to disclose that the calls were paid for by the Bloomberg campaign. They did not tell voters they were calling from inside a prison more than 1,500 miles away."[202]

Pulitzer Prize recipient Chris Hedges details the current state of prison labor in the United States and its massive scale:

> The roughly one million prisoners who work for corporations and government industries in the American prison system are a blueprint for what the corporate state expects us all to become. Corporations have no intention of permitting prison reforms to reduce the size of their bonded workforce. In fact, they are seeking to replicate these conditions throughout society.
>
> The American prison-industrial complex, which holds 2.3 million prisoners—22 percent of the world's prison population—makes money by keeping prisons full. It demands bodies, regardless of race, sex or ethnicity. As the system drains the pool of black male bodies, it has begun to incarcerate others. Women—the fastest growing segment of the US prison population—are swelling prisons, as are poor whites, Latinos, and immigrants.
>
> States, in the name of austerity, have stopped providing prisoners with essential items including shoes, blankets, and even toilet paper, while starting to charge them for electricity and room and board.
>
> Most of the prison functions once handled by governments have become privatized. Corporations run prison commissaries and, since the prisoners have nowhere else to shop, often jack up prices by as much as 100 percent. Corporations have taken over the phone systems and grossly overcharge prisoners and their families. They demand exorbitant fees for money transfers from families to prisoners. And corporations, with workshops inside prisons, pay little more than a dollar a day to prison laborers.[203]

The other distinctive feature of the US's prison system is its uniquely high detention of children. Thus, a recent, 2019 UN study concluded that the US has the highest rate of child detention on Earth, including 100,000 children being held in immigrant detention in violation of international law, including the Convention on the Rights of the

Child[204]—a Convention that every UN nation has ratified with one sole exception: the United States. This 100,000 figure is astounding, given that the total figure of children in detention worldwide is 330,000,[205] meaning that the US houses nearly one-third of all of the world's detained children.

Meanwhile, as the HRC explains, in the richest country on Earth, many citizens have no running water or proper waste disposal. Thus, "[i]n Alabama and West Virginia, a high proportion of the population is not served by public sewerage and water supply services. Contrary to the assumption in most developed countries that such services should be extended by the government systematically and eventually comprehensively to all areas, neither state was able to provide figures as to the magnitude of the challenge or details of any planned government response."

Of course, not all of these ills can be attributed to the US's grotesque amount of military spending—spending which starves critical social and infrastructure programs of much-needed revenue—but this is certainly a huge contributing factor.

Another factor, which the Human Rights Council singled out, is the US's almost total denial of the international law obligations of all nations to provide for and protect their citizens' social and economic rights. As the Human Rights Council explains:

> Successive administrations, including the current one, have determinedly rejected the idea that economic and social rights are full-fledged human rights, despite their clear recognition not only in key treaties that the United States has ratified, such as the Convention on the Elimination of All Forms of Racial Discrimination, but also in the Universal Declaration of Human Rights, which the United States has long insisted other countries must respect. But denial does not eliminate responsibility, nor does it negate obligations. International human rights law recognizes a right to education, a right to health care, a right to social protection for those in need and a right to an adequate standard of living. In practice, the United States is alone

> among developed countries in insisting that, while human rights are of fundamental importance, they do not include rights that guard against dying of hunger, dying from a lack of access to affordable health care or growing up in a context of total deprivation. Since the United States has refused to accord domestic recognition to the economic and social rights agreed by most other States in the International Covenant on Economic, Social and Cultural Rights and other treaties, except for the recognition of some social rights, and especially the right to education, in state constitutions, the primary focus of the present report is on those civil and political rights reflected in the United States Bill of Rights and in the International Covenant on Civil and Political Rights, which the United States has ratified.

This is a very important point when discussing the question of "humanitarian" intervention. First of all, no one with a straight face talks about the need to intervene in the US to protect its citizens' international social and economic rights, but this is not a frivolous issue.

Moreover, while the US demonizes, sanctions, and wages war against other countries who they find lacking in civil and political rights, those same countries are never given credit for the strides they may make in protecting the equally important economic and social rights. The UN Committee on Economic, Social, and Cultural Rights has denounced this selective concern about particular human rights, decrying "the shocking reality . . . that States and the international community as a whole continue to tolerate all too often breaches of economic, social and cultural rights which, if they occurred in relation to civil and political rights, would provoke expressions of horror and outrage and would lead to concerted calls for immediate remedial action,"[206] including, quite possibly, calls for armed intervention.

A great example of this selective concern about human rights is evidenced in the US's treatment of Cuba, which, even despite the US's undermining of its efforts through sanctions and a long-standing embargo, has managed to provide for its people in ways that other countries in Latin America have not been able to. As Jean Bricmont summarizes, "[i]n Cuba, life expectancy is six years longer than the rest of the continent. Under-five mortality is four times below the average. If Latin America could show the same results as Cuba, 250,000 children's lives could be saved every year. There are 5.7 million working children in Latin America. For the whole continent, there are 50 million street children. None of these situations are to be found in Cuba where all children go to school."[207]

In addition, Cuba has famously provided medical aid to around 70 poor countries throughout the world. Quite notably, even the *New York Times* itself recognized, Cuba has been at the frontline of the battle against cholera since the 2010 earthquake hit Haiti.[208] As the UN has explained:

> Cuban medical cooperation has saved thousands of lives in Haiti. Present in the country for the last 15 years and with over 700 people working closely with the Ministry of Health, the Cuban Medical Brigades have actively worked to fight cholera. The contingent has worked in 96 health care centers, 65 of which are part of a joint Cuban-Venezuelan program aimed at strengthening the health system in the country.[209]

Of course, it must be noted that the cholera that ravaged Haiti was brought there by a foreign intervention—that is, the UN troop intervention in Haiti. It is now certain that UN troops from Nepal created the cholera epidemic by defecating into water sources used for drinking.[210] At the same time, UN troops from Brazil have been guilty of numerous rapes and extrajudicial killings in Haiti.[211] Thus, the fact that a military intervention in a sovereign nation is carried out by the UN is hardly a guarantee against humanitarian and human rights violations.

The US's big contribution to Haiti during the same time, of course, was sending thousands of troops to keep the population down, proving the old adage that when you're a hammer, every problem looks like a nail.

There are several implications of all this. First of all, there is no doubt that the US could help save more lives in Cuba and around the world if it did what Article 2(1) of the ICESCR expressly calls upon the wealthier countries to do—that is, to lend assistance to poorer countries like Cuba in building up their (albeit already well-developed) domestic healthcare and other social security systems, and by helping Cuba as well as its medical solidarity efforts around the world.

Instead, the US, in the name of democracy and freedom, hampers these efforts with crushing sanctions and a cruel embargo that has been denounced year after year by the UN General Assembly. In November of 2019, all UN members voted in favor of the resolution condemning the embargo with the exception only of the US and Israel. Second, if Cuba's very real successes in protecting its own citizens' social and economic rights were taken into full account, one might conclude that they balance out the deficits there might be in protecting civil and political rights; in any case, one might conclude that the successes balance out the deficits at least enough to delegitimize any claimed right to intervene in Cuba on ostensible humanitarian grounds.

As the Human Rights Council also notes, moreover, the US isn't even doing a good job at protecting the rights it claims to recognize, such as those set forth in the ICCPR, including basic democratic rights and freedoms. As the HRC explains:

> The cornerstone of American society is democracy, but it is being steadily undermined, and with it the human right to political participation protected in article 25 of the International Covenant on Civil and Political Rights. The principle of one person, one vote applies in theory, but is increasingly far from the reality.
>
> In a democracy, the task of government should be to facilitate political participation by ensuring that all citizens can vote and that their votes will count equally. However, in the United States there is overt disenfranchisement of more than 6 million felons and ex-felons, which predominantly affects Black citizens since they are the ones whose conduct is often specifically targeted for criminalization. In

addition, nine states currently condition the restoration of the right to vote after prison on the payment of outstanding fines and fees. A typical outcome is that seen in Alabama, where a majority of all ex-felons cannot vote.

Then there is covert disenfranchisement, which includes the dramatic gerrymandering of electoral districts to privilege particular groups of voters, the imposition of artificial and unnecessary voter identification requirements, the blatant manipulation of polling station locations, the relocation of Departments of Motor Vehicles' offices to make it more difficult for certain groups to obtain identification, and the general ramping up of obstacles to voting, especially for those without resources. The net result is that people living in poverty, minorities and other disfavored groups are being systematically deprived of their right to vote.

It is thus unsurprising that the United States has one of the lowest turnout rates in elections among developed countries, with only 55.7 percent of the voting-age population casting ballots in the 2016 presidential election.

Again, all of this is quite relevant to the discussion about the US's claimed right to intervene in other countries in the name of protecting democracy and human rights. Certainly, it is hard to see how the US would have the moral right to intervene in other countries under the guise of protecting the very rights it is not protecting within its own national borders. And indeed, whether a country has moral authority to lead on human rights is seen as quite relevant to other matters, such as whether a country should be permitted to serve on a human rights oversight body such as the UN's Human Rights Council (formerly known as the Commission on Human Rights) itself. An Oxford University textbook on international human rights explains this well:

> As the US Ambassador put it in 2005, the members of the Commission "must be the firefighters of the world, not the arsonists".... In 2003

Human Rights Watch put forward a . . . set of criteria proposing that potential members "should have ratified core human rights treaties, complied with their reporting obligations, issued open invitations to UN human rights experts and not have been condemned by the Commission for human rights violations."[212]

As the same textbook notes,[213] the US itself, which has failed to ratify numerous core human rights covenants—including the International Covenant on Economic, Social, and Cultural Rights; the Rome Statute for the International Criminal Court; the Convention on the Rights of Persons with Disabilities; the Convention on the Elimination of All Forms of Discrimination Against Women; the Convention on the Rights of the Child; the International Convention on the Protection of the Rights of all Migrant Workers and Members of the Family; and the International Convention for the Protection of All Persons from Enforced Disappearance[214]—and which has been condemned, as seen above, for serious human rights abuses by the Human Rights Council, would have difficulty fulfilling these criteria. If the US could not fulfill the requisite criteria for serving on the Human Rights Council—a body that has little to no enforcement capability—how could it then legitimately purport to lead military operations that inflict lethal harm in the name of human rights? The answer, of course, is that it cannot, for the US is indeed the classic arsonist claiming to be putting out fires. Incredibly, though, this question is rarely asked, including by Human Rights Watch.

I would argue strongly that instead of worrying about what poor country the US should militarily invade in the name of democracy and freedom, Western human rights advocates would better spend their time, resources, and energies on encouraging the US to fix its own democracy deficits and, as required by international law, leave the rest of the world to work on theirs.

FOUR

The ICC, the Crime of Aggression, and Western Humanitarians

ANOTHER SEEMINGLY GREAT ADVANCE FOR human rights came in the form of the International Criminal Court (ICC), which was created by the Rome Statute of the ICC in 1998 and became effective in 2002.[215] The Rome Statute set up the ICC as a permanent tribunal empowered to try individuals criminally for international law violations, including Genocide, War Crimes and Crimes Against Humanity, and, relevant to our discussion, Crimes of Aggression. That is, the ICC is empowered to try individuals, including heads of state, for waging aggressive war and military interventions.

As a *Harvard International Law Journal* article[216] on the Crime of Aggression under the Rome Statute notes, while it took a while, the international community, as required by the Rome Statute, finally came up with a definition for the "Crime of Aggression" in 2010, thus allowing this section of the Statute to come into full force and effect. As the article explains, "[t]he Rome Statute defines the crime of aggression as 'the planning, preparation, initiation or execution, **by a person**

in a position effectively to exercise control over or to direct the political or military action of a State, of an act of aggression which . . . constitutes a manifest violation of the Charter of the United Nations.' (emphasis in original) The article continues, "[i]n essence, the crime of aggression as defined in the Rome Statute is a crime committed against the sovereignty of a state."

Not surprisingly, the United States—the greatest threat to world peace as confirmed in two international polls[217]—has always feared the ICC and the prospect of its leaders being prosecuted. Therefore, the US, under Bill Clinton, did its best to weaken the powers and jurisdiction of the ICC as much as possible in negotiations of the Rome Statute. And, in the end, the US never ratified the ICC anyway.

What may come as some surprise, however, is that Western human rights advocates have been quite sympathetic with the US's opposition to the ICC, though they understand that the US, with its substantial military and economic might, need not worry about such trifles.

For example, Kenneth Roth, longtime executive director of Human Rights Watch, wrote an article in the *New York Review of Books* back in 1998[218] seemingly to assure the US that it has nothing to be concerned with in the ICC, for the ICC, after all, is only for weak States. Roth's views on this are quite revealing of the prejudices, failings, and shortcomings of Western human rights practitioners and therefore deserve to be analyzed at length.

First of all, Roth colorfully relates that the US was nearly the only country in the world to oppose the ICC:

> As cheering broke out in the UN conference room on the Viale Aventino in Rome this past July, David Scheffer, the US ambassador-at-large for war crimes issues, was not pleased. While delegates from around the world celebrated a historic agreement to establish a new International Criminal Court (ICC), he sat stone-faced, arms folded. After three years of conferences and a final, five-week negotiating session in Rome, the participating nations voted by an

> overwhelming 120 to 7 to establish a new institution for bringing the world's worst human rights criminals to justice. In favor of the court were most of America's closest allies, including Britain, Canada, and Germany. But the United States was isolated in opposition, along with such dictatorships and enemies of human rights as Iran, Iraq, China, Libya, Algeria, and Sudan. It was an embarrassing low point for a government that portrays itself as a champion of human rights.
>
> This didn't have to happen. President Clinton had repeatedly endorsed the court. . . . But the President acceded to pressure from the Pentagon and its congressional allies to try to preclude any possibility of the court's prosecuting an American. Most other governments rejected this demand as inconsistent with their vision of equal justice for all.

Roth assumes that it is only other "rogue states" (invariably meaning non-Western states) that are "enemies of human rights"; never the US. It is also quite telling that Roth speaks of "other governments" and "their vision of equal justice for all" (as opposed to "our vision"), refusing to endorse what should be a very obvious vision for someone truly interested in human rights. And indeed, as discussed above, the UN and its Charter are built upon the proposition that all States are equal under the law and otherwise. As one UN expert panel explains, moreover, "[t]he credibility of any system of collective security also depends on how well it promotes security for all its members, without regard to the nature of would-be beneficiaries, their location, resources or relationship to great Powers."[219]

Meanwhile, Roth also laments in the same piece that the US has refused to sign on to other international agreements with near universal international buy-in, such as the antilandmine treaty and the treaty forbidding the use of child soldiers under eighteen. This is as far as Roth goes, however, in sounding like a true human rights advocate, rather than an apologist for Western imperialism.

Thus, Roth, no believer in the Crime of Aggression or even the concept of wrongful military intervention so long as it is carried out by the West, deals with the Crime of Aggression in his article only in passing, and in a footnote, assuring the US that it would never have to face the music for its serial crimes against peace given how the Rome Statute ended up being weakened on this score, of course through the pressing of the US. First of all, Roth states that "[a]s conceived in Rome, the new court will prosecute those responsible for future genocide, crimes against humanity, and war crimes." It is here that he drops his footnote about the Crime of Aggression, showing that, for the likes of Roth, it is nothing but a footnote at best in international law.

And Roth demonstrates one reason he believes this is to be a mere footnote—because, he wrongly claims, the burdens of "military intervention . . . fall mainly on the rank-and-file soldiers on the front line," rather than on civilians, which is actually the case. That an individual so tone-deaf to the realities of war has been the head of one of the major human rights organizations is both troubling and also quite telling.

In his footnote, Roth comforts would-be US war criminals, stating that "[s]ome of the court's US critics note that the court might also address the crime of aggression. But that will occur only if seven eighths of the governments that join the court can agree on a definition at a conference to be held seven years after the court is established. The only conceivable definition that could attract such broad support is one that would leave it to the Security Council to declare when aggression has occurred, meaning that the United States and the other permanent members of the Council could use their veto to prevent any such prosecution with which they disagreed." In other words, "don't worry," Roth assures us—the US can always use its veto power to opt itself out of prosecution for war.

In addition, Roth adds, the US can always bully its way out of any attempts to bring it to justice, just as it usually does. As Roth says comfortingly, "[t]he US government has many ways of dissuading governments from attempting to try an American—from diplomatic and economic pressure to the use of military force. But the administration fears such dissuasion would be less effective against the ICC. After all, the Pentagon could hardly threaten to bomb The Hague." Roth almost sounds sad that the US cannot threaten to bomb The Hague as it threatens to bomb its way out of every other problem it has. In the meantime, Roth seems to endorse the US's use of military force to evade justice though this would be a clear violation of the UN Charter, Article 2(4).

Roth digs himself in further, stating, "[t]he Clinton administration's opposition to the ICC stemmed in part from its fear, a plausible one, that hostile states like Cuba, Libya, or Iraq might try to convince the court to launch a frivolous or politically motivated prosecution of US soldiers or commanding officers." Here, Roth expresses sympathy for the fear that such countries might bring "a frivolous" case against US soldiers or officers, dismissing the possibility that these countries might in fact have a bona fide case against the US and its leaders.

Of course, at the time Roth wrote this piece in 1998, these countries had very legitimate reasons to bring a case against US officials for war crimes.

For example, Cuba would have an airtight case against US officials based upon the US's relentless economic and terrorist war against Cuba dating back to the early 1960s. In his book *The Economic War Against Cuba*, author Salim Lamrani, a professor at the Sorbonne in Paris, explains that the US war against postrevolutionary Cuba began on March 17, 1960, one month before Cuba established relations with Moscow.[220] Lamrani relates that this war, declared by President Eisenhower, was "built on several pillars: the cancellation of the Cuban sugar quota, an end to the deliveries of energy resources such as oil, the continuation of the arms embargo imposed in March 1958, the establishment of a campaign of terrorism and sabotage, and the organization of a paramilitary force designed to invade the island overthrow Fidel Castro."

This war would then be expanded by President Kennedy in 1962 to include the unprecedented economic blockade against Cuba—a blockade that continues to this day, years after the collapse of the Soviet Union. This relentless, decades-long economic war has cost Cuba more than $751 billion and has "affected all sectors of Cuban society and all categories of the population, especially the most vulnerable: children, the elderly, and women. Over 70 percent of all Cubans have lived in a climate of permanent economic hostility."

This economic war, moreover, has been combined with decades of violent, terrorist attacks by the United States—attacks intentionally devised to provoke a violent response by Cuba that could justify a full-scale invasion, but that violent response never came due to the incredible restraint of the Cuban government and people.[221]

As Noam Chomsky details, these attacks came very shortly after the January 1, 1959, Cuban Revolution and with incessant frequency. As Chomsky relates, "[i]n May [1959], the CIA began to arm guerrillas inside Cuba. During the winter of 1959-1960, there was a significant increase in CIA-supervised bombing and incendiary raids piloted by exiled Cubans based in the US."[222]

These assaults against Cuba continued for decades. In addition to the infamous 1961 Bay of Pigs invasion, Chomsky details that these included: attacks on a Cuban seaside hotel, killing a number of Russians and Cubans; attacks on British and Cuban cargo ships; the contamination of sugar shipments; an attack which blew up a Cuban industrial facility and killed 400 workers; the bombing of a Cubana airliner which killed all seventy-three civilian passengers; various attacks on fishing boats and upon Cuban embassies and other foreign offices; and a machine-gun attack upon a Spanish-Cuban tourist hotel in 1989 on the 30th Anniversary of the Revolution.[223]

There were more attacks into the 1990s, including a number of bombings in Cuba organized by Luis Posada, who was financed from Miami and given significant help from the US to carry out his attacks. As Chomsky explains, Posada was a Bay of Pigs veteran, and his subsequent operations in the 1960s were directed by the CIA. When he later joined Venezuelan intelligence with CIA help, he was able to arrange for Orlando Bosch, an associate from his CIA days who had been convicted in the US for a bomb attack on a Cuba-bound freighter, to join him in Venezuela to organize further attacks against Cuba. An ex-CIA official familiar with the Cubana bombing identifies Posada and Bosch as the only suspects in the bombing, which Bosch defended as "a legitimate act of war." Generally considered the "mastermind" of the airline bombing, Bosch was responsible for thirty other acts of terrorism, according to the FBI. He was granted a presidential pardon in 1989 by the incoming Bush I administration after intense lobbying by Jeb Bush and South Florida Cuban-American leaders, overruling the Justice Department, which had found the conclusion "inescapable that it would be prejudicial to the public interest for the United States to provide a safe haven for Bosch [because] the security of this nation is affected by its ability to urge credibly other nations to refuse aid and shelter to terrorists."[224]

In short, despite what Roth might think, Cuba has more than a "frivolous" case for war crimes against the US. And so did Libya at the time that Roth wrote his piece.

Lest we forget, well before the NATO destruction of Libya in 2011, and the resulting sodomizing and murder of Muammar Gaddafi, the US had attacked Libya. Thus, in 1986, the US bombed targets in Tripoli, killing 37 individuals, including Gaddafi's stepdaughter, and wounding 93 others, including two of Gaddafi's sons.[225] The majority of the Libyan victims were civilian.[226] There is no doubt that President Ronald Reagan, despite knowing full well the illegality of attempting to kill a foreign head of state and his civilian family members, intentionally targeted the Gaddafi family's compound of Bab al-Aziziyah.[227] At a minimum, therefore, the murder of Gaddafi's stepdaughter was a war crime—just as much as the intentional targeting and murder of, say, Sasha or Malia Obama would have been. But, of course, in this world where Western lives are viewed as much more valuable than those in the Third World, this thought most likely would never occur to Roth.

Finally, Iraq too had an overwhelming case against the US for various crimes at the time Roth wrote his piece. However, Roth explicitly downplays any potential case Iraq would have, especially after the Clinton Administration had successfully watered down the ICC rules before then refusing to ratify the ICC. Roth seems to approve of this weakening of the ICC in favor of the US, stating:

> Of special concern was the so-called rule of proportionality under international law, which prohibits a military attack causing an incidental loss of civilian life that is "excessive" compared to the military advantage gained. This less precise rule could implicate activity that US military commanders consider lawful but the ICC might not. For example, the Gulf War bombing of Iraq's electrical grid **was claimed** to have killed a disproportionate number of civilians, including the thousands **said to have died** because of the resulting loss of refrigeration, water purification, and other necessities of modern life. What if the ICC had been in existence and had found such claims well founded? What about the wholesale burning of El Chorillo neighborhood in Panama City and the death of some three hundred civilians during the US invasion of Panama?
>
> **To avoid prosecution in such borderline situations**, US negotiators successfully redefined the proportionality rule to prohibit attacks that injure civilians only when such injury is "clearly excessive" in relation to the military advantage. The effect of this and other concessions to the US—including a broader definition of military advantage—was to tip the balance considerably against the ICC's finding a violation of the rule of proportionality. (emphasis added)

So, these are "borderline situations" of war crimes in Roth's expert opinion as a leading Western human rights advocate? Let's look at what happened in the "borderline situation" of the US's conduct in the first Gulf War. The terrible war crimes the US carried out are not just a matter of rumor and hearsay, as Roth seems to suggest.

The US crimes are well described by former US Attorney General Ramsey Clark, who traveled through Iraq for three weeks as Iraq, "essentially defenseless against US technological warfare and offer[ing] no real resistance," was being carpet bombed by United States forces, who were able to attack targets at will.[228] And they willingly and intentionally attacked civilian targets necessary for the sustaining of human life—a clear violation of the Geneva Conventions.

As Clark, citing the Commission of Inquiry for the International War Crimes Tribunal, of which he was a member, explains:

> In every city we visited, we documented severe damage to homes, electrical plants, fuel storage facilities, civilian factories, hospitals, churches, civilian airports, vehicles, transportation facilities, food storage and food testing laboratories, grain silos, animal vaccination centers, schools, communication towers, civilian government office buildings, and stores. Almost all facilities we saw had been bombed two or three times, ensuring that they could not be repaired. Most of the bridges we saw destroyed were bombed from both ends.
>
> Dr. David Levinson, who visited Iraq immediately after the war with the International Physicians for the Prevention of Nuclear War, said, "There were many direct civilian casualties from the bombings, but these numbers do not reflect the true horror of this war." Compounded by sanctions, the damage to life-support systems in Iraq killed more after the war than direct attacks did during the war.
>
> As Levinson testified at Commission hearings in San Francisco and Los Angeles, "It was clear that the bombing war against Iraq has been a war directed against the civilian population though massive destruction of the country's infrastructure."[229]

And, according to plan, as Clark explains, over a million Iraqis would die as a result of this vicious air campaign combined with brutal economic sanctions. This number of dead is undisputed. As mentioned herein already, Secretary of State Madeleine Albright did not dispute such figures, including 500,000 dead children; she simply agreed that "it was worth it."

But, for Roth, this is somehow a "borderline" case for a war crimes prosecution, and he seems relieved that the Rome Statute for the ICC, after being sufficiently watered down by the US, would allow the US to get off the hook for its misdeeds in Iraq even if the US were a party to the Statute. Meanwhile, Roth quotes Madeleine Albright for her assertion that the US is "'indispensable'" to "humanitarian activities" around the world, simply ignoring Albright's approval of half a million Iraqi children dying as a result of such "humanitarian" activities.

Sadly, Roth and his Human Rights Watch were not the only major Western Human Rights advocates who downplayed the US abuses in Iraq, and the results were disastrous.

For example, respected human rights professor and former board member of Amnesty International (AI), Francis A. Boyle, explained in 2012 how AI aided and abetted the campaign against Iraqi civilians waged by the West:[230]

> During the past eight years, about 1.5 million people in Iraq have died as a result of genocidal sanctions imposed upon them primarily at the behest of the United States and Britain, including in that number about 500,000 dead Iraqi children. While on the AIUSA Board of Directors, I tried to get them and AI/London to do something about this genocidal embargo against the People of Iraq, and especially against the Iraqi Children. Both AI/London and AIUSA adamantly refused to act.

Neither Human Rights Watch nor Amnesty International would perform any better with respect to the second invasion of Iraq in 2003.

Indeed, neither organization was willing to take a position at all on whether the invasion itself was illegal as an act of unprovoked, aggressive war, much less condemn it as such.[231] Amnesty International, in an article attempting to defend its position on the NATO invasion of Libya against criticisms I leveled against it, flatly stated: "Amnesty International generally takes no position on the use of armed force or on military interventions in armed conflict, other than to demand that all parties respect international human rights and humanitarian law."[232] That is, Amnesty International takes no position on the most important issue under the UN Charter and international law.

For his part, Kenneth Roth, still ensconced as the head of Human Rights Watch, publically declared that he assumed that the US did its best to avoid civilian casualties,[233] despite mounds of evidence to the contrary, including irrefutable evidence that the US used chemical weapons such as deleted uranium and white phosphorous, which have sent cancer rates in Iraq skyrocketing and which will cause birth defects for many years to come.[234]

According to the *Independent* of London:[235]

> Dramatic increases in infant mortality, cancer, and leukaemia in the Iraqi city of Fallujah, which was bombarded by US Marines in 2004, exceed those reported by survivors of the atomic bombs that were dropped on Hiroshima and Nagasaki in 1945, according to a new study.
>
> Iraqi doctors in Fallujah have complained since 2005 of being overwhelmed by the number of babies with serious birth defects, ranging from a girl born with two heads to paralysis of the lower limbs. They said they were also seeing far more cancers than they did before the battle for Fallujah between US troops and insurgents.
>
> Their claims have been supported by a survey showing a four-fold increase in all cancers and a 12-fold increase in childhood cancer in under-14s. Infant mortality in the city is more than four times higher than in neighbouring Jordan and eight times higher than in Kuwait.

As this article continues, it explains that a study, titled "Cancer, Infant Mortality, and Birth Sex-Ratio in Fallujah, Iraq 2005–2009," by Dr. Christopher Busby, Malak Hamdan, and Entesar Ariabi,

> concludes that anecdotal evidence of a sharp rise in cancer and congenital birth defects is correct. Infant mortality was found to be 80 per 1,000 births compared to 19 in Egypt, 17 in Jordan and 9.7 in Kuwait. The report says that the types of cancer are "similar to that in the Hiroshima survivors who were exposed to ionising radiation from the bomb and uranium in the fallout".
>
> Researchers found a 38-fold increase in leukaemia, a ten-fold increase in female breast cancer and significant increases in lymphoma and brain tumours in adults. At Hiroshima survivors showed a 17-fold increase in leukaemia, but in Fallujah Dr Busby says what is striking is not only the greater prevalence of cancer but the speed with which it was affecting people.

And yet, few Western pundits or "humanitarians" have shed tears over such atrocities.

Indeed, compare this silence to the hand-wringing over alleged chemical attacks in Syria, which, even as alleged, killed at most tens of people as opposed to the thousands sentenced to slow, painful deaths by US-dumped toxins in Fallujah.

Moreover, as for the alleged Syria attacks, it should be pointed out that the Western press and NGOs have been hell-bent on pinning these on the Assad government, even while there is credible evidence that the alleged attacks were staged in order to justify US attacks against Syria. Indeed, a reporter from *Newsweek*, Tareq Haddad, recently resigned his post from there because his editors refused to run his well-researched and documented story showing how the Organization for the Prohibition of Chemical Weapons (OPCW)—the international body responsible for investigating chemical weapons use—suppressed such evidence in order to favor the US's version of events.[236]

In response to Haddad's revelations, "[m]embers of the OPCW team have come forward, expressing their 'gravest concern' about the 'selective representation of the facts' and the 'intentional bias' 'undermining the credibility of the report.' Even former OPCW Director-General Dr. Jose Bustani[237] stated that the whistleblowers' testimonies have 'confirmed the doubts and suspicions' he already had about the organization and Syria."

But meanwhile, "the alleged chemical weapons attack was immediately used as a justification for foreign intervention in the conflict. Within days, the U.S., France, and the United Kingdom launched bombings campaigns on the country, risking a potential nuclear conflict with Russia to the great approval of corporate media. Not one of the top 100 American newspapers by circulation opposed the extremely hasty actions." On the contrary, there was near-universal support for these bombings, which were portrayed as some kind of humanitarian venture, and there has been virtually no questioning of the narrative of the alleged chemical weapons attacks that were used to justify the bombings. The response of *Newsweek* to any challenge of this narrative, moreover, is a good indicator that we will most likely never be treated to the truth on this issue.

All told, Roth's belief in the good intentions of the US notwithstanding, another 2.5 million Iraqis (and possibly as many as 3.5 million) died as a consequence of the 2003 invasion;[238] that's on top of the 1.5 million killed as a result of the first Gulf War and accompanying sanctions. Those are staggering figures, rarely reported in the Western press, and of little to no concern to Western human rights practitioners.

Of course, there is no doubt that the 2003 invasion of Iraq constituted an illegal aggressive war—the primary scourge of the world that the UN was created to prevent—as it was carried out in the absence of any armed attack by Iraq and without Security Council authorization. Indeed, it was carried out on the basis of a lie that, even if true, would not have justified the use of force—that Iraq allegedly possessed weapons of mass destruction (WMDs); WMDs, by the way, that it would have possessed in the first place because the US and other Western allies had armed it with them.

Former UN Special Expert Dr. Alfred de Zayas characterized the 2003 invasion of Iraq as follows:[239]

> It was a primal catastrophe. International law altogether was eliminated and replaced by the imperial dictatorship of the United States. Since 1945, there was never a more wholesale violation of universal international law norms and customs than in March 2003. . . .
>
> A completely unprovoked violation of a people by the US occurred with the criminal support of a so-called "Coalition of the willing," forty-three states that helped the aggression of the United States.
>
> States consciously pushed aside the UN Charter as though it was not relevant. That Article 2 paragraphs 3 and 4 of the Charter were blatantly violated was shocking. At that time, Hans Blix and Mohammed el-Baradei were UN inspectors in Bagdad and testified that no weapons of mass destruction were stockpiled. Both of them were commissioned by the UN Security Council. There was no UN resolution justifying military action. Nevertheless, forty-four states supported this primal violation of international law.

And, while George H. W. Bush, constantly shifting in his pretexts for the invasion, ultimately tried to argue that the invasion of Iraq was a humanitarian one meant to liberate Iraqis from Saddam Hussein's repressive rule, and while Western liberal intellectuals such as Christopher Hitchens applauded this goal, all of the evidence of the US's conduct in the war refutes this contention.

As explained in an excellent law review article titled "'The Supreme International Crime': How the US War in Iraq Threatens the Rule of Law"[240]—a piece that challenges the very legal legitimacy of "humanitarian" interventionist doctrine:

> Beyond bearing the burden of persuasion, the legitimacy of humanitarian interventions depends, at a minimum, on protecting civilian populations. The use of indiscriminate weapons such as cluster bombs,

napalm, and depleted uranium shells by the invading forces, however, suggests that the primary goal was not to protect Iraqi civilians, but to destroy the Iraqi army and topple the regime of a troublesome adversary. In other words, the real motives were no different from any another war of aggression. As Hilary Charlesworth . . . points out, "if the human rights of the Iraqis were the primary motive for the invasion, given the destruction of civilian life and infrastructure that it caused, questions can be raised about whether the means used to protect Iraqi human rights were proportionate." The destruction of Iraqi material and social order by occupation forces and a [massive] death toll . . . render the claim that Iraq was invaded for humanitarian reasons highly suspect. As Michael Mandel . . . asks, "where was the humanity to be found in a war that had destroyed so many human lives?"

In short, there was no basis in fact, law, or morality for the invasion that caused so much death and destruction, but the two major Western human rights groups had nothing to say about this. In their silence, they were complicit in this gross violation of international law and human rights norms.

And, even human rights groups, which at least took the position that the invasion of Iraq was not justified by the responsibility to protect the Iraqi population from the crimes of Saddam Hussein because his worst crimes were behind him by then (and, of course, had been aided and abetted by the West), could not bring themselves to actually condemn the invasion. As Edward S. Herman and David Peterson, analyzing the position of the International Coalition for the Responsibility to Protect (R2P), explain:

> in the judgment of this Coalition, the relevant question is whether the government of Iraq had been committing "gross human rights violations . . . at the time of the 2003 military intervention." Left unasked is whether the United States had been responsible for gross human rights violations during the years they enforced the "sanctions of mass

destruction" (1990–2003), whether they were on the verge of committing even more egregious human rights violations by invading Iraq (ca. 2002–early 2003), and whether they did in fact commit gross human rights violations from March 19–20, 2003, on, including a death toll that may top one million Iraqis, with millions more driven from their homes.... Thus in the global acid-test for R2P in the first decade of the 21st Century, these R2P advocates can freely debate the need for the US-UK invasion to protect Iraq's population against the Iraqi regime. But neither these nor any other R2P advocate can even raise the question of the need to protect Iraq's population against the US-UK invaders. The United States and its allies simply could not kill sufficiently large numbers of foreign nationals for R2P and ICC enthusiasts and spokesperson to suggest that R2P and the ICC be invoked to stop them.

How is it, one might ask, that major human rights groups could be so dismissive of what were clearly war crimes—in this case, the intentional assault on civilian targets resulting in the deaths of over a million civilians—and utterly silent on the issue of aggressive war? The answer is quite simple, and reflected in something else Roth stated in his 1998 *New York Review of Books* piece.

Roth's illuminating words, contained in what can only be described as a non sequitur, are: "[b]ecause genocide and crimes against humanity involve by their very nature widespread or systematic atrocities, the United States today is unlikely to commit them." Why or how this is so Roth does not explain, and that is because it is unexplainable, at least with logic and reason. What Roth states is something akin to a religious belief—the US cannot, by its nature, commit "widespread or systematic atrocities," end of discussion. Of course, as any honest student of history knows, the US has indeed committed and helped commit such atrocities, including genocide—e.g., of Native Americans, Filipinos, Vietnamese, Yemenis, and arguably of Iraqis, as well. Indeed, one might even argue that the US is, by its very nature, genocidal. But one need not accept that proposition either, to see how wrong people like Kenneth Roth are.

Such truths are not, as Roth would have us believe, simply in the eye of the beholder. But it is the selective perception of such facts by such people as Roth, a highly influential human rights figure, that allows such crimes to go on and on without censure. That itself is a crime.

What is true is that the US does commit egregious crimes, but because, as in the case of the Rome Statute of the ICC, the US helps write the rules in a self-serving way, and then exempts itself from the rules when it sees fit, it is rarely if ever held accountable for them. And, for the likes of Human Rights Watch and Amnesty International, that is just fine.

In the end, the history of the ICC so far has proven that the US, and Roth as well, got what they wanted in this organization. Thus, no Western country has ever been referred to the ICC for investigation. And, of the eleven active investigations the ICC has been involved in during its first twenty-plus years in existence, ten have been of Africans.[241] And it is only Africans who have actually been put on trial by the ICC.[242]

Writing upon the ICC's 20th Anniversary, Awol K Allo describes what has come to be known as the ICC's "African problem":[243]

> All arrest warrants and indictments so far issued by the ICC are for Africans, including two sitting heads of states—Omar Hassan al-Bashir of Sudan and Uhuru Kenyatta of Kenya.
>
> This curious and disproportionate focus of the court on Africa, particularly the cases against al-Bashir and Kenyatta, angered African leaders, leading to accusations of racist bias. In October 2013, the African Union called upon African states not to cooperate with the ICC, after the Security Council refused to defer the proceedings against the two leaders.
>
> The former Ethiopian PM Hailemariam Desalegn accused the tribunal of being a racist institution "hunting" Africans while Burundi, who became the first country to withdraw from the court, criticized it for being "a political tool used by [foreign] powers to remove whoever they want from power on the African continent."

For his part, former UN special expert Dr. Alfred de Zayas put it this way: "The ICC is occupied with the smaller crimes of Africans while the big criminals like George W. Bush, Tony Blair, Dick Cheney, Paul Wolfowitz, Richard Pearl, Donald Rumsfeld, and others [responsible for the 2003 invasion of Iraq] run about freely. Those who destroyed a whole people and have over a million casualties on their conscience are not punished in any way. Therefore, this is a primal catastrophe in the sense of the international order."[244]

Meanwhile, in the spring of 2019, President Trump revoked the US visa of the ICC's chief prosecutor, Fatou Bensouda (who herself happens to be African), because she has requested that the ICC open up an investigation into war crimes by the US in Afghanistan.[245] As Judge Bensouda has explained, "there's information that members of the US military and intelligence agencies 'committed acts of torture, cruel treatment, outrages upon personal dignity, rape, and sexual violence against conflict-related detainees in Afghanistan and other locations, principally in the 2003-2004 period.'"

As the *LA Times* relates:[246]

> The State Department confirmed that Bensouda's US visa had been revoked and said, "The United States will take the necessary steps to protect its sovereignty and to protect our people from unjust investigation and prosecution by the International Criminal Court."
>
> US Secretary of State Michael R. Pompeo said last month that Washington would revoke or deny visas to ICC staff seeking to investigate allegations of war crimes or other abuses committed by US forces in Afghanistan or elsewhere and that it may do the same with those who seek action against Israel.

What's more, the Trump Administration—starting to at least approach Roth's fantasy of the US bombing The Hague—has gone so far as to threaten to arrest ICC Judges if they even attempt to investigate US officials for war crimes in Afghanistan.[247] As former US National

Security Council Adviser John Bolton warned, if the ICC pursues such an investigation, "[w]e will ban its judges and prosecutors from entering the United States. We will sanction their funds in the US financial system, and we will prosecute them in the US criminal system. . . . We will do the same for any company or state that assists an ICC investigation of Americans."[248] One such war crime the ICC is interested in investigating, it should be noted, is the US's dropping of what is known as the "mother of all bombs"—the largest non-nuclear bomb in the US's arsenal—upon a target in Afghanistan's Nangarhar Province in April of 2017.[249] To this day, Afghanis in this Province are complaining of numerous diseases and other health problems as a consequence of this bombing.

Bolton warned that the US would sanction the ICC, which he announced was "already dead" to the United States, in similar ways if it pursues war crimes investigations against Israel arising out of its occupation of the Palestinian Territories.[250] Given that the ICC just announced that it would indeed open such an investigation,[251] Bolton's threats may soon be put to the test.

As Kenneth Roth explained with great relief in his piece in the *New York Review of Books*, the US has many means at its disposal to fend off pesky human rights investigations into its many misdeeds around the world, and the Trump Administration is not reluctant to use them. For, after all, what is good for the goose is not always good for the gander. In the view of the Western governments and their Western human rights apologists, sovereignty is something only for the benefit of the powerful nations and human rights enforcement only for use against the weak. But anyone truly interested in the rule of international law must realize that this amounts to no rule of law at all, but rather, the rule of the jungle; of might making right.

FIVE

The Anticolonial Nature of International Law

"The 'responsibility to protect' is a white supremacist construction—the 21st-century 'white man's burden.' It is used as a cover for U.S. & Western attacks on nations resisting Western dominance. NATO & the more than 800 U.S. military bases are used to enforce white supremacy."
—Ajamu Baraka

ANOTHER MAJOR GLOBAL PROCESS THAT informed the priorities of the United Nations and the development of international law was decolonization—a process that was quite possibly the truly defining one of the 20th century. Belgian philosopher Jean Bricmont puts it well when he explains:

> Westerners do not always appreciate that the major event of the 20th century, was neither the rise and fall of fascism, not the history of communism, but decolonization. One should remember that, about a century ago, the British could forbid the access of a park in Shanghai to "dogs

and Chinese." And, of course, most of Asia and Africa was under European control. Latin America was formally independent, but under American and British tutelage; military interventions were routine. All of this collapsed during the 20th century, through wars and revolutions.

Venezuela's revolutionary leader, Hugo Chavez, said the very same thing when I heard him speak in Caracas in 2010—that the 20th century was not, as many claim, the "American Century," but that it was, instead, the "Century of Revolution." And when he said "revolution," he meant anticolonial revolution.

Thus, the end of World War II saw the collapse of Western Empires, such as those of the British, German, Portuguese, Dutch, and French, and the independence of numerous formerly colonized nations, such as China, India, and Indonesia. As a panel of UN experts explained in 2004, this transformed the UN, for "[i]n the first 30 years of the United Nations, dozens of new States emerged from colonial systems that, until recent times, tied half of mankind to a handful of capitals. Assisting new States into being was a seminal contribution of the United Nations during this period. Decolonization in turn transformed the United Nations. At the creation of the United Nations in 1945, there were 51 members; today there are 191."[252]

But the old Empires did not always walk away from their colonies quietly. For example, the French would violently attempt to continue their domination over Algeria, fighting a brutal counterinsurgency war there from 1954 until being forced to withdraw in 1962. The French would also fight a counterindependence war against Vietnam after World War II until finally being defeated by the heroic efforts of the Vietnamese liberation forces in the legendary battle of Dien Bien Phu in 1954. The British fought for a time in vain to keep their hold over Palestine as well as their control over Egypt's Suez Canal, and, lest one forget, they successfully maintained their hold over Hong Kong until 1997. And, the South African people would be subjected to the Apartheid rule of the largely Dutch white population until 1992.

What's more, a new imperial power now emerged after World War II to step into the shoes of the old Empires—the United States. And so, the anticolonial Declaration was agreed to in the context of the Cuban Revolution of 1959, which the US would viciously oppose to and through the current time; the beginning of the US war on Vietnam that was waged to maintain domination over Vietnam after France's humiliating defeat; the independence struggle of Congo was quickly interrupted by the assassination of leader Patrice Lumumba in 1960 by forces backed by the US; Iran's struggle to overthrow British domination was crushed by US intervention in 1953; and the struggle of Guatemala to emerge from its role as a banana republic was violently interrupted by the US in 1954.

As for the US intervention in Guatemala in 1954, this would come to be known, in the words of then-UN Secretary General Dag Hammarskjöld, as "the most serious blow so far aimed at the United Nations."[253] This intervention, which overthrew a democratically elected president in Jacobo Arbenz, was orchestrated by the United States in order to protect the United Fruit Company (now Chiquita Brands International) from having its unused land in Guatemala from being bought by the Arbenz government at market rates and turned over to small farmers as part of Arbenz's modernizing land reform program.[254] As the *Washington Post* tells us, most of the key players in this operation had some personal interest in United Fruit, including Allen and John Foster Dulles, the head of the CIA and Secretary of State, respectively.[255]

Henry Cabot Lodge, the US Ambassador to the UN at the time, himself "was a stockholder, and had been a strong defender of United Fruit while a US senator."[256] It was Lodge who would personally make sure that the UN Security Council would not even consider a resolution being urged by Guatemala to send peace observers to Guatemala in an attempt to forestall the US-backed coup.[257] While the Soviet Union, Denmark, Lebanon, and New Zealand voted in favor of this resolution, it failed to pass as the result of Lodge's bullying of Britain and France to vote against, threatening to withhold support for their colonial machinations if they did otherwise.[258] Instead of the UN Security Council, Lodge urged that the Organization of American States (OAS) handle this issue, knowing full well that the OAS, then as now, was a willing pawn of the United States.[259] And, Lodge wanted the resolution at the UN Security Council to be voted down in a straight up-and-down vote rather than being forced to use the US's veto, for this would have exposed the truth about the US—that it was an enemy of the UN and international law.[260]

Ultimately, the US successfully deposed Arbenz and installed and supported a series of brutal military regimes that would terrorize the Guatemalan population. The Guatemalan military governments would kill 200,000, mostly Mayan, civilians, in what is now universally recognized as a genocide.[261] The US, and its usual partner in crime, Israel, backed the Guatemalan military and the genocide in the name of fighting communism and supporting democracy—a constant refrain with absolutely no basis in reality. As the *New York Times* explained in 1999:

> A truth commission report made public today concluded that the United States gave money and training to a Guatemalan military that committed "acts of genocide" against the Mayans during the most brutal armed conflict in Central America, Guatemala's thirty-six-year civil war.
>
> The report, by the independent Historical Clarification Commission, contradicts years of official denials of the torture, kidnapping, and execution of thousands of civilians in a war that the commission estimated killed more than 200,000 people.
>
> Although the outlines of American support for Guatemala's military have been well known, the nine-volume report confirms that the Central Intelligence Agency aided Guatemalan forces....
>
> The commission listed the American training of the officer corps in counterinsurgency techniques as a key factor that "had a

significant bearing on human rights violations during the armed confrontation."[262]

As this article notes, the US not only supported the Guatemalan army as it carried out genocide, but its training of its officer corps actually helped guarantee that the army would carry out mass human rights abuses. It is important to note that Elliott Abrams, who actively attempted to cover up the Guatemalan genocide and to hide it from the knowledge of Congress and the US public in order to keep US military aid to the Guatemalan regime flowing, is now in charge of the US's regime change efforts in Venezuela.[263] This is good evidence that the US's intervention in Venezuela is anything but "humanitarian."

It is also quite telling that Samantha Power does not even include the Guatemalan genocide in her Pulitzer Prize-winning case study on genocide, *A Problem from Hell*.[264] This is because the Guatemalan genocide, made possible by US intervention and support, cuts against her thesis that the West must intervene to prevent genocide. The reality, which she must ignore, is just the opposite. As Joseph Nevins opines in his piece, "On Justifying Intervention," "[b]ecause Samantha Power excludes cases like these from her analysis, she seems to have little problem endorsing American global dominance and, on the basis of such, calling for the United States to take the lead in battling genocide."[265] Nevins faults her as well for not including the US-backed slaughters in Indonesia in the 1960s in which over one million left-wing political opponents of the government were killed; in El Salvador in the 1980s, in which 75,000 innocents were killed; and the mass killings in East Timor in the mid-1970s, in which 200,000 civilians, accounting for one-third of the total population, were killed by the US-backed Indonesian military. Again, these interventions simply do not fit into her prointerventionist worldview.

It is worth noting here that Power, the Yale- and Harvard-trained intellectual and soccer mom, represents what Hannah Arendt, referring to Nazi leader Adolf Eichmann, termed "the banality of evil."

That is, she is a "normal," professional, well-educated, and well-spoken individual who, despite all appearances, helps facilitate terrible crimes. It is such individuals, indeed, who carry out most of the crimes of the West. Indeed, as the *Washington Post* explained in its article about the CIA-led coup against Arbenz in 1954, the predecessor of the CIA, the Office of Strategic Services (OSS), "liked to hire Wall Street lawyers and Ivy Leaguers to commit espionage," and this "hiring philosophy was embraced by the OSS's Cold War successor, the CIA. Its top ranks were filled with Wall Streeters, many of whom were OSS veterans, and academics from leading eastern colleges."[266] "Ivy Leagers" are perfect war criminals, after all, because they have been well educated in the prevailing ideology, making them believe in the righteousness of their actions even when there is nothing righteous about them, and helping them to be affable and effective apologists for empire. Power is one such "Ivy Leaguer," as are Obama, Susan Rice, the Clintons, and Henry Kissinger. The list goes on.

Meanwhile, it was in the context of the anticolonial struggle and the West's violent pushback, that an important international instrument underscoring the high priority given by the UN and the UN Charter to national sovereignty and nonintervention was agreed to— UN General Assembly Resolution 1514 (XV), the "Declaration on the Granting of Independence to Colonial Countries and Peoples," of December 14, 1960. This resolution is specifically referenced with approval in the International Convention on the Elimination of All Forms of Racial Discrimination, a Covenant with 180 state parties, including the United States, and is therefore now a legally binding agreement.

This Declaration reads as follow (emphasis added):

Mindful of the determination proclaimed by the peoples of the world in the Charter of the United Nations to reaffirm faith in fundamental human rights, in the dignity and worth of the human person, in the equal rights of men and women and of nations large and small, and to promote social progress and better standards of life in larger freedom,

Conscious of the need for the creation of conditions of stability and well-being and peaceful and friendly relations based on respect for the principles of equal rights and self-determination of all peoples, and of universal respect for, and observance of, human rights and fundamental freedoms for all without distinction as to race, sex, language or religion,

Recognizing the passionate yearning for freedom in all dependent peoples and the decisive role of such peoples in the attainment of their independence,

Aware of the increasing conflicts resulting from the denial of or impediments in the way of the freedom of such peoples, which constitute a serious threat to world peace,

Considering the important role of the United Nations in assisting the movement for independence in Trust and Non-Self-Governing Territories,

Recognising that the peoples of the world ardently desire the end of colonialism in all its manifestations,

Convinced that the continued existence of colonialism prevents the development of international economic co-operation, impedes the social, cultural and economic development of dependent peoples and militates against the United Nations ideal of universal peace,

Affirming that peoples may, for their own ends, freely dispose of their natural wealth and resources without prejudice to any obligations arising out of international economic co-operation, based upon the principle of mutual benefit, and international law,

Believing that the process of liberation is irresistible and irreversible and that, in order to avoid serious crises, an end must be put to colonialism and all practices of Segregation and discrimination associated therewith,

Welcoming the emergence in recent years of a large number of dependent territories into freedom and independence, and recognizing the increasingly powerful trends towards freedom in such territories which have not yet attained independence,

Convinced that all peoples have an inalienable right to complete freedom, the exercise of their sovereignty and the integrity of their national territory,

Solemnly proclaims the necessity of bringing to a speedy and unconditional end colonialism in all its forms and manifestations;

And to this end *Declares* that:

1. The subjection of peoples to alien subjugation, domination and exploitation constitutes a denial of fundamental human rights, is contrary to the Charter of the United Nations and is an impediment to the promotion of world peace and co-operation.
2. All peoples have the right to self-determination; by virtue of that right they freely determine their political status and freely pursue their economic, social and cultural development.
3. Inadequacy of political, economic, social, or educational preparedness should never serve as a pretext for delaying independence.
4. All armed action or repressive measures of all kinds directed against dependent peoples shall cease in order to enable them to exercise peacefully and freely their right to complete independence, and the integrity of their national territory shall be respected. . . .
5. Any attempt aimed at the partial or total disruption of the national unity and the territorial integrity of a country is incompatible with the purposes and principles of the Charter of the United Nations.
6. All States shall observe faithfully and strictly the provisions of the Charter of the United Nations, the Universal Declaration of Human Rights and the present Declaration on the basis of equality, non- interference in the internal affairs of all States, and respect for the sovereign rights of all peoples and their territorial integrity.

This anticolonial Declaration in many ways mirrored the ten principles enunciated at the 1955 Bandung, Indonesia, conference—a conference of formerly colonized Third World nations representing half of the world's population and intended to create a unified voice for the emerging Global South. The Ten Bandung Principles are as follows:[267]

1. Respect for fundamental human rights and for the purposes and the principles of the Charter of the United Nations.
2. Respect for the sovereignty and territorial integrity of all nations.
3. Recognition of the equality of all races and of the equality of all nations large and small.
4. Abstention from intervention or interference in the internal affairs of another country.
5. Respect for the right of each nation to defend itself singly or collectively, in conformity with the Charter of the United Nations.
6. Abstention from the use of arrangements of collective defense to serve the particular interests of any of the big powers, abstention by any country from exerting pressures on other countries.
7. Refraining from acts or threats of aggression or the use of force against the territorial integrity or political independence of any country.
8. Settlement of all international disputes by peaceful means, such as negotiation, conciliation, arbitration or judicial settlement as well as other peaceful means of the parties' own choice, in conformity with the Charter of the United Nations.
9. Promotion of mutual interests and cooperation.
10. Respect for justice and international obligation.

Note the frequency with which the UN Charter is referenced and its noninterventionist language is utilized in these ten principles. This is because the countries of the world that had been colonized by the great powers, and that were continuing to struggle against colonial domination, clearly saw the UN Charter and international law as formidable instruments of resistance in this struggle. In other words, the UN Charter, embodying the equality of all nations and the right of nations to chart their own course without outside interference, was seen as a protection of the poorer and weaker nations from the more powerful nations seeking to control and exploit them. And, I would assert, this is a correct interpretation of the UN Charter.

The anticolonial resolution, moreover, would be followed in 1965 by another important, anti-interventionist UN resolution—General Assembly Resolution 2131 (xx) of 21 December 1965 Declaration on the Inadmissibility of Intervention in the Domestic Affairs of States and the Protection of their Independence and Sovereignty.

It should come as little surprise that it was the Union of Soviet Socialist Republics that initiated this resolution, as the USSR played a critical role in the post-War period in supporting the anticolonial struggle. As philosopher Jean Bricmont explains, indeed, "the main lasting effect of the Russian Revolution is probably the Soviet Union's not insignificant support to the decolonization process. This process freed hundreds of millions of people from the most brutal forms of oppression. It is major progress in the history of mankind, similar to the abolition of slavery in the eighteenth and nineteen centuries."[268] It should also come as no surprise that the philosophy of "humanitarian interventionism" rose and became so influential only after the collapse of the USSR in 1991.

In pertinent part, this resolution provides that:

1. No State has the right to intervene, directly or indirectly, for any reason whatever, in the internal or external affairs of any State. Consequently, armed intervention and all other forms of interference or attempted threats against the personality of the State or against its political, economic and cultural elements, are condemned.

2. No State may use or encourage the use of economic, political or any other type of measures to coerce another State in order to obtain

from it the subordination of the exercise of its sovereign rights or to secure from it advantages of any kind. Also, no State shall organize, assist, foment, finance, incite, or tolerate subversive, terrorist, or armed activities directed towards the violent overthrow of the regime of another State, or interfere in civil strife in another State.

3. The use of force to deprive peoples of their national identity constitutes a violation of their inalienable rights and of the principle of non-intervention.

4. The strict observance of these obligations is an essential condition to ensure that nations live together in peace with one another, since the practice of any form of intervention not only violates the spirit and letter of the Charter of the United Nations but also leads to the creation of situations which threaten international peace and security.

5. Every State has an inalienable right to choose its political, economic, social and cultural systems, without interference in any form by another State.

6. All States shall respect the right of self-determination and independence of peoples and nations, to be freely expressed without any foreign pressure, and with absolute respect for human rights and fundamental freedoms. Consequently, all States shall contribute to the complete elimination of racial discrimination and colonialism in all its forms and manifestations.

As the official introductory note to this resolution explains, "Resolution 2131 (XX) of 1965, in historical terms, reflects the remarkable acceleration of the decolonization process in the few years since the adoption of Resolution 1514 (XV). Eighteen new States, all but one of these (Mongolia) 'colonies' in the classical international law sense, had been admitted to the United Nations in the meantime. With their new numbers, the informal coalitions or associations of the neutral States had taken on an extra political coherence and certainly tactical and often strategical legal sophistication."[269]

While the language in Resolution 2132 (XX) of 1965 is clear, the introductory note makes a point to say that this resolution was intended to respond to and prevent not only military intervention in sovereign states—and in particular former colonial nations—but also to prevent interference "of a financial or economic character not yet adequately defined in or fully reached by positive law—economic and financial coercion or extreme trade pressures or boycotts, and also covert, or sometimes direct and open, encouragement or incitement for dissident, political breakaway groups in a particular State or region." Again, these prohibitions are an obvious response to the rise of US intervention in the Third World via the Central Intelligence Agency.

At the same time, it is important to note that the anti-interventionist proscriptions in the resolution did not represent any change in international law. Rather, they really represented a restatement of the law as set forth in the UN Charter and other international instruments. Indeed, the drafters of the resolution made this clear by underscoring in the resolution that "the United Nations, in accordance with their aim to eliminate war, created an organization, based on the sovereign equality of States, whose friendly relations would be based on respect for the principle of equal rights and self-determination of peoples and on the obligation of its Members to refrain from the threat or use of force against the territorial integrity or political independence of any State."

The resolution further recalls that "in the Universal Declaration of Human Rights the General Assembly proclaimed the recognition of the inherent dignity and of the equal and inalienable rights of all members of the human family is the foundation of freedom, justice and peace in the world, without distinction of any kind."

Finally, the resolution makes it clear that "direct intervention, subversion and all forms of indirect intervention are contrary to these principles [prohibiting aggression and requiring co-operation between States] and, consequently, constitute a violation of the Charter of the United Nations."

The Nuremberg Trials formed the basis of the International Prohibition of Aggressive War

Nelson Mandela: the Civil Rights leader Amnesty International would not support

Henry Kissinger: Proof that western war criminals can receive Nobel Peace Prizes

HRW's Kenneth Roth: The Voice of Empire under the guise of Human Rights

The Brutal Shah of Iran: Installed by the US, 1953, in the CIA's first regime-change operation

Augusto Pinochet: The US-backed fascist who protected western business interests in Chile

Witness testifies during genocide trial of former Guatemalan military dictator Rios Montt, a favorite of Ronald Reagan and Elliott Abrams

The War in Congo for minerals rages on under the noses of UN "peacekeepers"

Hillary Clinton meets with Libyan National Security Advisor, Mutassim Gaddafi, the fourth son of Muammar Gaddafi. Not long after, both Gaddafis would be killed in the war Clinton helped unleash

President Barack Obama and First Lady Michelle Obama walk with King Salman of Saudi Arabia. President Obama would sell him weapons to carry out mass slaughter in Yemen

Resolution 2132 (XX) had some immediate effects. Thus, the introductory note explains that "Among the more spectacular successes of this post-Resolution 2131 (XX) operation was the achievement of decolonization and independence for the former German colony of South West Africa that had been converted into a League of Nations Mandated Territory under the terms of the 1919 Treaty of Versailles after World War I, but entrusted to the then white-minority ruled Union of South Africa by the League of Nations."

What's more, the introductory note to Resolution 2132 (XX) mentions that, after the NATO intervention in Yugoslavia in 1999, l'Institut de Droit international (Institute of International Rights) was tasked "to report on contemporary legal issues involving self-defense, humanitarian intervention, military intervention by invitation and authorization of the use of force by the United Nations." However, as the introductory note goes on to explain, years later "[a]t its 2007 session, the president of l'Institut de Droit international noted that it had been unable to agree to accepting 'the lawfulness of military actions which have not been authorized by the United Nations but which purport to have been taken to end genocide, large-scale crimes against humanity, or large scale crimes.'" The Institute could not agree to the lawfulness of such interventionist actions, of course, because they are clearly prohibited by the UN Charter and its progeny.

Meanwhile, the introductory note explains that "[i]n the mid-1980s, the International Court of Justice, seized of the issue by the Nicaraguan Government which had complained of active military, logistical and other support by the United States to Contras rebel groups within Nicaraguan territories and to other actions including the United States' mining of Nicaraguan ports and coastal waters, referred in its Judgement, inter alia, to Resolution 2131 (XX) (Military and Paramilitary Activities in and Against Nicaragua, I.C.J. Reports, 1986, p. 107, para. 203)." The ICJ did not only refer to this resolution, moreover, but it held that the obligations set forth in it constitute "'basic principles' of international law."

An examination of this landmark case further illuminates the parameters of the anti-interventionist nature of the UN Charter and International Law as well as the illicit nature of "humanitarian interventionism."

*　*　*

Before we move on from UN Resolution 2131 (XX), however, one more observation is appropriate. The introductory note to this resolution mentions a curious event in world history—Vietnam's invasion and occupation of Cambodia from 1978 to 1989. While the West universally decried these actions of Vietnam, there is a huge irony here. This is because Vietnam's actions in Cambodia are considered by some as a truly humanitarian intervention, as they rid Cambodia of Pol Pot and the Khmer Rouge. As commentator Gregory Elich opined, the Vietnamese 1978 campaign against the Khmer Rouge "was one of history's great liberations."[270] Historian Eric Hobsbawm agrees, pointing to the general "consensus" that this was an "obvious" case of "justified intervention."[271]

Moreover, Western humanitarians such as Samantha Power and Kenneth Roth, in talking about the Cambodian genocide, focus their ire and hand-wringing on the actions of Pol Pot and Khmer Rouge, which were certainly atrocious. However, as usual, these Western humanitarians gloss over critical historical facts to pin all of the crimes on Pol Pot and to relieve the West of any responsibility for what happened.

In this case, they tend to ignore three salient facts. First, they ignore how the US itself committed genocide in Cambodia before Pol Pot even arrived on the scene. Thus, beginning in 1969, the US began a merciless bombing campaign against the hitherto peaceful and quiet nation of Cambodia. As one source described this campaign, "'[t]he methodical sacking of economic resources, of rubber plantations and factories, of rice fields and forests, of peaceful and delightful villages which disappeared one after another beneath the bombs and napalm, has no military justification and serves essentially to starve the population.'"[272] All told, the US carpet bombing of Cambodia from 1969 until 1973 killed around 250,000 Cambodians and displaced a million more.[273]

Meanwhile, the CIA sponsored a right-wing coup in Cambodia in 1970 that brought Lon Nol to power. As Noam Chomsky and Edward Herman have related, "Lon Nol quickly organized a pogrom-bloodbath against local Vietnamese" who had fled the war in their home country.[274] Over 5,000 people were killed in this slaughter, with 330,000 more Vietnamese forced out of the country. The US and South Vietnam would then invade "to support the organizers of the slaughter, who were on the verge of being overthrown."

The second salient fact generally ignored by the Western humanitarians is that the US brutal intervention in Cambodia, not too surprisingly, radicalized the population, turning them toward Pol Pot and his Khmer Rouge, helping him come to power to do the terrible things he ended up doing.[275] Power at least mentions this fact in her book, *A Problem From Hell*, where she notes in passing that "US B-52 raids killed tens of thousands of civilians" and "indirectly helped give rise to a monstrous regime."[276] As Herman and Peterson astutely point out in *The Politics of Genocide*, "[n]otice that in Power's hands, the 'monstrous regime' is the one that arose after the other regime's bombers 'killed tens of thousands of civilians'—but no negative adjectives are applied to the regime that sent along those bombers from the other side of the planet."[277]

Finally, the Western "humanitarians" ignore the inconvenient fact that it was not the West, but instead Vietnam, that ended up ridding the world of Pol Pot.[278] Meanwhile, the US actually continued to support the Khmer Rouge after the Vietnamese invasion in order to continue to harass the new revolutionary government in Vietnam.

Similarly, the West's apologists fail to acknowledge the other two 20th century interventions that many true human rights advocates consider were actually "humanitarian"—"the military intervention by India in East Pakistan in 1971, which ended the slaughter of Bengali citizens by the Pakistan army and resulted in the proclamation of the independent state of Bangladesh"; and "the invasion by Tanzania in Uganda in 1979, terminating the murderous rule of dictator Idi Amin."[279] As Human Rights Professor Peter R. Baehr notes, '[n]one of the intervening states based their actions on humanitarian or human rights considerations," precisely because "recogniz[ing] the legitimacy of humanitarian intervention would create a precedent which at some other point in time could be used against the intervening state."[280]

And, of course, I do not cite these cases now to justify the idea of "humanitarian" interventionism. However, they are important to note because they certainly cut against the prevailing notion that it is the West's unique right and privilege to intervene in other nations in the interest of human rights, if for no other reason than the West has never shown in practice that it truly wishes to do so. Rather, the West has proven time and again that countries, such as the once-peaceful Cambodia, would have been better off had the West simply not intervened in the place. At the same time, these cases show that the Global South is fully capable of dealing with its own human rights and humanitarian issues without Western intervention.

SIX

Nicaragua v. US, and Lessons about Nonintervention

QUITE APPROPRIATELY, THE *NICARAGUA V. US*[281] case before the International Court of Justice (ICJ) (see Statute of the ICJ at Appendix B) grew out of Nicaragua's anticolonial struggle to overthrow the US-backed Somoza dictatorship, which had been installed by the US, after numerous Marine invasions, in 1936. The Nicaraguan people finally overthrew this dictatorship, against all odds, in 1979, only to face a violent attempt by the US to counter this revolution and reimpose control over Nicaragua. This counterrevolution took the form of the arming of a violent paramilitary force—largely made up of former National Guardsmen of the Somoza dictatorship, known as the Contras—and economic warfare and various acts of terrorism carried out directly by the US. Nicaragua brought a case against the US before the UN to try to halt this counter-revolutionary activity and to obtain compensation for the damages it had already suffered as a result.

As for the makeup of the Contras, whom Ronald Reagan famously described as "freedom fighters," the ICJ found that they were anything but. As the ICJ explained, "Certain opponents of the new Government, **primarily supporters of the former Somoza Government and in particular ex-members of the National Guard**, formed themselves into irregular military forces, and commenced a policy of armed opposition, though initially on a limited scale." (emphasis added) That is, the Contra force was largely made up of those who had governed Nicaragua, with staunch US backing, and with an iron hand, for over forty years. These Guardsmen-turned-Contras wanted to reestablish the old, dictatorial order, not to bring about democracy.

Lest one forget just how cruel Somoza and his National Guard henchmen were, it is worth recalling what they did to try to hold on to power before the Sandinista victory in 1979. As one commentator explains:

> In the waning months of the Somoza dynasty, the depths of the tyrannical tradition were on full display. Following an unsuccessful insurrection by the Sandinista National Liberation Front (FSLN) in September 1978, Somoza ordered the bombardment of six major cities in a vain and vicious attempt to keep the Sandinista guerillas from consolidating power. The air campaign left more than 50,000 dead (80 percent of them civilians), 100,000 wounded, and estimated 40,000 orphaned, and some 150,000 refugees.[282]

In a country of less than three million people at that time, these numbers are truly staggering.

And of course, the US supported the Somoza dynasty to the bitter end of his reign. And, even when he was finally overthrown, our "human rights President," Jimmy Carter, "flew [National] Guard commanders out of the country in planes with Red Cross markings (a war crime), and began to reconstitute the Guard on Nicaragua's borders," setting the stage for what would become the Contras.[283]

The means employed by the Contras demonstrated their evil aims. Thus, as the ICJ noted, "the contras have caused . . . considerable material damage and widespread loss of life, and have also committed such acts as killing of prisoners, indiscriminate killing of civilians, torture, rape and kidnapping." Meanwhile, just as the US had supported the Somoza dictatorship and its National Guard until the bitter end of their reign, including supplying them as they bombed their own urban areas to try in vain to stay in power, the US, with help from the Argentine fascist government, supported their Contra successors. Indeed, as the ICJ found, based upon the affidavit of a key Contra leader, the US CIA exercised "virtually a power of command" over the Contras and their operations. In the final analysis, the ICJ found that the evidence "established that the United States authorities largely financed, trained, equipped, armed and organized" the Contras.

In addition to the Contras, the ICJ accepted as true Nicaragua's claims that the US funded and directed other actors who engaged in various terrorist acts against Nicaragua and its population, including "the mining of certain Nicaraguan ports in early 1984, and attacks on ports, oil installations, a naval base, etc. Nicaragua has also complained of overflights of its territory by United States aircraft, not only for purposes of intelligence gathering and supply to the contras in the field, but also in order to intimidate the population."

As to the mining of the harbors, the ICJ found "it established that, on a date in late 1983 or early 1984, the President of the United States authorized a United States government agency to lay mines in Nicaraguan ports; that in early 1984 mines were laid in or close to the ports of El Bluff, Corinto, and Puerto Sandino, either in Nicaraguan internal waters or in its territorial sea or both, by persons in the pay and acting on the instructions of that agency, under the supervision and with the logistic support of United States agents; that neither before the laying of the mines, nor subsequently, did the United States Government issue any public and official warning to international shipping of the existence and location of the mines; and that personal and material injury was caused by the explosion of the mines."

Further, "[i]n the economic field, . . . the United States has . . . imposed a trade embargo; it has also used its influence in the Inter-American Development Bank and the International Bank for Reconstruction and Development to block the provision of loans to Nicaragua."

Meanwhile, the US, consistently taking the position that international law applies to everyone else but itself, did not make the work of the ICJ easy. Thus, the US did not make an appearance or give evidence in the case on the merits, though it did make a limited appearance initially to challenge jurisdiction. But the ICJ, wanting to be fair, made the US's case for it based upon the US government's jurisdictional objections as well as its public pronouncements on the subject.

In addition, because the US had made a general "reservation" to the exercise of ICJ jurisdiction to the effect that no multilateral treaties could be applied to render a judgment in a case in which it was involved unless all States potentially affected by the outcome of the case were actually parties to that case, this greatly limited what laws the ICJ could apply. This is so because the US was claiming that its actions in Nicaragua were part of its collective defense of El Salvador, whose FMLN rebels the US claimed were receiving arms from the Sandinista government in Managua, and El Salvador was not a party to the case. Therefore, even such laws as those set forth in the UN Charter, to which El Salvador is a signatory, could not be applied by the ICJ in the case.

However, while not actually applying the UN Charter directly, the ICJ did at least look to the Charter as evidence of "customary international law" given that the Charter had nearly universal buy-in from every nation in the world. Looking to the Charter as "customary international law," the ICJ drew some broad conclusions that are helpful in understanding the import of that instrument, particularly as it relates to the demands of nonintervention and respect for national sovereignty.

First of all, the ICJ found that the principle of nonintervention was one now so firmly established in international law as to constitute a *jus cogens* norm—that is, a norm (such as the norms against genocide and slavery) so universally agreed to, and of such gravity, that it allows for no exceptions or derogations.

It found, indeed, that Article 2(4) of the UN Charter and UN Resolution 2131 (XX) set forth prohibitions of intervention and aggression already accepted by the world community and already existing as customary international law. The ICJ thus held: "[t]he principle of non-intervention involves the right of every sovereign State to conduct its affairs without outside interference; though examples of trespass against this principle are not infrequent, the Court considers that it is part and parcel of customary international law. As the Court has observed: 'Between independent States, respect for territorial sovereignty is an essential foundation of international relations' (I.C.J. Reports 1949, p. 35), and international law requires political integrity also to be respected."

The ICJ also cited with approval a prior ICJ case, the *Corfu Channel* case of 1949, which held:

> the alleged right of intervention as the manifestation of a policy of force, such as has, in the past, given rise to most serious abuses and such as cannot, whatever be the present defects in international organization, find a place in international law. Intervention is perhaps still less admissible in the particular form it would take here; for, from the nature of things, it would be reserved for the most powerful States, and might easily lead to perverting the administration of international justice itself.

The ICJ did not stop there. Because the US, one of those "most powerful States" that always justifies interventions based on such lofty goals as human rights and democracy, the ICJ considered whether such ostensible goals could justify military intervention. In short, the ICJ found that they do not. First of all, the ICJ made it clear that one nation may not intervene in another to change another nation's political or economic system, even a system the intervening nation finds objectionable. As the ICJ held, the principle of nonintervention

> forbids all States or groups of States to intervene directly or indirectly in internal or external affairs of other States. A prohibited intervention must accordingly be one bearing on matters in which each State is permitted, by the principle of State sovereignty to decide freely. One of these is the choice of a political, economic, social, and cultural system, and the formulation of foreign policy. Intervention is wrongful when it uses methods of coercion in regard to such choices, which must remain free ones. The element of coercion, which defines, and indeed forms the very essence of, prohibited intervention, is particularly obvious in the case of an intervention which uses force, either in the direct form of military action, or in the indirect form of support for subversive or terrorist armed activities within another State.

To put a finer point on it, the ICJ held:

> The finding of the United States Congress also expressed the view that the Nicaraguan Government had taken "significant steps towards establishing a totalitarian Communist dictatorship." However the régime in Nicaragua be defined, adherence by a State to any particular doctrine does not constitute a violation of customary international law; to hold otherwise would make nonsense of the fundamental principle of State sovereignty on which the whole of international law rests, and the freedom of choice of the political, social, economic and cultural system of a State. Consequently, Nicaragua's domestic policy options, even assuming that they correspond to the description given of them by the Congress finding, cannot justify on the legal plane the various actions the Respondent complained of. The Court cannot contemplate the creation of a new rule opening up a right of intervention by one State against another on the ground that the latter has opted for some particular ideology or political system.

In other words, the ICJ made clear, there is no legal basis for "ideological intervention" in international law.

In addition, and quite relevant to more current Western interventions such as those in Syria and Libya wherein the Western powers financed and armed opposition forces, the ICJ made it clear that a request by an opposition group in a country cannot constitute a proper legal basis for intervention in that country. As the ICJ held:

> the principle of non-intervention derives from customary international law. It would certainly lose its effectiveness as a principle of law if intervention were to be justified by a mere request for assistance made by an opposition group in another State—supposing such a request to have actually been made by an opposition to the régime in Nicaragua in this instance. Indeed, it is difficult to see what would remain of the principle of non-intervention in international law if intervention, which is already allowable at the request of the government of a State, were also to be allowed at the request of the opposition. This would permit any State to intervene at any moment in the internal affairs of another State, whether at the request of the government or at the request of its opposition. Such a situation does not in the Court's view correspond to the present state of international law.

Finally, and most important, the ICJ held that there is no concept of "humanitarian intervention" in international law. Indeed, the ICJ was quite clear on this point, stating, "[i]n any event, while the United States might form its own appraisal of the situation as to respect for human rights in Nicaragua, the use of force could not be the appropriate method to monitor or ensure such respect. With regard to the steps actually taken, the protection of human rights, a strictly humanitarian objective, cannot be compatible with the mining of ports, the destruction of oil installations, or again with the training, arming, and equipping of the contras."

Applying these well-established legal principles to the case, the ICJ ultimately made the following findings against the US:

> the United States of America, by training, arming, equipping, financing, and supplying the contra forces or otherwise encouraging, supporting, and aiding military and paramilitary activities in and against Nicaragua, has acted, against the Republic of Nicaragua, in breach of its obligation under customary international law not to intervene in the affairs of another State; ...
>
> ... the United States of America, by certain attacks on Nicaraguan territory in 1983–1984, namely attacks on Puerto Sandino on 13 September and 14 October 1983 ; an attack on Corinto on 10 October 1983 ; an attack on Potosi Naval Base on 4/5 January 1984 ; an attack on San Juan del Sur on 7 March 1984 ; attacks on patrol boats at Puerto Sandino on 28 and 30 March 1984 ; and an attack on San Juan del Norte on 9 April 1984 ; and further by those acts of intervention referred to in subparagraph (3) hereof which involve the use of force, has acted, against the Republic of Nicaragua, in breach of its obligation under customary international law not to use force against another State; ...
>
> ... by laying mines in the internal or territorial waters of the Republic of Nicaragua during the first months of 1984, the United States of America has acted, against the Republic of Nicaragua, in breach of its obligations under customary international law not to use force against another State, not to intervene in its affairs, not to violate its sovereignty and not to interrupt peaceful maritime commerce.

The ICJ also found that "that the United States of America, by producing in 1983 a manual entitled *Operaciones sicologicas en guerra de guerrillas*, and disseminating it to contra forces, has encouraged the commission by them of acts contrary to general principles of humanitarian law." Here, the ICJ is referencing the CIA's infamous "Psychological Operations" manual that encouraged the Contras to carry out terrorist activities within Nicaragua.

The ICJ ordered the US to immediately cease and desist from such conduct against Nicaragua and to make reparations to Nicaragua done by such unlawful acts.

Not surprisingly, the US disregarded the ICJ decision in its entirety, continuing to wage war, including through the Contras, against Nicaragua until at least 1990, when the Sandinistas were voted out of office under threat of continued war, and refusing to even discuss with Nicaragua the issue of reparations.

The US's continued illegal campaign against the Sandinista government, even after the ICJ decision, was well detailed by a group of US military veterans, turned peace activists, who went to Nicaragua to observe the run-up to the elections and their aftermath. In their report, they explain:

> President Bush continued the US economic embargo against Nicaragua by again declaring on October 25, 1989, that Nicaragua posed an "unusual and extraordinary threat to the national security and foreign policy of the United States." The economic situation throughout Nicaragua continues to force the majority of people to live in painful depravity.
>
> The US Congress and the CIA have combined to finance, with what are believed to be unprecedented amounts of money, the so-called opposition political parties in an effort to defeat the majority Sandinista Party in the February 1990 elections.
>
> In effect, the US orchestrated and financed three-pronged attack through use of "low intensity" warfare against Nicaragua is in full force: (1) continued Contra terrorism throughout Nicaragua's rural areas, (2) continued economic strangulation, and (3) unprecedented efforts to purchase the internal political process and elections.[284]

As for the first prong of the attack—the continued war effort against Nicaragua—this report explains that Congress appropriated new funding for the Contras in April of 1989, and the funding was authorized at least until just after the February 1990 elections. And again, whether this funding continued thereafter would depend on the outcome. Lest there were any doubt as to the intentions of the timing of this aid package, "[t]he Contras are communicating to virtually all rural campesinos, through word of mouth, distribution of US funded leaflets, and direct threats, that they will 'make the war worse than ever if the FSLN wins the elections.' Dr. Summerfield [an English psychiatrist studying the effects of the Contra war on the Nicaraguan population] suggested that a lot of people may not vote because of the fear of terrorist reprisals, like murder and maiming."

Harold Pinter, in his 2005 Nobel Prize speech titled "Art, Truth & Politics,"[285] summed up the above history as only a man of letters can. As Pinter, who was a spokesperson for Nicaragua in opposing Congressional aid to the Contras in the 1980s, opined:

> The United States supported the brutal Somoza dictatorship in Nicaragua for over 40 years. The Nicaraguan people, led by the Sandinistas, overthrew this regime in 1979, a breathtaking popular revolution.
>
> The Sandinistas weren't perfect. They possessed their fair share of arrogance and their political philosophy contained a number of contradictory elements. But they were intelligent, rational and civilized. They set out to establish a stable, decent, pluralistic society. The death penalty was abolished. Hundreds of thousands of poverty-stricken peasants were brought back from the dead. Over 100,000 families were given title to land. Two thousand schools were built. A quite remarkable literacy campaign reduced illiteracy in the country to less than one seventh. Free education was established and a free health service. Infant mortality was reduced by a third. Polio was eradicated.
>
> The United States denounced these achievements as Marxist/ Leninist subversion. In the view of the US government, a dangerous example was being set. If Nicaragua was allowed to establish basic norms of social and economic justice, if it was allowed to raise the

standards of health care and education and achieve social unity and national self-respect, neighboring countries would ask the same questions and do the same things. . . .

The United States finally brought down the Sandinista government. It took some years and considerable resistance but relentless economic persecution and 30,000 dead finally undermined the spirit of the Nicaraguan people. They were exhausted and poverty stricken once again. The casinos moved back into the country. Free health and free education were over. Big business returned with a vengeance. "Democracy" had prevailed.

Meanwhile, Western human rights groups were not particularly helpful to the Nicaraguan cause for peace and national sovereignty, and this is largely due to their embrace of the very doctrine which the ICJ held is not contemplated in international law—"humanitarian" interventionism.

One of the few who has recognized the perversion of this doctrine is Jean Bricmont in his wonderful book, *Humanitarian Imperialism* (Monthly Review Press, 2006). Throughout this book, Bricmont explains how kind-hearted liberals and humanitarians have been hoodwinked by the new human rights ideology to support Western intervention against upstart revolutionary governments while largely remaining silent about threatened or ongoing Western interventions that are so clearly undermining human rights.

One example Bricmont gives of this is the strange phenomenon of liberal intellectuals, such as Bernard-Henri Levy, who lobbied for aid to the Contras in the name of human rights and of fighting what they viewed to be "a totalitarian party" in the Sandinistas. Bricmont points out the obvious—that it was the Sandinistas that overthrew a US-backed dictatorship to begin with and that then peacefully stepped down from power in 1990 after losing an election. "Hardly a model 'totalitarian party,'" quips Bricmont.

Meanwhile, Bricmont explains that these same self-described "human rights defenders" simply ignored the brutal tactics of the

Contras—tactics taught to them by the CIA in its infamous "Psychological Operations" manual. Such tactics, which can only be described as terrorism, included kidnapping and "neutralizing" (meaning "killing") key Sandinista judges, police, and other officials, preferably in the presence of a mob; hiring professional criminals to carry out dirty deeds as required; and sabotaging key civilian infrastructure, such as roads, power generators, and food supplies. It is worth noting, by the way, that the very same CIA-developed tactics were used on a large scale during the recent crisis in Nicaragua in the summer of 2018 by the opposition forces so romanticized by many in the Western left.

That such conduct could somehow be considered "humanitarian" is incredible, and so the pro-Contra intellectuals simply ignored it, and they ignore it still. At the same time, much greater humanitarian crises are being ignored in the region as self-described human rights defenders obsess about Nicaragua.

SEVEN

The Right of Self-Defense

NEARLY EVERY WAR THE US fights is a war of choice, meaning that the US fights because it wants to, not because it must do so in order to defend the homeland. This means that nearly every war the US fights is illegal, because, as we have already learned, the UN Charter, and in particular Article 51, specifically provides only one exception to Article 2(4)'s prohibition on the use of force—self-defense in the case of an armed attack.

And, the ICJ made it clear in the *Nicaragua v. United States* case that Article 51, which itself restates the international customary law norms allowing for self-defense, means what it clearly states: only an "armed attack" directly against a State (i.e., individual self-defense), or against another State that has asked the former for help in repelling an attack (i.e., collective self-defense), allows that State to use force. Professor Ryan T. Williams boils down the self-defense proviso of the Charter as follows: "the state may resort to force (1) in self-defense, (2) pursuant to a UN Security Council resolution, or (3) with the consent from the leader of the host state."[286]

In addition, the ICJ made it clear that the response the State in question uses in response to the armed attack must comport with the limitations of necessity and proportionality. Defining these terms succinctly, Professor Mary Ellen O'Connell of the University of Notre Dame writes, "[n]ecessity refers to force being used only as a last resort and where there is a reasonable likelihood of accomplishing the objective. The force used must not claim more lives or create more damage than is proportionate to the injury."[287] These limitations will rarely allow for the defending State, for example, to attempt to change the regime of the attacking State, for this will rarely represent proportional or necessary force.

As the ICJ explains:

> With regard to the characteristics governing the right of self-defense, since the Parties consider the existence of this right to be established as a matter of customary international law, they have concentrated on the conditions governing its use. . . . The Parties also agree in holding that whether the response to the attack is lawful depends on observance of the criteria of the necessity and the proportionality of the measures taken in self-defense. . . .
>
> In the case of individual self-defense, the exercise of this right is subject to the State concerned having been the victim of an armed attack. Reliance on collective self-defense of course does not remove the need for this. There appears now to be general agreement on the nature of the acts which can be treated as constituting armed attacks. In particular, it may be considered to be agreed that an armed attack must be understood as including not merely action by regular armed forces across an international border, but also "the sending by or on behalf of a State of armed bands, groups, irregulars or mercenaries, which carry out acts of armed force against another State of such gravity as to amount to" (inter alia) an actual armed attack conducted by regular forces, "or its substantial involvement therein."

Summing up these legal principles, Professor O'Connell explains, "Article 51 permits individual and collective self-defense *if* an armed attack occurs. A US delegate to the 1945 San Francisco drafting conference made clear that 'the intention of the authors of the original text was to state in the broadest terms an absolute all-inclusive prohibition... there should be no loopholes.'"[288] Citing the *Nicaragua v. US* case, she further relates that "[t]he United Nations Charter permits unilateral self-defense only in cases where objective evidence of an emergency exists for the entire world to see, namely, evidence of an armed attack or an action amounting to an armed attack."

Applying the foregoing legal principles to the *Nicaragua v. United States* case, the ICJ concluded that the allegation that Nicaragua was supporting the FMLN guerillas in El Salvador did not provide a sufficient basis for the assertion of either individual or collective self-defense permitting the US to act against Nicaragua because even if this alleged conduct constituted an armed attack against El Salvador, it certainly did not constitute one against the US. Therefore, the US had no basis for claiming individual self-defense.

Moreover, there was no case for claiming collective self-defense either because (1) El Salvador had not declared itself attacked by Nicaragua as a consequence of this alleged conduct; and (2) El Salvador had not asked the US to come to its assistance in defending it. Thus, the two prerequisites for collective self-defense were not met. As the ICJ made clear, "At all events, the Court finds that in customary international law, whether of a general kind or that particular to the inter-American legal system, there is no rule permitting the exercise of collective self-defense in the absence of a request by the State which regards itself as the victim of an armed attack. The Court concludes that the requirement of a request by the State which is the victim of the alleged attack is additional to the requirement that such a State should have declared itself to have been attacked."

In addition, even if the exception of self-defense had been properly triggered by this alleged conduct, it would not have, according to the ICJ, allowed the US to try to overthrow the Sandinista government, for this would not have constituted proportional or necessary force to repel the "attack" alleged.

These principles are important, for they show how the US has acted illegally in nearly every one of its post-WWII war efforts abroad. Indeed, the only time the US could properly invoke Article 51, after WWII, was after 9/11, which of course was an armed attack and which the Security Council, in SC Resolution 1368, deemed was an armed attack and a threat to international peace and security permitting armed self-defense.[289] But again, this does not end the discussion.

First of all, against whom was the US authorized to defend itself? Of course, those who attacked the US on 9/11 and who, we were told, were associated with Al Qaeda. We were also told that Al Qaeda and its leader, Osama bin Laden, the US's one-time ally in the fight against the secular Afghan state, were being harbored by Afghanistan and its Taliban government. But no one claims that the Taliban itself had attack the US, though that is strongly implied even to this day to justify what came next.

Right after 9/11, the US threatened to attack Afghanistan if the Taliban government did not turn over Osama bin Laden. Did the Taliban refuse to do this? No. Rather, they said that they would indeed comply with this request on the sole condition that the US supply them with the evidence showing that Osama bin Laden was indeed involved in the 9/11 attacks.[290] President George W. Bush refused to provide such evidence and invaded Afghanistan. As we know, Osama bin Laden— who, by the way, never made the FBI Most Wanted list for his alleged involvement in the 9/11 attacks due to lack of evidence[291]—escaped to Pakistan, where he was later killed in cold blood in 2011. And yet the US continued fighting in Afghanistan first to topple the Taliban, which it did rather quickly, then to ward off the Taliban counteroffensive, and is there to this day, now eight years after bin Laden's death.

In light of these facts, the US invasion of and war in Afghanistan was and is illegal. Thus, as is quite typical, the US simply eschewed the pacific means available to avoid armed conflict—that is, providing evidence to the Taliban of Osama bin Laden's 9/11 culpability. The US was obligated to avail itself of this peaceful avenue to avoid the use of force but simply chose not to because it wanted the war in Afghanistan regardless of what happened with bin Laden.

But even assuming that the US's initial invasion had some justification as an act of self-defense, there is no doubt that its continued war in that country is contrary to the UN Charter. As Professor Ryan T. William writes:

> The most relatable justification to the general public appears to be self-defense. There is little doubt America was attacked on 9/11, and the perpetrators were members of al Qaeda. But, bin Laden's death and the subsequent troop withdrawal raise some concerns about the viability of self-defense as a legal justification for the war in Afghanistan. If America begins withdrawing from Afghanistan because the leader of al Qaeda was shot and killed in Pakistan, how was (and is) the war against the Taliban in Afghanistan self-defense against al Qaeda?[292]

The quick answer is that this war was and is not legal. But again, the US is rarely concerned about legal niceties. But Western "humanitarians" should be.

Meanwhile, as the US overplays its hand in claiming self-defense as a justification for its wars of aggression, it absolutely denies the right of other countries to defend themselves from armed attack. And when they do defend themselves, the US points to this as but another justification for its own warfare.

For example, former UN Ambassador Nikki Haley, in an attempt to gin up war against Iran, went before the United Nations to try to prove that Iran had provided the Houthi rebels in Yemen with short-range missiles, which, she and the Saudis claimed, were fired upon Saudi Arabia a total of two times, doing no damage.[293] Haley declared that "the fight against Iranian aggression is the world's fight. The US is acting today in the spirit of transparency and international cooperation that is necessary to defeat this threat."[294]

Even putting aside the fact that the "evidence" of the Iranian supplying of such missiles is at best equivocal, with some UN experts serious expressing doubts about this claim,[295] what if this allegation were true? In a *Guardian* article, the authors state the obvious—that is, that "the Saudi-led coalition leading the fight against the Houthis in Yemen, which has been supplied with weaponry by the US, the UK and other allies, has been accused of the indiscriminate killing of civilians through its aerial bombing campaign and by its blockade of rebel-controlled areas of the country." The truth is that the "war" in Yemen is really a one-sided assault by the Saudi Coalition, with the support of the United States and the United Kingdom, against the Yemeni people. The fact is that morality, international law (including Article 51 of the UN Charter), and just plain common sense allow Yemen to defend itself against this incessant attack. And armed forces in Yemen have every right to attack Saudi Arabia in order to engage in such self-defense, and to enlist the support of others, like Iran, to help them do so.

However, since the founding of our nation, such self-defense is not permitted of those we designate as our enemies, even if, as is almost always the case, they are much weaker than ourselves. As Vietnam veteran and longtime peace activist Brian S. Willson has explained, "imperial US military principles" were set forth centuries ago with George Washington's orders of 1789 to Major General Sullivan to "lay waste to all [indigenous] settlements around . . . that the [native] country not be merely overrun but destroyed. . . . You will not by any means listen to any overtures for peace before the total ruin of their settlements. . . . Our future security will be in their inability to injure us . . . and in the terror which the severity of the chastisement they receive will inspire in them."[296]

From this order, Willson and others have gleaned a number of principles, including the "crime of self-defense." The United States and its allies may brutalize and attempt to decimate an entire nation or people, but those people are never allowed to fight back. Such fighting back is indeed cause for even more brutality on the part of the United States.

We see this time and again, for example in the Vietnam War, when the claim that the Vietnamese attacked two US military vessels (this claim turned out to be untrue) in the Gulf of Tonkin enraged US Congressional representatives, who then voted overwhelmingly in response to fund the war efforts that, up till then, they had been reluctant to do. Again, forget the fact that the allegations were not factually true. And even if they were, the idea that somehow the Vietnamese could not fight back as the United States was demolishing their country with aerial bombs, napalm, and Agent Orange seems preposterous. And yet, that was in fact the overwhelming opinion of our leaders. Indeed, it would have been completely justifiable for Vietnam to attack the continental United States in order to defend itself (which of course never happened), but this seems unthinkable. Surely, the United States would have wiped it off the map if it had dared to do such a thing.

Similarly, I remember quite vividly when, at the outset of the US invasion of Iraq in 2003, the two spokespeople for the Defense Department described in horror how the badly outgunned Iraqis were using guerilla tactics to try in vain to repel the invasion. One example given was how a pregnant Iraqi woman lured a US convoy into halting, whereupon she threw a grenade in its direction. The Defense spokespeople declared, without any tongue in cheek or any irony in their voice, that such tactics were actually proof of why the invasion was necessary to begin with. Surely, we were told, any people who would engage in such self-defense tactics deserved to be attacked.

Numerous examples of such strained reasoning abound. Most notably, in her recent memoir, Samantha Power attempted to justify the NATO assault on Libya and consequent brutal murder of Muammar Qaddafi on the basis of of what she suspected would be Qaddafi's response to the West's call for him to step down from power. As she explained, "many US analysts predicted that, since Qaddafi viewed Western government's call for his departure as a betrayal, he would return to sponsoring terrorism as he had in the past."[297]

In short, the US has turned Article 51, which is meant to be a shield of last resort, into a sword, interpreting any response (or even merely presumed response) of others to US and allied attack as justification to attack them in the first place. This shows the absurd lengths to which the US will go to bend and distort international law to their deadly advantage.

And the "humanitarian" apologists for the US, as well as the mainstream press, lend great support to the efforts of the US in this regard. Political commentator Tom Englehardt expresses well the marvel of the US propaganda system in successfully fostering the belief that the US is somehow always under attack and thus justified in responding with military force nearly everywhere:

> So here's the strange thing, on a planet on which, in 2017, US Special Operations forces deployed to 149 countries, or approximately 75 percent of all nations; on which the United States has perhaps 800 military garrisons outside its own territory; on which the US Navy patrols most of its oceans and seas; on which US unmanned aerial drones conduct assassination strikes across a surprising range of countries; and on which the United States has been fighting wars, as well as more minor conflicts, for years on end from Afghanistan to Libya, Syria to Yemen, Iraq to Niger in a century in which it chose to launch full-scale invasions of two countries (Afghanistan and Iraq), is it truly reasonable never to identify the United States as an "aggressor" anywhere?

What you might say about the United States is that, as the self-proclaimed leading proponent of democracy and human rights (even if its president is now having a set of love affairs with autocrats and dictators), Americans consider ourselves at home just about anywhere we care to be on planet Earth. It matters little how we may be armed and what we might do. Consequently, wherever Americans are bothered, harassed, threatened, attacked, we are always the ones being provoked and aggressed upon, never provoking and aggressing. I mean, how can you be the aggressor in your own house, even if that house happens to be temporarily located in Afghanistan, Iraq, or perhaps soon enough in Iran?[298]

Of course, the only way to accomplish this hat trick is by dispensing with all conceivable notions of international law, and that is exactly what the US and its intellectual class have done.

A very good example of this hat trick has been the justifications given for the recent US assassination of Iranian General Qassem Soleimani in Baghdad, Iraq. Thus, the Trump Administration has claimed that the US was legally justified in killing General Soleimani as a matter of self-defense because he had allegedly been responsible for killing American servicemen in the past in helping Iraq resist the 2003 US invasion and the occupation that followed, and because he allegedly was planning future attacks against American targets. This argument simply does not find support in international law even if we assume that the factual assertions of Trump are true, and this is a big assumption, especially given the fact that Soleimani was killed while on a mission to ratchet down regional tensions between Iran and Saudi Arabia; that is, he was actively engaged in a mission of peace rather than planning for war.[299] Indeed, he may have been killed precisely to prevent peace from breaking out in the Middle East—always a grave threat to the war profiteers.

Moreover, this all ignores the fact that the US invasion of Iraq in 2003, based as it was upon the lie of weapons of mass destruction, was itself illegal. Again, it was Iraq that had the right to resist this invasion as a bona fide matter of self-defense, and to enlist Iran to aid in this self-defense. While the US government and press passionately believe that other nations lack this right to self-defense, they are simply wrong as a matter of law and morality. In any case, General Soleimani's aid of Iraq in defending itself against the US's illegal invasion—and also against ISIL and Al Qaeda, by the way—does not trigger the US's right of self-defense. This would be like arguing that a gang involved in a violent home invasion is justified in killing the family members living therein because they attempt to defend themselves. No rational individual would take this position. And the legal system, which actually gives such family members the right to use lethal force against the invaders, certainly does not, either. But this is exactly the type of twisted reasoning the US position on such issues demands that we accept.

In addition, the claim that the US had the right of "preemptive" or "preventive" self-defense against General Soleimani because, we are vaguely told, he was allegedly planning attacks sometime in the future upon US targets somewhere in the world has been roundly rejected by the UN as one contemplated by Article 51 of the UN Charter.[300] Rather, Article 51 only permits the exercise of force as self-defense against "actual" or "imminent" attack, which does not appear to be the case here.[301] Indeed, it turns out that Trump green-lighted the assassination of Soleimani—someone the US has actually worked with to fight ISIS—seven months before he was actually killed,[302] demonstrating that whatever threat he posed was certainly not imminent. And Trump, appearing to concede that there was not an imminent threat, is now arguing that it simply does not matter whether the claimed threat was imminent.[303] While this may be his view, he is certainly not correct as a matter of law.

Indeed, if such "preventive" self-defense were permitted, numerous US officials, up to the president himself, would be fair targets for attack by numerous nations given that such officials are daily involved in the planning of aggressive wars and war crimes on a global scale (as evidenced by the fact, for example, that Trump and Secretary of State Mike Pompeo have explicitly threatened to destroy historical cultural sites in Iran—a clear violation of the Geneva Conventions), but very few Americans would accept this proposition.

I am not alone in the view that this assassination was unlawful. Thus,

> Oona Hathaway, an international law expert and law professor at Yale University, told Reuters the available facts "do not seem to support"

the assertion that the strike was an act of self-defense, and concluded it was "legally tenuous under both domestic and international law."

The UN special rapporteur on extrajudicial executions, Agnes Callamard, said the US assassination was outside the context of active hostilities.

"The targeted killings of Qasem Soleiman and Abu Mahdi Al-Muhandis are most likely unlawful and violate international human rights law: Outside the context of active hostilities, the use of drones or other means for targeted killing is almost never likely to be legal," she wrote on Twitter.[304]

And, the results of this killing could be truly catastrophic. As Pulitzer-Prize recipient Chris Hedges explains:[305]

> The assassination by the United States of Gen. Qassem Soleimani, the head of Iran's elite Quds Force, near Baghdad's airport will ignite widespread retaliatory attacks against US targets from Shiites, who form the majority in Iraq. It will activate Iranian-backed militias and insurgents in Lebanon and Syria and throughout the Middle East. The existing mayhem, violence, failed states and war, the result of nearly two decades of US blunders and miscalculations in the region, will become an even wider and more dangerous conflagration. The consequences are ominous. Not only will the US swiftly find itself under siege in Iraq and perhaps driven out of the country—there is only a paltry force of 5,200 US troops in Iraq, all US citizens in Iraq have been told to leave the country "immediately" and the embassy and consular services have been closed—but the situation could also draw us into a war directly with Iran. The American Empire, it seems, will die not with a whimper but a bang.

Meanwhile, a terrible and almost immediate consequence of the murder of General Solemaini was the accidental shooting down of the Ukrainian civilian aircraft by Iranian defense forces, killing 176 passengers, most of whom were Iranian, but a number Canadians, as well. It is clear that this happened because of the increased tensions and fears raised by the assassination. Indeed, many in Canada recognize this, with a number of family members and friends of the victims putting the blame for this tragedy firmly upon President Trump.[306]

It is because such unilateral attacks as the one carried out by the US upon Iran's General Soleimani can result in these types of dire consequences, predictable and not, that the UN Charter so strictly forbids them and so narrowly defines the right to self-defense.

Would that our leaders understand the importance of such international law norms in preserving the peace. But of course, even despite the prospect for such catastrophes, there are those amongst our leaders who are already benefiting from the threat of war. Thus, some of those arms companies I mentioned above that are making huge profits from the war in Yemen—Lockheed Martin and Raytheon—saw their stocks jump after the assassination of Soleimani, as the prospect of war is seen as but another opportunity for giant financial gains.[307] As long as our government and our nation are held captive by such interests, war will be inevitable, and it will have nothing to do with advancing the interests of human rights.

EIGHT

The UN and the Responsibility to Protect

"Every time the US 'saves' a country, it converts it into either an insane asylum or a cemetery."
—Eduardo Galeano

AS AN INITIAL MATTER, IT must be pointed out that the UN has not issued any binding legal instruments that permit, much less require, "The Responsibility to Protect" (R2P)—that is, the doctrine that one State or States may intervene in another for humanitarian purposes. With that said, there have been a number of recommendations made through various UN panels over the years related to this doctrine. However, even these recommendations fall far short of authorizing the type of wide-ranging interventions advocated, and at times carried out, by Western powers.

For example, from September 15 to 17, 2005, "the largest

gathering of world leaders" to date was held in New York City in what was termed the World Summit 2005.[308] While many now consider this Summit and the resulting UN General Assembly Resolution (60/1) as one advancing the notion of the "Responsibility to Protect," this is far from the case.

Thus, the main purpose of this Summit was to reaffirm the goals of the Millennium Development Declaration—a Declaration focusing on the reduction of poverty and the economic development of the Third World.[309] The GA Resolution that came out of this Summit reflected the attempt of the majority of the world nations—that is, the nations of the developing world—to push back against the attempts of the United States to undermine the Millennium Development Declaration.

Thus, as commentator Anup Shah, citing news reports by the *Washington Post* and *Guardian*, explains,[310] the US, through President George W. Bush's UN Ambassador John Bolton (a right-wing hawk who would later serve as President Trump's National Security Adviser), "introduced more than 750 amendments that would, amongst other things, eliminate new pledges of foreign aid to poor nations; scrap provisions that call for action on climate change and nuclear proliferation; delete the mention of the Millennium Development Goals; eliminate any mention of the ICC; delete references to respecting nature, the rights of self-determination of peoples, and the rights of people under colonial domination and foreign occupation; delete references to corporate responsibility; and eliminate requirements of pharmaceutical companies to provide cheap AIDS and HIV drugs to poor nations."

As Shah further related, "the *Post* also added that in meetings with foreign delegates, Bolton has expressed concern about a provision of the agreement that urges wealthy countries, including the United States, to contribute 0.7 percent of their gross national product in assistance to poor countries."

To the extent the US made proposals related to the Responsibility to Protect, it was to weaken such a notion, for example by opposing "language that urges the five permanent members of the Security Council not to cast vetoes to block action to halt genocide, war crimes, or ethnic cleansing."

In the end, the GA Resolution that came out of this World Summit reflected the main goals of the majority of participants—that is, reaffirming the goals of eradicating world poverty and assisting the Third World in economic development.[311]

In addition, as Professor Mary Ellen O'Connell explains correctly, this resolution also affirmed the UN's "support for the regime of peace and the prohibition on the use of force."[312] Professor O'Connell points, for example, to Paragraphs 78 & 79 of the resolution, which provide:

> 78. We reiterate the importance of promoting and strengthening the multilateral process and of addressing international challenges and problems by strictly abiding by the Charter and the principles of international law, and further stress our commitment to multilateralism.
>
> 79. We reaffirm that the relevant provisions of the Charter are sufficient to address the full range of threats to international peace and security. We further reaffirm the authority of the Security Council to mandate coercive action to maintain and restore international peace and security. We stress the importance of acting in accordance with the purposes and principles of the Charter.

There are numerous other resolution provisions that affirm this commitment to peace and the prevention of war, most notably the following section:

> **Pacific settlement of disputes**
> 73. We emphasize the obligation of States to settle their disputes by peaceful means in accordance with Chapter VI of the Charter, including, when appropriate, by the use of the International

Court of Justice. All States should act in accordance with the Declaration on Principles of International Law concerning Friendly Relations and Cooperation among States in accordance with the Charter of the United Nations.

74. We stress the importance of prevention of armed conflict in accordance with the purposes and principles of the Charter and solemnly renew our commitment to promote a culture of prevention of armed conflict as a means of effectively addressing the interconnected security and development challenges faced by peoples throughout the world, as well as to strengthen the capacity of the United Nations for the prevention of armed conflict.

75. We further stress the importance of a coherent and integrated approach to the prevention of armed conflicts and the settlement of disputes and the need for the Security Council, the General Assembly, the Economic and Social Council and the Secretary-General to coordinate their activities within their respective Charter mandates.

76. Recognizing the important role of the good offices of the Secretary-General, including in the mediation of disputes, we support the Secretary-General's efforts to strengthen his capacity in this area.

The following resolution paragraphs also emphasize the UN's commitment to peace, the rule of law, and prevention of the use of force: Par. 2, reaffirming the "faith in the United Nations and our commitment to the purposes and principles of the Charter of the United Nations and international law, which are indispensable foundations of a more peaceful, prosperous and just world, and reiterate[ing] our determination to foster strict respect for them"; Par. 9, acknowledging the principle "that peace and security, development and human rights are the pillars of the United Nations system and the foundations for collective security and well-being," and recognizing "that development, peace and security and human rights are interlinked and mutually reinforcing"; Par. 72, reaffirming "the commitment to work towards a security consensus based on the recognition that many threats are interlinked, that development, peace, security and human rights are mutually reinforcing"; Par. 77, reaffirming, inter alia, "the obligation of all Member States to refrain in their international relations from the threat or use of force in any manner inconsistent with the Charter"; Pars. 92 to 95, resolving to strengthen the UN's Peacekeeping capabilities and urging compliance with disarmament agreements; Pars. 97 to 105, establishing a Peacebuilding Commission; and Par. 134(a), reaffirming "the commitment to the purposes and principles of the Charter and international law and to an international order based on the rule of law and international law, which is essential for peaceful coexistence and cooperation among States."

Moreover, only two of the resolution's 178 paragraphs deal specifically with the "Responsibility to Protect," and these paragraphs are not supportive of the notion of R2P advanced by the Western Humanitarians such as Samantha Power and Kenneth Roth. They read as follows:

Responsibility to protect populations from genocide, war crimes, ethnic cleansing, and crimes against humanity

138. Each individual State has the responsibility to protect its populations from genocide, war crimes, ethnic cleansing, and crimes against humanity. This responsibility entails the prevention of such crimes, including their incitement, through appropriate and necessary means. We accept that responsibility and will act in accordance with it. The international community should, as appropriate, encourage and help States to exercise this responsibility and support the United Nations in establishing an early warning capability.

139. The international community, through the United Nations, also has the responsibility to use appropriate diplomatic, humanitarian and other peaceful means, in accordance with Chapters VI

and VIII of the Charter, to help to protect populations from genocide, war crimes, ethnic cleansing, and crimes against humanity. In this context, we are prepared to take collective action, in a timely and decisive manner, through the Security Council, in accordance with the Charter, including Chapter VII, on a case-by-case basis and in cooperation with relevant regional organizations as appropriate, should peaceful means be inadequate and national authorities are manifestly failing to protect their populations from genocide, war crimes, ethnic cleansing, and crimes against humanity.... We also intend to commit ourselves, as necessary and appropriate, to helping States build capacity to protect their populations from genocide, war crimes, ethnic cleansing, and crimes against humanity and to assisting those which are under stress before crises and conflicts break out.

The takeaways from these provisions do not support the Western humanitarians' notion of R2P as an unbridled right to militarily intervene in other nations based upon humanitarian concerns, real, imagined, or made up. Thus, this section emphasizes that it is each individual state that is responsible for ensuring the human rights of its own people, and it calls upon the international community to help individual States to build their own capacity to protect their populations and guarantee their rights. Moreover, to the extent the international community is called upon to assist individual States to deal with active threats to their populations, it is required that the international community attempt to use "diplomatic, humanitarian, and other peaceful means" to do so.

Finally, there is no explicit call upon the international community to use force to protect human rights inside a sovereign State. Rather, the resolution simply calls upon the international community to refer human rights emergencies within a State to the Security Council to decide "on a case-by-case basis" how to handle the situation. In other words, the UN Charter and its methods for maintaining international peace and security are not augmented, diminished, or changed one iota. And certainly, no end-around is provided to allow one nation to intervene in another in contravention of the UN Charter or without Security Council authorization.

Meanwhile, another set of recommendations often pointed to by R2P enthusiasts is contained in a document titled "A More Secure World: Our Shared Responsibility, Report of the High Level Panel on Threats, Challenges and Change."[313] As the introduction to the report, then-UN Secretary General Kofi Annan explains that it is the result of the meeting of 15 international experts to address a number of issues of pressing concern for the international community.

It is curious to note that one of the "experts" who helped to draft this report was Australian Gareth Evans. What is significant about him is that while he is a huge proponent of R2P, he was also an individual who helped to solidify the illegal occupation and annexation of East Timor by Indonesia and to help firms from his country profit from the genocide committed against the East Timorese people.

As explained in the penetrating book, *The Politics of Genocide:*[314]

> Perhaps no single individual has done more to raise the profile of R2P and to place it on the UN's agenda than Evans. He is the author of a 2008 book on R2P, serves as the co-Chair of the International Advisory Board of the Global Center for the Responsibility to Protect at the City University of New York was co-Chair of the International Commission on Intervention and State Sovereignty, which produced the 2001 report *The Responsibility to Protect* that helped bring this phrase into common usage, and is past president of the International Crisis Group.
>
> Before all of this, Evans served as the Foreign Minister of Australia (1988–1996). It was while performing in this role that he was instrumental to Australia's completion of the 1989 Timor Gap Oil Treaty that granted Australian firms the right to explore and drill in the oil-rich "Indonesian province of East Timor," in the treaty's terms. With this treaty, Evans placed Australia squarely in that rare

camp of states that recognized Indonesia's illegal conquest of East Timorese territory by force in 1975—despite some 200,000 deaths in East Timor as a "result of the Indonesian invasion and occupation," roughly a "third of the population, or proportionately more than were killed in Cambodia under Pol Pot."

This goes to show, I suppose, that one man's genocide is another man's opportunity. And, after all, what is a little genocide to someone like Evans when there is oil profiteering to be made?

Meanwhile, these are the six specific issues dealt with in the 2004 report:

- Economic and social threats, including poverty, infectious diseases, and environmental degradation
- Inter-State conflict
- Internal conflict, including civil war, genocide, and other large-scale atrocities
- Nuclear, radiological, chemical, and biological weapons
- Terrorism
- Transnational organized crime

It is, of course, the section related to the third issue above that is most germane to R2P.

This 2004 report makes it clear in the text that it's content reflects "recommendations" that, it is hoped, would lead to further debate about how to handle a number of threats confronting the world. The report does not purport to alter existing international law, nor could it given the ad hoc nature of the panel put together to draft it.

The body of the report opens with the following words: "The United Nations was created in 1945 above all else 'to save succeeding generations from the scourge of war'—to ensure that the horrors of the World Wars were never repeated." The report also makes clear that the UN Charter is the prime, governing international law instrument, and that it is up to the task of dealing with the pressing issues confronting the world. As the report states:

> We address here the circumstances in which effective collective security may require the backing of military force, starting with the rules of international law that must govern any decision to go to war if anarchy is not to prevail. It is necessary to distinguish between situations in which a State claims to act in self-defense; situations in which a State is posing a threat to others outside its borders; and situations in which the threat is primarily internal and the issue is the responsibility to protect a State's own people. In all cases, we believe that the Charter of the United Nations, properly understood and applied, is equal to the task: Article 51 needs neither extension nor restriction of its long understood scope, and Chapter VII fully empowers the Security Council to deal with every kind of threat that States may confront. The task is not to find alternatives to the Security Council as a source of authority but to make it work better than it has.

The report further reaffirms that "[t]he Charter of the United Nations, in Article 2.4, expressly prohibits Member States from using or threatening force against each other, allowing only two exceptions: self-defense under Article 51, and military measures authorized by the Security Council under Chapter VII (and by extension for regional organizations under Chapter VIII) in response to 'any threat to the peace, breach of the peace or act of aggression.' At the same time, the report noted with concern the fact that "[f]or the first 44 years of the United Nations, Member States often violated these rules and used military force literally hundreds of times, with . . . Article 51 only rarely providing credible cover."

And quite importantly, the report contains a Section that reaffirms the vitality to Article 51 and the long-standing interpretation of it as a very narrow exception to the rules against the use of force. Specifically, the report rejects the push by some States—the US has been a notable one of these—that claim to have the right of "preventive" or "anticipatory" self-defense, meaning that they can attack a State before actually being attacked because they believe an attack may be possible. As the report makes clear:

> The short answer is that if there are good arguments for preventive military action, with good evidence to support them, they should be put to the Security Council, which can authorize such action if it chooses to. If it does not so choose, there will be, by definition, time to pursue other strategies, including persuasion, negotiation, deterrence and containment—and to visit again the military option.
>
> For those impatient with such a response, the answer must be that, in a world full of perceived potential threats, the risk to the global order and the norm of nonintervention on which it continues to be based is simply too great for the legality of unilateral preventive action, as distinct from collectively endorsed action, to be accepted. Allowing one to so act is to allow all.
>
> **We do not favor the rewriting or reinterpretation of Article 51.**
> (emphasis in original)

This recommendation could not be clearer that States do not have the right of "preventive" self-defense under the UN Charter, and the panel of experts does not believe they should.

In addition, before getting to the question of the use of force to deal with international conflicts, the report contains a section titled "Preventive diplomacy and mediation," which, as the title suggests, focuses on "the appointment of skilled, experienced and regionally knowledgeable envoys, mediators and special representatives, who can make as important a contribution to conflict prevention as they do to conflict resolution." Again, this is very much in keeping with the UN Charter's focus on the pacific management and resolution of disputes.

There is also a strong focus in the report on the need to reduce nuclear and chemical weapons proliferation in order to maintain international peace and security.

When it comes to the so-called "responsibility to protect," the report prefaces this section by again reaffirming that "[t]he Security Council is fully empowered under Chapter VII of the Charter of the United Nations to address the full range of security threats with which States are concerned. The task is not to find alternatives to the Security Council as a source of authority but to make the Council work better than it has."

The report also underscores the fact that, as required by the UN Charter, when confronting a threat to international peace and security, "the primary focus should be on assisting the cessation of violence through mediation and other tools and the protection of people through such measures as the dispatch of humanitarian, human rights, and police missions. Force, if it needs to be used, should be deployed as a last resort."

And again, it is the Security Council that must authorize such force, and only in very limited circumstances. Indeed, the report recommends five specific criteria that should be considered by the Security Council in authorizing. As the report recommends:

> In considering whether to authorize or endorse the use of military force, the Security Council should always address—whatever other considerations it may take into account—at least the following five basic criteria of legitimacy:
>
> (a) *Seriousness of threat*. Is the threatened harm to State or human security of a kind, and sufficiently clear and serious, to justify prima facie the use of military force? In the case of internal threats, does it involve genocide and other large-scale killing, ethnic cleansing or serious violations of international humanitarian law, actual or imminently apprehended?
>
> (b) *Proper purpose*. Is it clear that the primary purpose of the proposed military action is to halt or avert the threat in question, whatever other purposes or motives may be involved?

(c) *Last resort.* Has every non-military option for meeting the threat in question been explored, with reasonable grounds for believing that other measures will not succeed?

(d) *Proportional means.* Are the scale, duration and intensity of the proposed military action the minimum necessary to meet the threat in question?

(e) *Balance of consequences.* Is there a reasonable chance of the military action being successful in meeting the threat in question, with the consequences of action not likely to be worse than the consequences of inaction?

In my view, these criteria, which again are merely recommendations, have much merit and, if truly considered and followed, would have invalidated nearly every "humanitarian" intervention since WWII.

Before evaluating some of these interventions against these criteria, however, one must ask (though few if any do) what the burden of proof should be to prove that such criteria are met before lethal military force is carried out in the ostensible cause of human rights. I would strongly argue that, given that the consequences of such military interventions invariably include the massive loss of life and civilian infrastructure, if not the destruction of whole nations, those who wish to engage in a "humanitarian" intervention have the burden of proving beyond a reasonable doubt—the burden of proof in a criminal proceeding—that these criteria are met.

Let's now take, for example, the NATO intervention in Yugoslavia in the 1990s—the quintessential "humanitarian" intervention and the intervention that inaugurated the R2P era. As one commenter summed up about this intervention upon its 17th anniversary, the NATO "attack—38,400 sorties, including 10,484 strike sorties—lasted 78 days and destroyed infrastructure, commercial buildings, schools, health institutions, media houses, and cultural monuments." As he continued with obvious sarcasm, "NATO 'deeply' regretted killing at least seventeen people when a bomb hit a bus packed with women and children.

It also supposedly regretted killing fifteen people after it targeted a hospital with a cluster bomb and killed three diplomats at China's embassy in Belgrade. After Serbian television criticized Albright and Clinton, it was bombed as well, killing sixteen people."[315]

This hardly sounds like a humanitarian effort, and it was not, though one of the main purposes of this intervention was to set the precedent that the West could intervene at will as long as it cited humanitarian concerns as a fig leaf. As Karen Talbot, then-Director of the International Center for Peace and Justice (ICPJ), explains,

> United States and its NATO underlings clearly were emboldened by their "success" in bombing Yugoslavia, by their earlier bombing of the Serb areas of Bosnia, and by their victories in the other remnants of Yugoslavia: Croatia, Slovenia, and Macedonia. . . . The assault against Yugoslavia threw open the floodgates for new wars, including wars of competition among the industrial powers. President Bill Clinton praised NATO for its campaign in Kosovo, saying the alliance could intervene elsewhere in Europe or Africa to fight repression. "We can do it now. We can do it tomorrow, if it is necessary, somewhere else," he told US troops gathered at the Skopje, Macedonia, airport (*Agence France Presse*, 1999).[316]

As an initial matter, the 1999 intervention did not have UN Security Council authorization and thus was illegal from the get-go, again even if the report were binding law, for this report recommends no change to the UN Charter's proviso that the Security Council have a monopoly on the authority to authorize the use of force. As Professor Adam Roberts explains, this was "the first sustained use of armed force by the NATO alliance in its 50-year existence; [and] the first time a major use of destructive armed force had been undertaken with the stated purpose of implementing UN Security Council authorization but without Security Council authorization," as Russia and China made it clear they would not give such authorization.[317]

And again, a number of commentators, including longtime journalist covering the Balkans, Diana Johnstone, have opined that this was the point of the intervention, to prove that the West could do an end-around the Security Council at will. As she explained, "a major motivation for the 1999 'Kosovo war' was to demonstrate that the United States and NATO could wage a unilateral, unauthorized (by the UN Security Council) and thus illegal aggressive war and get away with it."[318] In other words, the point of this intervention was to undermine, if not destroy, the primary prohibition of international law—that against the unilateral use of force. And this plan worked swimmingly, with William Rockler, former prosecutor of the Nuremberg War Crimes Tribunal opining, "[t]he [1999] bombing war violates and shreds the basic provisions of the United Nations Charter and other conventions and treaties; the attack on Yugoslavia constitutes the most brazen international aggression since the Nazis attacked Poland to prevent 'Polish atrocities' against Germans." [319]

Certainly, the unilateral use of force carried out to set the precedent for carrying out future unilateral uses of force cannot be considered a "Proper Purpose" within the meaning of this report. And the other true purpose for the intervention—corporate profits and the spread of neoliberal economic policies—also does not pass muster as a "Proper Purpose." Karen Talbot, quoting President Bill Clinton's own words at the time, as well as Thomas Friedman's, reveals this true purpose:

An article by Thomas Friedman in the *New York Times* tells it all. Illustrated by a US flag on a fist and entitled "What the World Needs Now," the article states:

For globalism to work, America can't be afraid to act like the almighty superpower that it is. . . . The hidden hand of the market will never work without a hidden fist—McDonald's cannot flourish without McDonnell Douglas, the designer of the F-15. And the hidden fist that keeps the world safe for

Silicon Valley's technologies is called the United States Army, Air Force, Navy, and Marine Corps (Friedman, 1999: 40).

There could not be a better description of how the US armed forces are seen as the military arm of globalizing transnational corporations. President Clinton said in a speech delivered the day before his televised address about Kosovo in April 1999: **"If we're going to have a strong economic relationship that includes our ability to sell around the world, Europe has got to be a key. . . .. That's what this Kosovo thing is all about"** (Schwarz and Layne, 1999: 11). (emphasis added)

Indeed, it is important to remember how the West was intervening in Yugoslavia well before the 1999 war in ways that gave rise to the humanitarian issues that ended up being used to justify this war. Thus, it is no secret that the West (most notably the US, Germany, and the UK), in order to destroy the last socialist state in Europe and to prime the Western world for a post-Soviet unipolar world order in which capitalism would rule all, began to actively support the partitioning of Yugoslavia, by encouraging first the secession of Slovenia and Croatia and then the breaking away of Bosnia-Herzegovina (again, hardly a proper purpose)—events that would inevitably lead to the internecine violence that followed.[320]

In other words, the West laid the groundwork in which the different ethnic groups of Yugoslavia would be at one another's throats and then used the ensuing interethnic violence to justify further intervention. This is a very typical trope of Western intervention and cannot be ignored in assessing such intervention. Arguably, had the West left Yugoslavia alone to begin with, we would have no need to be discussing whether NATO should or should not have bombed the Balkan States, which may have continued to be happily united into one country.

In short, the very fact that the West helped set the fire that it then claimed to want to put out with flame throwers also cuts against any claim of "Proper Purpose."

In addition, while I'll assume for purposes of this book that one, and only one, of the recommended R2P criteria was present here—that of the "Seriousness of the Threat"—there was a selectiveness in combating certain humanitarian threats and violations over others. Thus, NATO claimed to want to protect Kosovars from violations (both real and exaggerated) by Serbs, while aiding and abetting the violations committed by Kosovars (and in particular the terrorist KLA shock troops) against Serbs and other ethnic groups. Karen Talbot explains this hypocrisy well:

> We were told that this war was for a noble, humanitarian purpose and people wanted to believe this explanation. Yet the most obvious and glaring contradiction was the absence of any similar concerns about hundreds of thousands of Serbs expelled from the Krajina region of Croatia by the Croatian military in 1995, described as "the largest ethnic cleansing" of the Yugoslav civil war (Bonner, 1999: A17). Thousands died in that "Operation Storm." . . . There were a million Serb refugees even before the bombing of Kosovo Metohija began. . . . After the NATO forces moved into Kosovo, there was a further vast exodus, particularly of Serbs, as the KLA swiftly stepped up the drive for an ethnically pure Kosovo. NATO troops stood by and took no real steps to prevent it. As journalist Rick Rowden argued, "Americans should question the administration's stated objective to 'stop the killing' in Kosovo. [It] should give us reason to ask, 'Why can the US support Croatian ethnic cleansing in Croatia but oppose Serbian ethnic cleansing in Kosovo?' The answer likely has little to do with 'stopping the killing' and much to do with the expansion of NATO and its post-Cold War global role" (Rowden, 1999).

NATO's selective "humanitarianism" further cuts against any claim that its purpose in the former Yugoslavia was proper. And, it should be noted, the West's concern about human rights is always selective. This is well reflected in an internal US State Department memo titled "Balancing Interests and Values." Thus, this May 17, 2017, advice memo from foreign policy aide to then-Secretary of State Rex Tillerson states:

> One useful guideline for a realistic and successful foreign policy is that allies should be treated differently—and better—than adversaries. Otherwise, we end up with more adversaries, and fewer allies. The classic dilemma of balancing ideals and interests is with regard to America's allies. In relation to our competitors, there is far less of a dilemma. We do not look to bolster America's adversaries overseas; we look to pressure, compete with, and outmaneuver them. For this reason, we should consider human rights as an important issue in regard to US relations with China, Russia, North Korea, and Iran. And this is not only because of moral concern for practices inside those countries. It is also because pressing those regimes on human rights is one way to impose costs, apply counter-pressure, and regain the initiative from them strategically.[321]

Such a selective, and quite cynical, policy of handling human rights concerns cuts across all US Administrations and is applied as well by Western human rights groups, which also tend to show more concern with the human rights practices of Western adversaries than with Western allies.

This selective concern for human rights, moreover, is reflected in our mainstream media, which, not coincidentally, has the very same policy as the US State Department in treating international human rights issues, thus incessantly highlighting the flaws of our ostensible enemies, such as China and Russia, while downplaying or outright ignoring our own flaws and the flaws of our allies. This was brought home recently by a study done by Fairness and Accuracy in Reporting (FAIR) on the coverage of recent protests by the *New York Times* and CNN on protests in Hong Kong against mainland China as compared to the coverage of protests in countries with governments allied with the US (Ecuador, Haiti, and Chile). As FAIR explained:

> In total, there have been 737 stories on the Hong Kong protests, twelve on Ecuador, twenty-eight on Haiti and thirty-six on Chile. . . . [B]oth the *Times* and *CNN* had similar ratios of coverage.
>
> This enormous disparity cannot be explained by the other protests' size or significance, nor the severity of the repression meted out by security services. After barely a week's worth of turmoil, the death toll in Ecuador was eight, according to that government's own Human Rights Defender, while the UN confirms that forty-two Haitians have been killed in the last two months alone. And in Chile, where right-wing President Sebastian Piñera literally declared war on the population, sending tanks through the streets, twenty-six have died and over 26,000 have been arrested. In contrast, no one has died at the hands of the Hong Kong security forces, although one protester died after falling from a building, and a seventy-year-old man was killed by a brick thrown by protesters, both deaths occurring in November after months of demonstrations.[322]

In Chile, moreover, the state security forces have had a policy of intentionally blinding protestors by shooting them in the eye, with over 350 protestors blinded in this way so far.[323] But, apparently, this is barely worth a mention by the US press. As for the US State Department, in keeping with its selective concern about human rights, it has vowed to help countries like Chile, Haiti, and Ecuador put down the protests in their country.[324]

Meanwhile, as for the "Last Resort" criterion, this one is easily dispensed with in regard to the NATO bombing of Libya. The incontrovertible fact is that the West, and in particular the US, not only failed to explore "every non military option" to avoid armed conflict, it in fact made sure that viable non-military options were eschewed. Thus, on two occasions, when a peace deal was nearing finality, the US intervened to ensure that the deal be scuttled.

First, the US, through Ambassador Warren Zimmerman, convinced Bosnian leader Alija Izetbegovic to renounce the 1992 Lisbon Agreement, which could have prevented the civil war from breaking out in the first place and which Izetbegovic had already signed. As Jean Bricmont explains, "of the Lisbon agreements of February 1992, the Canadian Ambassador to Yugoslavia at that time, James Bissett, has written, 'The entire diplomatic corps was very happy that the civil war had been avoided—except the Americans. The American Ambassador, Warren Zimmerman, immediately took off for Sarajevo to convince [the Bosnian Muslim leader] Izetbegovic not to sign the agreement.'" As Bricmont relates, Zimmerman would later admit this, and an anonymous, high-ranking State Department would tell the *New York Times* that Zimmerman was not acting on his own, that "[t]he policy was to encourage Izetbegovic to break the partition plan."

Second, the US also undermined the peace deal that could have averted the 1999 NATO bombing on the eve of this intervention. Thus, it is pretty clear that Slobodan Milosevic would have accepted an agreement pursuant to which Serbian troops would be removed from Kosovo—allegedly the goal of the bombing that ultimately ensued—but the US inserted a poison pill in the agreement (the 1999 Rambouillet Accord) in the form of Appendix B, which would have required Serbia to essentially give up its sovereignty to NATO occupation. As Lewis MacKenzie in the *Globe & Mail* puts it so well: "unfortunately—but intentionally," the March 18, 1999 accord contained a requirement "that Mr. Milosevic could never accept, making war or at least the allied bombing of a sovereign state inevitable." To wit, the agreement "demanded that NATO have freedom of movement throughout the entire land, sea and airspace of the former Federal Republic of Yugoslavia."[325]

No self-respecting country, of course, would have accepted such an arrangement. The other predictably unacceptable portion of the agreement, MacKenzie explains, would have required that "a referendum be held within three years to determine the will of those citizens living in Kosovo regarding independence. The fact that Kosovo's population was overwhelmingly Albanian Muslim guaranteed that the outcome of any such referendum would be a vote for independence and the loss of the Serbian nation's historic heart." As a consequence, "Mr. Milosevic refused to sign the accord, and NATO began bombing Serbia on March 24, 1999, without a Security Council resolution, citing a 'humanitarian emergency'—a decision still widely challenged by many international legal scholars."[326]

So, in short, the 1999 NATO bombing was not a "last resort" of exhaustive peace negotiations, but rather the intentional effort of the US to prevent peace.

The major bombing campaign of NATO then occurred in 1999 and lasted for eleven weeks. The NATO bombing seemed to only intensify the very human rights abuses against the Kosovars that the bombing was allegedly intended to prevent, with Professor Adam Roberts explaining that

> [I]t is not disputed that, in the words of a White House spokesman on 26 March, the situation in Kosovo took "a dramatic and serious turn for the worse" in the day after the bombing commenced. Many refugees fleeing from Kosovo saw the Serb onslaught against them as a direct consequence of the NATO action. . . . Within one month of the start of the bombing campaign, over half a million people had fled from Kosovo into neighboring countries, and many thousands were displaced within Kosovo itself. During the whole period of the bombing, according to NATO figures, almost one million inhabitants left

Kosovo, and a half-a-million were internally displaced. Thousands of Kosovar Albanians were killed.[327]

In addition, the NATO bombing, in which, of course, no NATO soldiers risked their lives in what amounted to shooting fish in a barrel, did much damage to the civilian population and infrastructure of Serbia. Roberts quotes then-UN High Commissioner for Human Rights, Mary Robinson, who complained, "[i]n the NATO bombing of the Federal Republic of Yugoslavia, large numbers of civilians have incontestably been killed, civilian installations targeted on the basis that they are or could be of military application, and NATO remains the sole judge of what is or is not acceptable to bomb."[328]

Mary Robinson also expressed grave concern for whether the international humanitarian law norm requiring proportionality was being followed. The quick answer is no, and the details of how the NATO bombing violated the rules of proportionality also goes to another R2P criterion—the "Balance of Consequences." As Karen Talbot opines:

> In the United States, we were told that the relentless US-led NATO *blitzkrieg* (23,000 "dumb" bombs and "smart" missiles rained upon Yugoslavia for 79 days) was necessary to protect the human rights of ethnic Albanians in Kosovo. The US Senate labeled Serbia a "terrorist state" (Weiner, 1999: A6). Yet what could be more "terrorist" than dropping upon civilians—from the sanctuary of high altitude, and from computer-guided missiles—radioactive depleted-uranium weapons and outlawed cluster bombs designed to rip human flesh to shreds? Was it not terrorism to deliberately target the entire infrastructure of this small nation, including the electrical and water filtration systems critical to the survival of civilians? Was it not terrorism to obliterate 200 factories and destroy the jobs of millions of workers? What of the constant air assault—"fire from the sky"— against cities, villages, schools, hospitals, senior residences, TV

towers and studios, oil refineries, chemical plants, electrical power plants, transmission towers, gas stations, homes, farms, marketplaces, buses, trains, railroad lines, bridges, roads, medieval monasteries, churches, historic monuments—destruction amounting to more than $100 billion? What of the incalculable destruction of the environment, including the deliberate bombardment of chemical plants. Above all, was it not terrorism to kill, maim, traumatize, impoverish, or render homeless tens of thousands of men, women, and children?

The questions posed by Talbot are rarely asked when assessing such interventions as the one in the former Yugoslavia, and yet, they must be asked if one wants to determine if the intervention is truly "humanitarian," as we are so often told. And once these questions are asked, as recommended by the UN expert report, they immediately answer themselves, and the answer is not pretty. Targeting civilians and civilian infrastructure for weeks against a country utterly unable to defend itself does not constitute "proportional" force; does not comply with the rules of war as set forth in the Geneva Conventions; creates more harm than it could possibly prevent; and, in this case, only accelerates attacks against the very people (the Kosovars) claimed to be the beneficiaries of the intervention.

Given all of this, the 1999 NATO intervention was not indeed "humanitarian," as we have been told, and did not comport even with the R2P rules the Western intervention enthusiasts point to in order to justify their interventions.

And other Western "humanitarian" interventions fare no better when exposed to scrutiny. Another example of such a Western intervention is that of NATO in Libya, which, as discussed above, was an explicitly "humanitarian" project urged by three self-described "humanitarians"—Hillary Clinton, Samantha Power, and Susan Rice.

This intervention too utterly failed to meet the criteria for R2P set forth by the expert UN panel. Thus, as for "Proper Purpose," there simply was none. As set forth in more detail above, the NATO Allies all had their own, quite self-interested purposes for this military campaign, ranging from the US's desire for access to oil and infrastructure profiteering, to France's desire for Gaddafi's gold reserves and French President Sarkozy's desire to get rid of Gaddafi as a witness to the latter's huge contribution to Sarkozy's presidential campaign, to Italy's desire to extricate itself from the agreement it made with Gaddafi for reparations for its former colonial crimes in Libya.

In addition, Sidney Blumenthal—the chief Hillary Clinton adviser on Libya who continuously pushed for total victory over Gaddafi, and apparently to good effect—had his own self-interested reasons for this. As a letter by US Congressman Trey Goudy detailed,

> [b]etween the start of the Libyan uprising and the time when American missiles first hit Tripoli, Blumenthal lobbied tirelessly for a US military intervention against the Libyan dictator Muammar Qaddafi. . . . Perhaps more disturbing is that at the same time Blumenthal was pushing Secretary Clinton to war in Libya he was privately pushing a business interest of his own in Libya that stood to profit from contracts with the new Libyan government—a government that would exist only after a successful US intervention in Libya that deposed Qaddafi.
>
> Blumenthal owned a financial stake in Osprey Global Solutions, a military contractor seeking to do business with the Libyan rebels. Using intelligence from Cody Shearer, another longtime Clinton hanger-on, and Tyler Drumheller, an ex-CIA spy, he urged then-Secretary Clinton to support the Libyan rebels' plans to hire Western military contractors.[329]

As for "Seriousness of Threat," the Hillary Clinton team privately acknowledged that there was no threat at all of human rights abuses justifying the NATO operation. Thus, while the main justification for the NATO operation was the protection of Benghazi, Hillary Clinton's adviser Huma Abedin was passing on intelligence as early as February 21, 2011—that is, before the NATO operation even began—that Benghazi was within opposition control, that the top military leader there was now on the side of the opposition, and that the mood there was "celebratory." For his part, Sidney Blumenthal admitted to Hillary Clinton within days of the beginning of the bombing in March of 2011 that the ostensible human rights concerns were a thing of the past by then. As Blumenthal explained just eleven days into the bombing, any **"humanitarian motive offered is limited, conditional and refers to a specific past situation."** (emphasis added)

Similarly, in terms of "Last Resort," it is well known that the Gaddafi government made several overtures to the West to try to discuss a peaceful settlement to the Libyan conflict.[330] Indeed, as explained to me by Khaled Kaim, Gaddafi's last foreign minister, whom I met in Venezuela, he personally urged US representatives at the UN Security Council to hold off the first planned bombing raid for a mere hour so that UN observers already on the ground could confirm his claim that Benghazi was not under threat (a fact that, as we know from the Clinton emails, was already known by US officials). But as usual, the NATO countries leading the charge, wanting war at all costs to advance their own nonhumanitarian interests, simply ignored these overtures. Indeed, the swiftness of the NATO blitzkrieg, beginning on March 19, 2011—only a few short weeks after the very first signs of any unrest in Libya on February 15, 2011—seemed intended to leave absolutely no time for peaceful means of dispute resolution to be explored much less exhausted. In other words, the NATO attack was clearly not a "Last Resort"; rather, it was the first, desired resort, just as the Yugoslavia operation was.

In terms of "Proportionality," again, the many months of bombing of Libya until October of 2011, which ended with the brutal murder of Muammar Gaddafi, was disproportionate to the claimed threat allegedly motivating the bombing given that any true human rights concerns were already dispensed with months before. Moreover, the leveling of defenseless towns like Sirte by NATO had no true military, much less human rights, purpose and certainly could not be considered "proportional" force.

Finally, as for the "Balance of Consequences," this criterion clearly and predictably weighed against the NATO operation in Libya. Indeed, contrary to Samantha Power's claim in her memoir that they would have needed a "crystal ball" to know the disastrous nature of the outcome of the operation, US intelligence revealed quite early on that the risk of disaster was a near certainty. Again, Sidney Blumenthal, in a memo to Hillary Clinton in April of 2011, openly warned that the NATO bombing could very well give rise to a "jihadist resurgence" in Libya—a resurgence that eventually took place, with predictably awful consequences for Libya and the region.[331]

Pulitzer Prize-winning journalist Chris Hedges sums up this sorry state of affairs well:

> The NATO airstrikes on the city of Sirte expose the hypocrisy of our "humanitarian" intervention in Libya. Sirte is the last Gadhafi stronghold and the home to Gadhafi's tribe. The armed Libyan factions within the rebel alliance are waiting like panting hound dogs outside the city limits. They are determined, once the airstrikes are over, not only to rid the world of Gadhafi but all those within his tribe who benefited from his forty-two-year rule. The besieging of Sirte by NATO warplanes, which are dropping huge iron fragmentation bombs that will kill scores if not hundreds of innocents, mocks the justification for intervention laid out in a United Nations Security Council resolution. The UN, when this began six months ago, authorized "all necessary measures. . . to protect civilians and civilian populated areas under threat of attack." We have, as always happens in war, become the monster we sought to defeat. We destroy in order to save. Libya's ruling National Transitional Council estimates that the number of Libyans killed in the last six months, including civilians and combatants, has exceeded 50,000. Our intervention, as in Iraq

and Afghanistan, has probably claimed more victims than those killed by the former regime. But this intervention, like the others, was never, despite all the high-blown rhetoric surrounding it, about protecting or saving Libyan lives. It was about the domination of oil fields by Western corporations.[332]

In short, as with the NATO carpet bombing of Yugoslavia, the "humanitarian" bombing of Libya was not so humanitarian and certainly did not comport with any possible interpretation of governing international law. These two quintessential test cases of the R2P doctrine stand as monuments to the failure and indeed cynical nature of this ideology.

NINE

The US Military Is Not a Feminist Organization

THE MAIN INTERNATIONAL TREATY DOCUMENT designed to protect women's rights worldwide is the Convention on the Elimination of All Forms of Discrimination against Women (CEDAW). As Amnesty International explains, CEDAW "provides an international standard for protecting and promoting women's human rights and is often referred to as a 'Bill of Rights' for women. It is the only international instrument that comprehensively addresses women's rights within political, civil, cultural, economic, and social life."[333]

With 187 signatories, nearly all of the 194 countries of the United Nations have agreed to CEDAW.[334] The United States is not one of those countries. As Amnesty International decries, "The United States is among a small minority of countries that have not yet ratified CEDAW, including Iran and Sudan. The United States has the dubious distinction of being the only country in the Western Hemisphere and the only industrialized democracy that has not ratified this treaty."

CEDAW, in keeping with the spirit of the UN Charter and all of the other instruments that followed, recognizes war, and in particular imperial war, as the greatest threat to the rights and well-being of women. As the parties to CEDAW state in the Preamble, "the eradication of . . . colonialism, neo-colonialism, aggression, foreign occupation and domination and interference in the internal affairs of States is essential to the full enjoyment of the rights of men and women." The Preamble further states that

> the strengthening of international peace and security, the relaxation of international tension, mutual co-operation among all States irrespective of their social and economic systems, general and complete disarmament, in particular nuclear disarmament under strict and effective international control, the affirmation of the principles of justice, equality and mutual benefit in relations among countries, and the realization of the right of peoples under alien and colonial domination and foreign occupation to self-determination and independence, as well as respect for national sovereignty and territorial integrity, will promote social progress and development and as a consequence will contribute to the attainment of full equality between men and women . . . .

In short, the drafters of CEDAW realized what should be obvious to most—that women are especially devastated by armed conflicts, particularly in the form of sexual violence, and that preventing war and imperial intervention are critical to protecting women. And history indeed supports these views.

It is well known that during the US war on Vietnam, for example, rape was, according to the testimony of US soldiers themselves, "standard operating procedure" (SOP), and men who served and killed in Vietnam were considered by their fellow soldiers to be "double veterans" if they raped Vietnamese women and girls, all of whom were considered enemies and thus fair targets of rape.[335] And again, "comrades-co-members of the same military units . . . are [also] raped in theaters of combat. A preliminary study of female Vietnam veterans estimated that as many as 29 percent of the American military women who served in Vietnam were the victims of attempted or completed sexual assaults."[336]

And the Vietnam War is not anomalous in this regard. Even in the "Good War," WWII, Allied Forces, including US forces, engaged in rapes even of "allied nationals." For example, as a *Duke Law Journal* article explains, "rape of French women by American soldiers in World War II was sufficiently pervasive to cause General Eisenhower's headquarters to issue a directive in December 1944 to US Army Commanders announcing the General's "grave concern" and instructing that speedy and appropriate punishments be administered."[337]

Indeed, rape in France went up a whopping 260 percent after the US landed in Normandy, France, on D-Day. As the official history of the Office of the Judge Advocate General for the US's European Theater of Operations explains: "the number of violent sex crimes enormously increased with the arrival of our troops in France. . . . Generally speaking, the rape cases of the French Phase fell into one broad pattern characterized by violence, though of different degrees. The use of firearms was common in perpetrating the offense."[338]

While getting little to no coverage, more recent conflicts have also seen widespread US military abuse of civilian women in theater. For example, as antiwar feminist Elizabeth Mezok explains:

Since the US invasion of Iraq in 2003, there have been reports of women assaulted during home raids and at checkpoints. On March 12, 2006, fifteen-year-old Abeer Qasim Hamza al-Janabia was gang-raped by five US Army soldiers, murdered, and burned, following the murder of her mother, father, and seven-year-old sister. . . . Such acts of sexual military violence are, of course, not exclusive to women, and further, are always already racialized. As the 2003 photographs documenting the Abu Ghraib prison scandal reveal, Iraqi men were subjected to sexual violence including rape, being stripped naked and humiliated, and being forced to simulate homosexual acts on other male detainees. . . . Importantly, as Anne McClintock makes clear, the events at Abu Ghraib were not an aberration, but a snapshot of a much larger and longer history of US imperialism dependent on sexual torture.[339]

As Mesok further relates, while none of the thousands of photos from Abu Ghraib depicted the abuse of women, women are nonetheless being victimized in Iraqi prisons. Thus, "a note written by an Iraqi woman held at the prison and smuggled out claimed, US prison guards had been systematically raping women detainees, many of whom ended up pregnant. Iraqi women lawyers including Amal Kadham Swadi claim that this sexual violence is not exclusive to Abu Ghraib but rather has been 'happening all across Iraq.'

As the *Duke Law Journal* article concludes, "[i]n sum, rape in war is pervasive. It may be officially permitted or forbidden. Its victims include civilians as well as troops, allies, and sometimes even nationals as well as enemies."

But it is not only during wartime that the presence of the US military leads to rape. As Elizabeth Mesok writes in a piece critiquing liberal feminists (including luminaries such as Gloria Steinem) who believe that promoting the equal opportunity and status of women in the military will somehow cure the problem of sexual violence by US servicemen:

> Entirely erased from the campaign against internal military sexual violence is the global violence of the US military, both sexual and imperial. US bases in Okinawa, South Korea, and the Philippines have, respectively, long historical legacies of sexual violence wrought by US military personnel, with the accused rapist often protected by the impunity offered through Status of Force Agreements and Visiting Forces Agreements. . . . In 1995, for instance, Suzuyo Takasato established the organization Okinawa Women Act Against Military Violence following the gang rape of a twelve-year-old girl by three US soldiers; the organization has compiled an extensive list of

the victims of sexual violence perpetrated by US military personnel stationed in Okinawa, documenting 139 reported incidents since 1945. . . . GABRIELA, a Filipino network of grassroots organizations, has argued that US military personnel have "diplomatic license to violate our women and children," referring to the approximately 2,000 reported cases of sexual assault by US military personnel since World War II that were never adjudicated by Filipino courts. According to the Korea International War Crimes Tribunal, between 1967 and 1987, eighty-four US soldiers were convicted of rape; this number does not account for violence predating 1967, as the Status of Force Agreements had yet to go into effect.

In addition to the problem of rape is that of prostitution and modern-day "comfort women." Thus, nearly every one of the US's hundreds of foreign military bases (and many domestic ones, as well) is serviced by brothels. As David Vine, the author of *Base Nation*, explains,

Commercial sex zones have developed around US bases worldwide. Many look much the same, filled with liquor stores, fast-food outlets, tattoo parlors, bars and clubs, and prostitution in one form or another. The evidence is just outside the gates in places such as Baumholder and Kaiserslautern in Germany, and Kadena and Kin Town on Okinawa. Even during the US wars in Afghanistan and Iraq, there have been multiple reports of brothels and sex trafficking involving US troops and contractors.[340]

Vine explains that "the problems associated with the sex trade are particularly pronounced overseas—especially in South Korea, where 'camptowns' that surround US bases have become deeply entrenched in the country's economy, politics, and culture. Dating to the 1945 US occupation of Korea, when GIs casually bought sex with as little as a cigarette, they are at the center of an exploitative and profoundly disturbing sex industry." Vine relates:

As World War II came to a close, US military leaders in Korea, just like their counterparts in Germany, worried about the interactions between American troops and local women. "Americans act as though Koreans were a conquered nation rather than a liberated people," wrote the office of the commanding general. The policy became "hands off Korean women"—but this did not include women in brothels, dance halls, and working the streets. . . .

Most troublingly, US military authorities occupying Korea after the war took over some of the "comfort stations" that had been central to the Japanese war machine since the nineteenth century. During its conquest of territory across East Asia, the Japanese military forced hundreds of thousands of women from Korea, China, Okinawa and rural Japan, and other parts of Asia into sexual slavery, providing soldiers with "royal gifts" from the emperor. With the assistance of Korean officials, US authorities continued the system absent formal slavery, but under conditions of exceedingly limited choice for the women involved.

Again, international law understands that such evils flow from war and foreign, colonial occupation, and that is why international instruments such as CEDAW call explicitly for the prevention and end to war and occupation.

However, judging by media coverage of the US's seemingly endless war in Afghanistan, one would be forgiven for thinking that the US military somehow defies the logic of international law norms, and that it somehow functions as a feminist organization that goes around the world protecting women's rights.

As just one of many examples, NPR's Scott Simon read an on-air piece of his on February 2, 2019, titled "Opinion: As US Seeks To Withdraw Troops, What About Afghanistan's Women?"[341] In this piece, which is reflective of much of the mainstream liberal opinion on the subject, Simon expressed his concern over the future of Afghan women in the event the US leaves Afghanistan pursuant to an agreement that would leave the Taliban back in power—an opinion that assumes, of course, that women are so much better off now with the US military occupying the country.

Human Rights groups have joined in to magnify such themes. For example, in 2012 Amnesty International organized a poster campaign showing a young Afghan girl being escorted by two women in blue burqas with the caption: "Human Rights for Women and Girls in Afghanistan. NATO: Keep The Progress Going!"

But what progress are Amnesty International and our media talking about? History and the facts—things we are constantly asked to ignore in order to believe wild fairy tales about our foreign policy—point to no such progress. Thus, according to Sonali Kohlhatkar, the vice-president of the Afghan Women's Mission, the US did not advance women's rights in Afghanistan by its invasion or ever for that matter.[342]

First of all, lest we conveniently forget, as our compliant press apparently has, the Taliban came to power in Afghanistan, and much progress for women was destroyed, due directly to the US actions of supporting the fanatical Mujahadeen, one of whose leaders was of course Osama bin Laden. As Kohlhatkar notes, the US supported this terrorist group in order to bring down a secular socialist government that had been doing much to advance women's rights, including by progressive reforms to marriage laws and the opening of educational opportunities for women and girls. The US, with the intention to destroy this secular state and to draw the Soviets into a disastrous war (yes, the support of the Mujahadeen came *before* the Soviet invasion and was intended to bring it about), had no problem interrupting this progress with the support of right-wing fanatics.

As Kohlhatkar explains:

In April 1979, six months prior to the Soviet invasion, seven different Afghan groups of men called Mujahadeen ("Soldiers of God") began meeting with, and receiving weapons and military training from, CIA officials. Washington's aid to these so-called "freedom-fighters" consisted of billions of dollars in sophisticated weapons and small arms throughout the 1980s. This was matched dollar-for-dollar by Saudi Arabia. The US and its ally apparently ignored the extremist ideology of the Mujahadeen, including their utter disregard for the rights of women. Gulbuddin Hekmatyar, the Afghan warlord who received the bulk of funding, was famous for throwing acid in the faces of Afghan women who refused to wear the veil. Even the CIA admitted to his "vicious" and "fascist" tendencies.

Kohlhatkar continues, "[a]s Mujahadeen leaders fought the Soviets for a decade with foreign supplied weaponry, their stronghold on the Afghan landscape grew. Women's groups like RAWA [the Revolutionary Association of Women of Afghanistan] denounced the fundamentalists and their 'foreign masters' and accused them of waging a war against their own people. . . . With the Soviet withdrawal in 1989, the Mujahadeen increased their control over Afghanistan, eventually toppling the Soviet's puppet regime headed by Mohammed Najibullah. The Mujahadeen then instituted laws banning alcohol and requiring that women be veiled. Both of these new crimes were punishable by floggings, amputations, and public executions." The US continued to support the Mujahadeen for three years after the Soviet withdrawal, guaranteeing their rise to power on April 28, 1992. But this rise to power was not uncontested, and civil war continued in Afghanistan.

As Kohlhatkar tells us, "[w]hat followed [under Mujahadeen rule from 1992 to 1996] is the darkest period in Afghan history, especially for women," as women were subject to "rape and ill-treatment by armed personnel" on a huge scale.

Ultimately, in 1996, the Taliban, another fundamentalist group backed by Pakistan, emerged as the victors in the civil war that had been raging since 1979 and established themselves as the government of Afghanistan. Meanwhile, the Mujahadeen regrouped into the Northern Alliance—a group we have been lead to believe was a moderate alternative to the Taliban—which continued to fight the Taliban until the 2001 US invasion, when it was brought to power by the United States.

Meanwhile, the Taliban, which the US helped come to power of course through its intentional destabilization of Afghanistan, were no friends to women or women's rights. Still, this did not prevent the US from supporting the Taliban government. Few may remember that the United States was not only playing ball with the Taliban until just shortly before 9/11, but was in fact helping to bankroll it. And the reason was the desire to help Unocal (now Chevron) fulfill its dream of running a pipeline from the Caspian Sea region through Afghanistan and into Asia.[343]

As Central Asian expert Ahmed Rashid explains, "Impressed by the ruthlessness of the then-emerging Taliban to cut a pipeline deal, the [US] State Department and Pakistan's Inter-Services Intelligence agency agreed [back in 1994] to funnel arms and funding to the Taliban in their war against the ethnically Tajik North Alliance. As recently as 1999, US taxpayers paid the entire salary of every single Taliban government official,"[344] though the Taliban was not even recognized by the United Nations as the government of Afghanistan.

The United States continued to aid the Taliban, pledging a total of $124 million in aid to them in early 2001, just several months before 9/11.[345] However, when negotiations between the United States and the Taliban began to sour over the pipeline project, the United States threatened to "carpet bomb" Afghanistan.[346] Finally, the United States decided to invade Afghanistan even prior to 9/11 in light of the impasse over the oil pipeline, telling both India and Pakistan in early 2001 that they planned to invade Afghanistan in October. *Jane's Defense Newsletter* reported as early as March 2001 that the United States was planning such an invasion.[347]

In short, the invasion of Afghanistan was not carried out because the US wanted to rid the country of a retrograde regime, or to fight terrorism, and it certainly wasn't carried out to advance women's rights. And indeed, women's rights have not been advanced by the invasion.

As *Time* magazine explained in December, 2018:[348]

> As in all war-torn societies, women suffer disproportionately. **Afghanistan is still ranked the worst place in the world to be a woman.** Despite Afghan government and international donor efforts since 2001 to educate girls, an estimated two-thirds of Afghan girls do not attend school. 87 percent of Afghan women are illiterate, while 70-80 percent face forced marriage, many before the age of sixteen. A September watchdog report called the USAID's $280 million Promote program—billed the largest single investment that the US government has ever made to advance women's rights globally—a flop and a waste of taxpayer's money.
>
> Government statistics from 2014 show that **80 percent** of all suicides are committed by women, making Afghanistan one of the few places in the world where rates are higher among women. Psychologists attribute this anomaly to an endless cycle of domestic violence and poverty. The 2008 Global Rights survey found that nearly 90 percent of Afghan women have experienced domestic abuse. (emphasis added)

As this *Time* magazine piece notes, echoing international law, war and occupation hurt women, and the US war in that country is no exception to this rule.

What's more, the US military is, as in all theaters it operates in, a party to violating the rights of women and children on a daily basis. For example, as the *New York Times* reported in 2015, the US military has a policy of looking the other way as their Afghan military allies—the Mujahadeen, now reorganized as the Northern Alliance—rape children. As the *Times* explained:

Rampant sexual abuse of children has long been a problem in Afghanistan, particularly among armed commanders who dominate much of the rural landscape and can bully the population. The practice is called *bacha bazi*, literally "boy play," and American soldiers and Marines have been instructed not to intervene—in some cases, not even when their Afghan allies have abused boys on military bases, according to interviews and court records.

The policy has endured as American forces have recruited and organized Afghan militias to help hold territory against the Taliban. But soldiers and Marines have been increasingly troubled that instead of weeding out pedophiles, the American military was arming them in some cases and placing them as the commanders of villages—and doing little when they began abusing children.

"The reason we were here is because we heard the terrible things the Taliban were doing to people, how they were taking away human rights," said Dan Quinn, a former Special Forces captain who beat up an American-backed militia commander for keeping a boy chained to his bed as a sex slave. "But we were putting people into power who would do things that were worse than the Taliban did—that was something village elders voiced to me."[349]

As Thameena Faryal, a women rights advocate in Afghanistan, puts it, "It is, of course, richly ironic that the first achievement of the war on terrorism has been to install in Kabul the Northern Alliance, for whom terrorism has been the entire line of business and way of life for more than twenty years."[350]

Meanwhile, of course, US military forces have themselves engaged in rape in Afghanistan—of both Afghanis and, as is quite common in all theaters, of their own comrades (both male and female). Thus, "according to the Revolutionary Association of Women of Afghanistan, there have been reports of US soldiers and marines raping Afghan women and girls since the occupation of Afghanistan began in 2001."[351]

Again, all of this is the predictable result of war and colonial occupation, and that is why international law, including CEDAW, forbids such war and occupation. Putting it quite succinctly, Malalai Joya, a former member of the Afghan parliament and celebrated Afghan women's rights advocate, has stated: **"[w]e have many problems in Afghanistan—fundamentalism, warlords, the Taliban. But we will have a better chance to solve them if we have our self-determination, our freedom, our independence. NATO's bombs will never deliver democracy and justice to Afghanistan or any other country."**[352] (emphasis added)

All of this recalls to mind a story I heard recently about what was viewed as a recent victory for women's rights—the agreement of BMC Toys, the manufacturer of the iconic "green army men," to create "green army women," as well.[353] The owner of BMC Toys stated that "[w]hether it's a dinosaur, or Davy Crockett, or an Army man, maybe having a set of plastic Army women will help some kid somewhere be the hero of their own story at playtime. And I think that's a good thing for everybody." Of course, I am all for the equality between the sexes and full inclusivity, but maybe, in light of the brutal nature of warfare that includes rape, including of female soldiers by their male comrades, people should question whether there should be "green army people" at all to play with, and whether we should instead encourage boys and girls alike to imagine being "the hero of their own story" in a way that does not involve war and violence. I think that would be a good idea for everybody. The alternative is the regret, as Martin Luther King once expressed, of having "integrated my people into a burning building."

Meanwhile, the US war in Afghanistan has had another adverse consequence for women and girls (and for men and boys, as well)—the massive increase of poppy production and the consequent skyrocketing of heroin use even amongst young Afghani children. Whatever one might think of the Taliban, it had nearly eradicated poppy production by the time the US invaded in September of 2001.

Indeed, the Taliban were lauded for this feat just a few months before the US invaded. As the *New York Times* explained in a June, 2001 article:[354]

> The unexpected success of the Taliban in Afghanistan in eradicating three-quarters of the world's crop of opium poppies in one season is leading experts to ask where production is likely to spring up next. . . .
>
> The chairman of the Central Asia Institute at Johns Hopkins, Frederick Starr, said the West, especially Europe, had been inexplicably slow in recognizing developments in Afghanistan. "The reduction is probably the most dramatic event in the history of illegal drug markets, not only in scale, but also in the fact that it was done domestically, without international assistance," he said.

The US invaded Afghanistan shortly after this piece was written, and, within a short time after the invasion, the Taliban's drug-eradication progress was wiped out, with Afghanistan now producing more poppies than ever in its history and supplying the world with 85 percent of its heroin.[355] This sort of tragedy is another result of war, if even an unintended consequence. (I'll assume for purposes of this book that this was an unintended consequence.)

Not surprisingly, this development is devastating Afghan society and is disproportionately hurting women. As NPR recently reported, in an October 2019 piece titled "Women And Children Are The Emerging Face Of Drug Addiction In Afghanistan":[356]

> From an estimated 200,000 opium and heroin addicts in 2005, the number rose to nearly a million in 2009 and reached between 1.9 million to 2.4 million in 2015, the United Nations reported. The growing number of addicts reflects the octopus-like reach of opium and heroin. Husbands often addict wives, and mothers often addict children—by using opium while pregnant, by exposing the children to secondhand opium smoke and by using a pinch of opium to calm them when they are fussing.

"Many children become dependent on drugs, mainly opiates, at an alarmingly young age while in the care of drug-dependent parents or family members," the UN reported.

At least three percent of women were drug addicted in 2009, a number the UN considered to be low, because addiction can be easily concealed and underreported. By 2015, it had risen to 9.5 percent. Addiction among children wasn't properly counted until 2015, when the UN reported that 9.2 percent of children up to fourteen years old tested positive for one or more type of drugs and were likely to be active drug users.

Four years on, "the number of women addicted is definitely increasing. It's on the rise compared to even two or three years back," said Anubha Sood, a senior program officer for the United Nations Office on Drugs and Crime in the Afghanistan country office.

As the NPR story explains, "[t]he growing rates of addiction reflect the increased availability of drugs. Afghanistan is the world's largest opium producer." And of course, with growing drug addiction come other social ills like prostitution, and young girls being sold into marriage by fathers who use the money to feed their heroin habit.

Of course, NPR fails to link the US invasion and war to this tragic situation—this would be asking too much. And, without any pause, NPR will continue to ask what the fate of women will be if the US leaves Afghanistan, pretending that the US military presence is somehow protecting and benefiting Afghan women now.

And just as NATO and the US are not benefiting women in Afghanistan, they will not bring justice or women's rights to Syria, either. This was underscored by the recent murder of the woman some have called "the loudest voice that fought for women's rights in Syria," Hevrin Khalaf. According to the London-based International Observatory of Human Rights (IOHR),

On the afternoon of the 12th of October [2019], Hevrin Khalaf was pulled from her vehicle, beaten and shot in an execution style murder on the side of a road, south of the Syrian town of Tel Abyad, also known as Gire Spi. She was also raped, and her body was mutilated. Her murderers were male troops belonging to the Free Syrian Army, a Syrian rebel group that is actively supported by Turkey, a member of NATO. We know all of this, because her murder, also now considered a war crime by many human rights organizations, was filmed by the executors. They can be heard laughing and jeering as she died.[357]

The IOHR report of Ms. Khalaf's death is typical of the Western media and human rights reports that have covered it in that they all try to pin her brutal rape and murder on Turkey and Trump's recent withdrawal from Syria that allowed Turkey to enter from the North.

Of course, this ignores the fact that Turkey is, as at least the IOHR article notes, itself a NATO member that receives huge amounts of military assistance from the US and other Western countries. But this is only the tip of the iceberg, for as the article also notes, it was not Turkish forces who carried out this horrible crime, but instead, the Free Syrian Army (FSA). And what is notable about them, as one may recall, is that they were the umbrella group of the "moderate rebels" that President Obama, with Samantha Power at his side in the National Security Council and then as US Ambassador to the UN, supported with financial and lethal military assistance beginning in 2013.

The *New York Times* explained this inconvenient fact back in 2017 when President Donald Trump finally ended the program of arming these rebels, who most pundits and politicians had to concede by then were never really moderate to begin with. As the *Times* related,[358] Obama began the covert program of arming these rebels, with strong urging by Secretary of State Hillary Clinton, "in 2013 in concert with the CIA's counterparts in Saudi Arabia, Turkey, and Jordan." The plan, of course, was to topple Syrian President Bashar al-Assad with the help of these rebels, a plan that ultimately failed, but not through lack of trying.

In short, it was Obama's "moderate" rebels who raped and

murdered possibly the most prominent feminist in Syria. And it gets worse. Thus, the Obama Administration helped to arm the FSA through a "rat line" running from Libya, to Syria after the disastrous intervention in Libya which, of course, the troika of Susan Rice, Hillary Clinton, and Samantha Power helped to instigate.

As Pulitzer-Prize winning journalist Seymour Hersh explains:[359]

> The full extent of US co-operation with Turkey, Saudi Arabia, and Qatar in assisting the rebel opposition in Syria has yet to come to light. The Obama administration has never publicly admitted to its role in creating what the CIA calls a "rat line," a back channel highway into Syria. The rat line, authorized in early 2012, was used to funnel weapons and ammunition from Libya via southern Turkey and across the Syrian border to the opposition. Many of those in Syria who ultimately received the weapons were jihadists, some of them affiliated with al-Qaida.

Hersh explains that a classified part of the Senate Committee Report on the 2012 attack on the US Embassy in Benghazi, Libya, reveals the truth about this. As Hersh relates:

> A highly classified annex to the report, not made public, described a secret agreement reached in early 2012 between the Obama and Erdoğan administrations. It pertained to the rat line. By the terms of the agreement, funding came from Turkey, as well as Saudi Arabia and Qatar; the CIA, with the support of MI6, was responsible for getting arms from Gaddafi's arsenals into Syria. A number of front companies were set up in Libya, some under the cover of Australian entities. Retired American soldiers, who didn't always know who was really employing them, were hired to manage procurement and shipping. The operation was run by David Petraeus, the CIA director who would soon resign when it became known he was having an affair with his biographer.

In his article on this "rat line," Hersh also gives revealing details exposing the fact that some of the devastating chemical attacks that were blamed on President Assad to justify further US intervention were most likely carried out by the Syrian rebels that the US and its friends Turkey, Saudia Arabia, and Qatar were supporting.

In addition to arms, hundreds of fighters from Libya—fighters that the US and NATO backed to overthrow Libyan leader Muammar Qaddafi—joined the ranks of the FSA in Syria, entering from the North through Turkey, shortly after Qaddafi was killed.[360]

In her memoir, Samantha Power alludes to all of this in a mere two sentences that attempt to conceal more than reveal what truly happened. Thus, attempting to defend her support of the Libya invasion, she opines what might have happened if Qaddafi had managed to hold on to power, surmising that "some opposition forces could have teamed up with extremist financiers and arm suppliers outside Libya, deepening the chaos. This very scenario would soon unfold in Syria." (pp. 307–308). This is an incredibly disingenuous statement, for this "unfold[ed] in Syria" (somehow magically Power would have us believe) precisely because the US teamed up with jihadists in Libya to topple Qaddafi, and these jihadists, once in power, then helped spread extremism and terror to Syria through the FSA.

In short, the FSA, which raped and murdered Hevrin Khalaf, was a monstrous creature created through US direct support and intervention, both in Syria and in Libya. To ignore this is to ignore how US intervention is doing no service to women in Syria or anywhere else. But in the "United States of Amnesia," as historian Gore Vidal liked to refer to the USA, ignoring such inconvenient facts is part of the American pathology—a pathology that allows the Western "humanitarians" to literally get away with rape and murder and still be considered humanitarians.

TEN

The Genocide Convention and Selective Justice

ONE OF THE WORST THINGS one can be accused of today is being a "genocide denier"—that is, of questioning whether a generally recognized genocide has taken place or even whether it took place in the precise way we are told to believe it did. At the same time, there is absolutely no stigma attached to denying that a particular event is a genocide so long as the opinion makers do not consider that event, though absolutely horrible, to constitute a genocide. Indeed, there is no stigma attached to even carrying out the latter type of genocide. Indeed, it is still possible to be awarded a Nobel Peace Prize in spite of being the intellectual author of such a genocide. This seemingly incredible situation is made possible by a selective application of the law on genocide. And so, it is important to take a close look at that law.

One of the key Conventions to emerge directly from the ravages of WWII and The Holocaust was, of course, the Convention on The Prevention and Punishment of Genocide ("Genocide Convention"). As the UN Office on The Prevention of Genocide and The Responsibility to Protect explains, "[t]he Genocide Convention was the first human rights treaty adopted by the General Assembly of the

United Nations on 9 December 1948 and signified the international community's commitment to 'never again' after the atrocities committed during the Second World War. Its adoption marked a crucial step towards the development of international human rights and international criminal law as we know it today."[361]

The language of the Genocide Convention[362] is quite brief and straightforward. The heart of this Convention reads as follows:

Article I
The Contracting Parties confirm that genocide, whether committed in time of peace or in time of war, is a crime under international law which they undertake to prevent and to punish.

Article II
In the present Convention, genocide means any of the following acts committed with intent to destroy, in whole or in part, a national, ethnical, racial, or religious group, as such:
  (a) Killing members of the group;
  (b) Causing serious bodily or mental harm to members of the group;
  (c) Deliberately inflicting on the group conditions of life calculated to bring about its physical destruction in whole or in part;
  (d) Imposing measures intended to prevent births within the group;
  (e) Forcibly transferring children of the group to another group.

While the five types of acts constituting genocide under this Convention tend to be readily identifiable and proven, it is the required intent of those committing these acts that is the difficult thing to prove. This is because the particular acts against a particular national, ethnical, racial, or religious group must be committed with the "intent to destroy" that group (entirely or in part) "as such." The "as such" language is key because this means that there must be "specific intent," as we say in the legal field, to destroy the particular group being targeted—that is, the destruction of the group cannot merely be incidental to whatever project the violent acts are intended to carry out.

To take a simple example, while the Allies in WWII could only win the war by killing vast numbers of Germans, no one claims that they were killing Germans because they wanted to get rid of the German national group; they did so in order to win the armed conflict against Nazi Germany. Therefore, the killing of Germans in this context, though massive, could not be considered genocide. The Nazis' killing of Jews, on the other hand, was intended quite explicitly to remove Jews from Europe and indeed the Earth. Therefore, the killing of the Jews in this context was genocide.

However, the Nazi's genocide against the Jews was unique in that the Nazis were very open in their writings and speeches about their intent to wipe out the Jews as a people, and the method used to carry out this genocide—camps in which Jews were gathered from around Europe in huge numbers and systematically killed—lent further proof of this intent. Outside this very specific event, however, this type of intent is often concealed and hard to prove, and consequently, few have ever been successfully prosecuted under the Genocide Convention.

And in the few cases in which genocide has been successfully prosecuted against individuals, the specific intent requirement, while being paid lip service to, has been watered down considerably in order to obtain a conviction. Of course, this watering down of the intent requirement has never been used to prosecute Western leaders for genocide; it has only been used against people, some of whom could barely be called "leaders," of the Global South and East.

Let's take, for example, one of the genocide convictions that arose from the violence in the former Yugoslavia. It must first be pointed out that, not surprisingly, no NATO officials were ever charged, tried, or convicted of any crimes for their 79-day bombing spree that largely targeted civilians and civilian infrastructure. The very idea of trying NATO officials for such things indeed seems preposterous, at least in the real world we inhabit.

Instead, former Bosnian Serb leader Radovan Karadžić was tried by the International Criminal Trial for Yugoslavia (ICTY) for a number of alleged offenses, including genocide, most notably arising from the so-called "Srebrenica massacre"—one of the key casus belli of the NATO bombing raid—in which 7,000 to 8,000 adult males were allegedly rounded up and killed. The evidence against Karadžić was quite weak, as many commentators have recognized, though almost all with approval, and the evidence of "specific genocidal intent" required by the Genocide Convention was next to nil. And yet, he was convicted of genocide just the same.

Summarizing this situation, Professor Milena Sterio explains

> As other commentators have already noted, the most striking finding of the ICTY Trial Chamber was that Karadžić had specific genocidal intent regarding the Srebrenica killings. During the Karadžić trial, the Prosecution had not been able to provide "smoking gun" evidence that Karadžić knew about the killings in Srebrenica as they were taking place; instead, the Prosecution's case was essentially circumstantial. The Trial Chamber accepted the Prosecution's reasoning and drew inferences from indirect evidence. It found that Karadžić was a participant in a JCE [joint criminal enterprise], sharing its common purpose: to eliminate Bosnian Muslims from Srebrenica. This common purpose eventually evolved to encompass the agreement to kill all Bosnian adult males and to forcibly transfer women and children. The most important item of evidence that the Trial Chamber took into account was a conversation that Karadžić had with another official, Miroslav Deronjić. From this conversation, the Trial Chamber inferred first that Karadžić knew about the killings at Srebrenica as they were taking place and second that Karadžić, because he did not do anything after this conversation, must have

shared Deronjić's (and others') intent to kill Bosnian Muslims at Srebrenica.

As Sterio concludes, "[t]his interpretation of the intent requirement under the Genocide Convention and the customary law definition of genocide is novel and had not been espoused by other tribunals in the past." The reason, of course, that this interpretation of the Genocide Convention's "intent requirement" was "novel" and had never before been "espoused" is that it is clearly wrong. There is no question that the ICTY Prosecutors lacked sufficient evidence to prove that Karadžić had specific, or even vague, genocidal intent. Indeed, they did not even have sufficient evidence that he had the intent to kill anyone. All they had was evidence of a phone call that, at worst, showed that he knew killings were taking place and then did nothing to stop them. This is pretty weak tea indeed.

In the end, however, the Prosecutors desperately wanted a conviction, and so they simply bypassed the requirements of the Genocide Convention, again with much approval from Western commentators, including Professor Sterio herself who believes, as she wrote in her article, that the outcome of the Karadžić trial was good (if completely unlawful) because it will pave the way for more genocide convictions in the future. Quite tellingly, I emailed Professor Sterio about her article and told her that I too hoped this would lead to more genocide convictions, but specifically against United States officials. She did not respond to my email because, I suspect, she believed that I had taken away the wrong lesson from her argument, which was meant to be used only against non-Western leaders.

In their book *The Politics of Genocide*, Edward S. Herman and David Peterson dissect this phenomenon of Western leaders being let off the hook, both legally and in the court of public opinion, for mass killings that arguably amount to genocide while non-Western leaders are put on trial for much smaller killings. In treating the Srebrenica massacre, Herman and Peterson first challenge the claim that thousands were killed in this event, arguing that the case for so many being killed "is extremely thin . . . ." Moreover, in describing the Karadžić case itself, Herman and Peterson write, the ICTY Prosecutors successfully "argued that genocide could occur in one 'small geographical area' (the town of Srebrenica), even one where the villainous party had taken the trouble to bus all the women, children and the elderly men to safety. . . ."

They then quote Michael Mandel, an esteemed Canadian jurist who brought an unsuccessful complaint before the ICTY against NATO, for the proposition that "'Genocide was transformed in this judgment, not into mere ethnic cleansing but into killing of potential fighters during a war for military advantage. . . . In the Karadžić case, the concept of genocide, except as pure propaganda, lost all contact with the Holocaust—a program of extermination of a whole people." But the ICTY's genocide conviction of Karadžić, as Herman and Peterson argue, did its trick—it helped pave the way for the military assault that NATO was pushing for.

Meanwhile, as Herman and Peterson note, even if we were to believe that 7,000 to 8,000 males of military age were killed in Srebrenica, this still pales in comparison, say, to the nearly two million Iraqis (including men, women, and children) that they estimated had been killed by the US's two wars in, and sanctions against, that country. How could the former event, they properly question, amount to genocide, but the latter not? Of course, the answer is clear: because the characterization of the killings in the first instance served the Western purposes of waging war, while characterizing the latter as genocide would undermine the West's moral authority and its desire to engage in future armed conflicts. In the end, international law is mutilated beyond recognition to allow for this selective categorization of events. But again, few Western lawyers seem to care.

Another apt comparator here is the US War on Vietnam, which, as Herman and Peterson note, Samantha Power barely mentions in her book on genocide, *A Problem from Hell*, and she certainly does not even entertain the idea that this war was genocidal. Meanwhile, Power's bare mention of Vietnam in her new memoir reveals either her complete ignorance of what happened there, or her outright deceptiveness about it.

Thus, Power, in attempting to defend the indefensible—the NATO destruction of Libya—invokes the war on Vietnam. Essentially throwing up her hands, she states:

> As a young foreign service officer in Vietnam, Richard Holbrooke had clipped and shared a Peanuts cartoon showing a disconsolate Charlie Brown after his baseball team was thumped 184–0. "I don't understand it," Charlie Brown says, "How can we lose when we're so sincere?" . . . Whatever our sincerity, we could hardly expect to have a crystal ball when it came to accurately predicting outcomes in places where the culture was not our own.[363]

As an initial matter, what Power fails to recognize here is that aggressive war is illegal precisely because it has horrible consequences, even if many are unintended. The fact that the aggressor does not know what terrible results its aggression will have does not relieve it of moral and legal responsibility for those results. "Oops" is not a very good response, after all, to the laying of waste to an entire nation. But this is exactly Power's response.

But even more to the point, Power's suggestion that the US was somehow "sincere" in its efforts in Vietnam is simply baffling. Was it "sincere" in killing millions of people (men, women, and children) and dumping millions of gallons of poisons upon the country's farms and forests? I understand, however, from the use of "sincere" by Power that she actually means to say, "well-intentioned," but she knows that this proves too much. And indeed it does, for the War on Vietnam, while being portrayed in humanitarian terms as a war for freedom and democracy, was anything but. Indeed, I would submit, the war was genocidal as that term is used in the Genocide Convention.

After World War II, during which the US had received significant help from Ho Chi Minh and his Viet Minh guerilla fighters to fight off Japan, the US turned on its Viet Minh allies to defend French colonialism against their liberation struggle. And, as has been quite typical of the US's willing collaboration with fascists and even Nazis after WWII, the US allied with recently defeated Japan in helping to defeat the Vietnamese independence effort against the French. As John Marciano explains, "[i]n a stunning shift in history, US vessels brought French troops [many of themselves who had just fought on the side of Vichy France] so they could join recently released Japanese troops to support France's attempt to crush the Vietnamese independence movement." Marciano notes that this aroused the very first antiwar protests against the American intervention in Vietnam, this time by US sailors who could not stomach the hypocrisy of what the US was doing and with whom they were doing it.

Ultimately, of course, the Viet Minh triumphed against the French in the battle of Diem Bien Phu on May 7, 1954. As Marciano relates, the Viet Minh "had organized and inspired a poor, untrained, ill-equipped population to fight and ultimately win against a far better equipped and trained army." One might believe (and Ho Chi Minh in fact did at one point) that the US, in the Spirit of '76, would welcome and support such an independence victory. Ho Chi Minh even cited the American Declaration of Independence in declaring the independence of Vietnam from France.

Indeed, according to the *New York Times*, in a 1971 article based on the infamous Pentagon Papers, "in late 1945 and early 1946, Ho Chi Minh wrote at least eight letters to President Truman and the State Department requesting American help in winning Vietnam's independence from France." In one of these letters, Ho Chi Minh wrote,

> I assure you of the admiration and friendship we feel toward American people and its representatives here. That such friendly feelings have been exhibited not only to Americans themselves but also

to impostors in American uniform is proof that the US stand for international justice and peace is appreciated by the entire Vietnamese nation and "governing spheres".

I convey to you Mr. President and to the American people the expression of our great respect and admiration.[364]

Sadly, none of these letters were ever responded to. Instead, silence was the rude reply.

Meanwhile, after the Viet Minh victory at Diem Bien Phu, the French and the Viet Minh signed what came to be known as the Geneva Accords—an agreement intended to end the conflict and to guarantee Vietnam's independence. As the *New York Times* explains, an important part of this 1954 agreement provided that Vietnam would be temporarily divided between north and south pending elections to be held in 1956 that would unite Vietnam under one elected leadership.[365] The accord further provided that "[t]he introduction of foreign troops or bases and the use of Vietnamese territory for military purposes were forbidden. The United States, which did not join with the nations that endorsed the accords, issued a declaration taking note of the provisions and promising not to disturb them."[366] But no sooner was this promise made than the US began to actively, and violently, act to unravel the accords and to replace the French as the colonial occupier of Vietnam.

Again, the *New York Times*:

> The secret Pentagon study of the Vietnam war discloses that a few days after the Geneva accords of 1954, the Eisenhower Administration's National Security Council decided that the accords were a "disaster" and the President approved actions to prevent further Communist expansion in Vietnam.
>
> These White House decisions, the Pentagon account concludes, meant that the United States had "a direct role in the ultimate breakdown of the Geneva settlement." . . .

According to the Pentagon writer, the National Security Council, at a meeting on Aug. 8, 1954, just after the Geneva conference, ordered an urgent program of economic and military aid—substituting American advisers for French advisers—to the new South Vietnamese Government of Ngo Dinh Diem.[367]

The accords were seen as a "disaster" by the Eisenhower Administration, moreover, because it was quite aware that US ally Diem was horribly unpopular and that Ho Chi Minh was almost universally beloved. US intelligence revealed that if free elections were held, Ho Chi Minh would be elected the president of a unified Vietnam with about 80 percent of the vote. Democratic elections in Vietnam, therefore, had to be stopped at all costs.

Thus, as the *Times* explains, "the Eisenhower Administration sent a team of agents to carry out clandestine warfare against North Vietnam from the minute the Geneva conference closed," and to lay the groundwork for future operation. Thus, the team "spent the last days of Hanoi in contaminating the oil supply of the bus company for a gradual wreckage of engines in the buses, in taking actions for delayed sabotage of the railroad (which required teamwork with a CIA special technical team in Japan who performed their part brilliantly), and in writing detailed notes of potential targets for future paramilitary operations."

And while the *Times* also explains that the US also began massive economic and military support for the hated Diem regime, it neglected to mention what few are willing to: that the US began to work with Diem in violently assaulting the civilian population, not of North Vietnam, but of its ostensible ally, South Vietnam.

Noam Chomsky has made this point over and over: that especially in the early part of the war on Vietnam, it was South Vietnam that was the target, and not North Vietnam. As he and Edward S. Herman have written, "[u]nder our tutelage, Diem began his own 'search-and-destroy' operations in the mid- and late-1950s, and his prison camps and the torture chambers were filled and active. In 1956 the official figure for political prisoners in South Vietnam was fifteen to twenty thousand."

In addition, Diem engaged in a "pacification program" in South Vietnam. In one "pacification" campaign, according to one-time Diem supporter and adviser Joseph Buttinger, "[h]undreds, perhaps thousands of peasants were killed. Whole villages whose populations were not friendly to the government were destroyed by artillery. These facts were kept secret from the American people." And this took place at a time, it should be noted, when the Viet Minh in the North were concentrated on political work and were quite restrained in military operations.

As Chomsky and Herman point out,

> Diem's extensive use of violence and reprisals against former Resistance fighters was in direct violation of the Geneva Accords (Article 14c), as was his refusal to abide by the election proviso. The main reason for Diem's refusal to abide by this mode of settlement in 1955–56 was quite evident: the expatriate mandarin imported from the United States had minimal popular support and little hope for winning in a free election. . . . Diem was a typical subfascist tyrant, compensating for lack of indigenous support with extra doses of terror. Violence is the natural mode of domination for those without local roots or any positive strategy for gaining support, in this instance the United States and its client regime.[368]

The US and its henchman Diem thereby managed to scuttle the 1954 Geneva Accords and to prevent the election in 1956, which could have brought peace, democracy and independence to Vietnam. Instead, Vietnam would be subjected to an unforgiving war fought on a scale never seen before or since.

The gruesomeness of the US war effort in Vietnam is best typified by the My Lai Massacre, which Obama has recently tried to whitewash as the "My Lai Incident." In case the reader never heard of this incident, or possibly forgot about it, here is a little summary of that event as it is described in detail in Nick Turse's recent book, *Kill Anything That Moves: The Real American War in Vietnam*:[369]

> On the evening of March 15, 1968, US soldiers from Company C, or, "Charlie Company" entered the village of My Lai where they were ordered to "kill everything in the village"; "to kill everything that breathed." This admonition included women and children. Indeed, Charlie Company met no armed adversaries that day—just women, children and the elderly. And so, the Americans "gunned down old men sitting in their homes and children as they ran for cover. Tossed grenades into homes. Shot women and babies at close range." For good measure, "they raped women and young girls, mutilated the dead, systematically burned homes, and fouled the area's drinking water." General Westmoreland congratulated these brave soldiers for their "heavy blows" against the enemy, and their "aggressiveness." All told, over 500 civilians were killed in this massacre.

As Turse explains, there were many My Lais during the war. For this proposition, he cites a letter from a Vietnam veteran named Charles McDuff in which he expressed his disgust over the war in Southeast Asia, saying that My Lai was merely the tip of the iceberg.[370] Indeed, My Lai-type incidents were encouraged by the US military's designation of "free fire zones" in which "everyone, men, women, children, could be considered [a fair target]; you could not be held responsible for firing on innocent civilians since by definition there were none there."[371]

Another example of such wanton destruction of human life can be seen in the operations led by General Julian Ewell, the US 9th Division commander who would become known as "the butcher of the Delta." General Ewell initiated what he termed "Speedy Express."[372] Speedy Express, which would run from December of 1968 to May of 1969, was an operation intended to subdue the Mekong Delta region of South Vietnam, and it became a massive blood bath by design.

Turse notes that in carrying out this operation, "the United States brought to bear every option in its arsenal" to attack the Delta, increasing the kill rate, mostly of civilians, dramatically, from twenty-four Vietnamese to one US serviceman at the beginning of the operation to 134 to one by the end. Many of the kills were had through aerial attacks at night that did not distinguish between combatants or noncombatants, men or women, adults or children.

In addition to such atrocities, the US subjected Vietnam to the equivalent of 640 Hiroshima-sized atomic bombs—*the lion's share on South Vietnam, which was the US's ally*. A 1967 letter from a US Marine to Senator William Fullbright explains:

> I went to Vietnam, a hard charging Marine 2nd Lieutenant, sure that I had answered the plea of a victimized people in their struggle against communist aggression. That belief lasted about two weeks. Instead of fighting communist aggressors I found that 90 percent of the time our military actions were directed against the people of South Vietnam. These people had little sympathy or for that matter knowledge of the Saigon Government. We engaged in a war in South Vietnam to pound a people into submission to a government that has little or no popular support among the real people of South Vietnam.[373]

The US even bombed Catholic churches throughout South Vietnam for good measure.

All told, according to Nick Turse, the US, with its superior air and fire power, killed approximated 3.8 million Vietnamese (eight percent of its total population) and created over 14 million refugees. Meanwhile, Vietnam continues to feel the effects, in terms of environmental degradation and horrible birth defects, from the "millions of gallons of chemical defoliants, millions of pounds of chemical gases, [and] endless canisters of napalm" that the US dumped on that country.

In short, the US War on Vietnam was antidemocratic, undoubtedly in violation of the UN Charter's ban on the unilateral use of force and marked by untold numbers of war crimes and crimes against humanity. And there is ample evidence that it was genocidal, for the massive killings of civilians carried out were done for the specific purpose of destroying, at least in very large part, the Vietnamese national group, and they indeed accomplished this end.

The racist nature of the War on Vietnam could be seen in the very training US soldiers were given. Thus, the Vietnamese were never referred to as such in training, but instead as "dinks, gooks, slopes, slants, rice-eaters, everything that would take away humanity."[374] All Vietnamese were suspect, and "even women and small children were possible foes or outright enemies—a particularly sinister attitude in the context of a war that was supposedly being fought to protect Vietnamese from communist aggression." As Nick Turse relates, "[o]ne veteran told me that his training made it clear that the 'enemy is anything with slant eyes who lives in the village. It doesn't matter if it's a woman or child.'"

This racist policy was in fact given a name by the US military—the "Mere Gook Rule" (MGR), which meant that if someone of any age or gender was a "Gook" (meaning Vietnamese), they could legitimately be abused, raped, and/or killed.[375] And the abusing, raping, and killing was carried out on a systematic and mass scale. And again, the death toll of this racist policy was certainly in the millions. This is hardly the stuff worthy of a comparison with a Charlie Brown comic, but Samantha Power has no trouble drawing this analogy.

Moreover, it is hard to argue against that such an overtly racist war was not genocidal, and again, much less has resulted in genocide convictions, just not of anyone from the West. In addition to the case of Radovan Karadžić, take for example the infamous case of Jean-Paul Akayesu, who was successfully convicted of genocide by the International Criminal Tribunal for Rwanda.[376]

First of all, as Professor Sterio explains, again with approval, the victims at issue in the ICTR cases—the Tutsis, which is really more of a socioeconomic grouping in Rwanda which people can move in and out of—did not even constitute one of the victim groups enumerated in the Genocide Convention, as they cannot really be considered a national, ethnic, racial, or religious group. As historian Tony Sullivan explains: "[i]n the western media the [Rwandan] killings were widely portrayed as tribal hostilities. But the Tutsis and Hutus are not 'tribes'. They belong to the same Banyarwanda nationality. They share the same language, religions, and kinship and clan systems. Before white rule the Tutsis simply constituted a privileged social layer, about 15 percent of the population, with control of cattle and arms. The Hutus were farmers. Most of the land was ruled by a Tutsi king, though some Hutu areas were independent."[377]

But again, the law was simply thrown out the window in the ICTR cases in order to obtain a conviction against the Africans being targeted for punishment.

This is a good time to point out that while the Rwandan genocide is an example often cited by devotees of R2P, such as Samantha Power, as an event the West should have intervened in to prevent genocide, the truth is that the West, and particularly the US, did intervene in this event.

First of all, it is well accepted that the Western powers, running their tried-and-true divide-and-conquer strategy, had been stirring up animosities between the Tutsis and Hutus for years before the genocide began, working through the minority Tutsis as the governing class in Rwanda to govern over the majority Hutus in order protect the West's interests.[378] This began with Germany in 1894 and continued with Belgium beginning in the 1920s.[379] Before Germany left Rwanda in 1916, it set up coffee as the cash crop of Rwanda, establishing Rwanda as a virtual "coffee republic"—a situation that would become important later in the events leading up to the 1994 genocide.

As Tony Sullivan explains, "Belgian policy was openly racist. Early in its mandate, the Belgian Government declared: 'The government should endeavour to maintain and consolidate traditional cadres composed of the Tutsi ruling class, because of its important qualities, its undeniable intellectual superiority, and its ruling potential.' Belgium educated only male Tutsi.... In the 1930s Belgium instituted Apartheid-like identity cards, which marked the bearer as Tutsi, Hutu, or Twa (pygmy)."[380] As Sullivan explains, "Hutu resistance was brutally suppressed. Amputations and other mutilation were standard punishments decreed by the Belgians authorities, and administered by Tutsis."

Then, in 1961, Rwanda was granted formal independence with the Hutu majority coming to power. However, the West's imperial machinations did not end there. As Sullivan relates, "with staggering hypocrisy, the colonialists [then] encouraged a violently anti-Tutsi atmosphere to divert the fury of the Hutus from themselves." And the new majority Hutu government would engage in violent and grisly reprisals against the Tutsis in the initial years of its rule, with many Tutsis fleeing to neighboring countries, including Uganda.

Meanwhile, in neighboring Burundi, a country carved out of Rwanda by the colonial powers and subject to the same divide-and-rule tactics by the Western powers as those carried out in Rwanda, there was a genocide of 200,000 Hutus by the Tutsi-led government there in 1972. This came to be known "as the 'Genocide against Hutus' [and] it was a turning point in the ethnic divisions that later plunged even the neighboring countries such as Rwanda into a cycle similar to what happened in Burundi."[381]

Few in the West, which is so invested in the vilification of the Hutus and in deflecting all blame from the colonial powers, know or care about this particular genocide in Burundi. And needless to say, no Germans or Belgians were ever brought to justice for the abuses they inflicted upon the people of Rwanda or Burundi under their colonial rule or for helping to lay the groundwork for the genocide that would ultimately follow.

If this were not enough, in 1989, the West again inserted itself in ways that would be devastating to the Rwandan people. Thus, nine Western governments that dominated the global coffee market backed out of the long-standing International Coffee Agreement—an agreement that had kept world coffee prices stable, to the great benefit of producing countries in the Global South, such as Rwanda. As John Smith in his *Imperialism in the 21st Century* relates:

> The destruction of the International Coffee Agreement in 1989 played a crucial but almost unacknowledged role in the creation of the conditions for genocide in Rwanda. This poor African nation relied almost exclusively for its export earnings. As the world market price of coffee plummeted so did the Rwandan economy, bringing famine, hyperinflation, and government collapse down on the heads of the Rwandan people. When the Rwandan government begged the IMF for emergency assistance, the latter duly responded with a stingy loan and a savage structural adjustment program that only intensified the misery and insecurity of the Rwandan people. Isaac Kamola, in his aptly named *The Global Coffee Economy and the Production of Genocide in Rwanda*, adds that "these economic stresses created the conditions in which state-owned enterprises went bankrupt, health and education services collapsed, child malnutrition surged, and malaria cases increased by 21 percent." Michel Chossudovsky, in *The Globalization of Poverty*, comments that "no sensitivity or concern was expressed [by the IMF] as to the likely political and social repercussions of economic shock therapy applied to a country on the brink of civil war. . . . The deliberate manipulation of market forces destroyed economic activity and people's livelihood, fueled unemployment and created a situation of generalized famine and social despair."[382]

For its part, "Oxfam reported that 'there has never been such a dramatic collapse in the coffee market,' and urged immediate action to mitigate the devastating effects on coffee producers and coffee-producing nations, pleas that were completely ignored."[383]

And yet, the worst still was to come. Thus, in 1990, a wing of the Ugandan military known as the Rwandan Patriotic Front (RPF), invaded Rwanda with at least tacit US approval.[384] These RPF forces were led by Paul Kagame, a Rwandan Tutsi leader who had been trained in the US at Fort Leavenworth, Kansas, and immediately began to attack and displace Hutus in Rwanda.[385] As Edward S. Herman and David Peterson explain:

> To accept the standard model of "The Genocide," one must ignore the large-scale killing and ethnic cleansing of Hutus by the RPF long the before April-July 1994 period, which began when Ugandan forces invaded Rwanda . . . on October 1, 1990. . . . The Ugandan invasion and resultant combat were not a "civil war," but rather a clear case of aggression. Yet this led to no reprimand or cessation of support by the United States and Britain—and . . . the [Security] Council took no action on the Ugandan invasion of Rwanda until March 1993 and did not even authorize an observer mission . . . until late June 1993; the RPF by then occupied much of northern Rwanda and had driven out several hundred thousand Hutu farmers.[386]

Then, at a critical moment in 1994, the US actively intervened in Rwanda, this time in a way that guaranteed that the genocide could take place. Thus, even as it was becoming quite evident that genocide was taking place, President Bill Clinton moved affirmatively to have the UN peacekeepers, who could have halted the killings, out of Rwanda.

Indeed, even Samantha Power's own account of events confirms this. Thus, as she wrote in the *Atlantic*,[387] at a time when the Clinton Administration was receiving reports that genocide was being carried out, that "the United States did much more than fail to send troops. It led a successful effort to remove most of the UN peacekeepers who were already in Rwanda. It aggressively worked to block the subsequent authorization of UN reinforcements." That is, even by Power's own account, the US "did much more than" turn away from the genocide; it actually intervened to ensure it. This is but another example of how a country would have been better off had the US not intervened in the first place. However, unable to face the full truth about the US's active role in the Rwandan genocide, or the obvious anti-interventionist lessons to be drawn from it, Power still tries to portray the US's role as merely passive, titling her *Atlantic* piece, "Bystanders to Genocide."

Meanwhile, it must also be noted, by the way, that while the ICTR was tasked to prosecute all those guilty of genocide, it did not prosecute anyone responsible for killing Hutus during the 100-day conflict in Rwanda in 1994 even though the best evidence available is that of the 800,000 people killed during this period, the majority were in fact Hutus.[388] Indeed, an internal US State Department document from 1994 concludes that the allies of the US and the forces we are told were the "good guys" in all of this—the forces of Paul Kagame's Rwandan Patriotic Front (RPF), a Tutsi organization—were killing 10,000 Hutus a month and were responsible for 95 percent of the killing.[389]

However, this reality has been purposefully concealed by a narrative that was crafted to paint Paul Kagame as a human rights hero, and the Hutus as genocidal maniacs. As former UN human rights investigator Timothy B. Reid explains:

> On the ground, the reality of the Rwandan genocide was very different from that which is often portrayed in Western media. The "Hollywood version" of good Tutsis massacred by evil Hutus is a grossly distorted one, which ignores comprehensive and credible reports of massacres conducted by Tutsi forces against Hutu civilians.
>
> The story of the Rwandan genocide cannot be reduced to one of "good versus evil". It is far more complicated, and more nuanced, than that. However, Western politicians such as Tony Blair, Bill and Hillary Clinton, and former British development secretary Claire Short have consistently glossed over these 'complications' to portray a one-sided and largely inaccurate picture of what happened in Rwanda.[390]

I interviewed Paul Rusesabagina about all of this. Mr. Rusesabagina was of course the hero of the movie *The Hotel Rwanda* and was played in that movie by Don Cheadle, who was nominated for an Oscar for his portrayal of Rusesabagina. This movie, of course, solidified the fairytale version of the Rwandan genocide in the minds of Americans, but Mr. Rusesabagina does not himself accept this version of events.

Indeed, Mr. Rusesabagina is in exile now precisely because he has challenged the prevailing narrative of the Rwandan genocide—a crime in Rwanda under President Paul Kagame. Mr. Rusesabagina summarized what happened as follows:[391]

> In 1990, the RPF, consisting mostly of Tutsis living in exile, invaded Rwanda from Uganda. So, when they invaded Rwanda, there was a civil war for four years. In that civil war, that army, those rebels, we called them rebels at that time, were killing each and every person, every Hutu on their way. People fled their homes. They were occupying slowly. And, by 1993, early 1994, before the genocide, we had about 1.2 million displaced people who were surrounding Kigali the capital city, having to bathe in town, going to sleep in the open air in camps, dying every day, hungry. So, in 1994, these rebels, who had already signed a peace accord with the government, killed the President. That is a fact which almost everyone knows. So, when they killed him, the genocide broke out. Now, we were in a civil war where civilians were being killed by both sides. The civil war never stopped. The genocide happened within a civil war. Both sides killed, and now, afterwards, in July 1994, when the period of the genocide ended, after three months, ninety days, the Tutsi rebels took power. They took power in blood from both sides. And, the international community gathered the United Nations, and they decided to put up a tribunal for Rwanda. That tribunal was supposed to try and convict Rwandans who killed Rwandans for a period of time from January 1 through December 31 of that year [1994]. From January 1 through December 31 of that year, I saw myself with my own eyes, this [RPF] army tying people with their hands behind their

backs and beating their chests, breaking it, throwing them into containers, burning their bodies, and spraying their ashes into the national game preserve. I am a witness to this. But, because the Hutus lost the war, they are the only ones being tried and convicted. So, the international tribunal, the international criminal court for Rwanda, is a court for the losers.

The ICTR acknowledged this complaint of selective prosecution but simply shrugged it off. As the Appeals Court explained, "Akayesu submits that the Tribunal is prosecuting only the 'losers' in the Rwandan conflict by failing to prosecute the perpetrators of 'crimes of extermination of the Hutu' who enjoy 'complete immunity' from prosecution" (Par. 93). The Appeals Court simply concluded that "[a]ssuming that the Prosecutor pursues a discriminatory prosecutorial policy, Akayesu has failed to show any causal relationship between such a policy and the alleged partiality of the Tribunal" (Par. 96). And that was the end of that.

Meanwhile, the evidence of Akayesu's genocidal intent was based on very similar evidence present in the US War on Vietnam. Thus, one of the key pieces of evidence of this intent was a gathering that preceded the killings in Akayesu's town. The Trial Chamber found, and the Appeals upheld this finding, that Akayesu urged the population during this gathering "to eliminate the accomplices of the RPF," and, the Chamber concluded, this call "could be construed as one to kill the Tutsi in general" (Par. 225).

As noted above, the training and orders given to US forces in Vietnam were even more explicitly genocidal in that the troops were explicitly told that all Vietnamese (man, woman, and child) were legitimate military targets who could and should be killed in as large numbers as possible. Indeed, there was an explicit "Body Count Mentality" encouraged among US forces, in which soldiers were rewarded for racking up the death tally of Vietnamese nationals, regardless of whether these nationals were armed, unarmed, two years old, or elderly—they all counted toward the total.[392] As just one example of this, in the "battle" of Bin Dinh, US forces proudly recorded 5,576 "enemy casualties," even though only 354 weapons were obtained from the dead.[393]

One might compare, for example, the case of Akayesu, who is alleged to have actually participated in very few killings of Tutsis, to the case of US Sergeant Roy Bumgarner (of course, no actual case was ever brought against him), who, in his zealousness to meet the body count admonition, proudly killed more than 1,500 Vietnamese, including many who he knew were innocent of any misdeeds.[394] But, of course, they were not innocent of being Vietnamese, and that was the point.

In addition, as Professor Milena Sterio summarizes well, the ICTR lacked direct evidence of genocidal intent and therefore, in its prosecution of Akayesu and other accused genocidaires, inferred such intent from their actions. As Professor Sterio explains, the ICTR held that "factors to take into account when examining whether genocidal intent exists include: the scale and nature of the atrocities, the discriminatory targeting of only particular groups, methodical and systematic planning of the killings and other genocidal acts, weapons employed and the extent of victims' injuries, and documents which may reflect participation in or knowledge of the atrocities."[395]

Again, if we consider these factors in the case of the US conduct of the War on Vietnam, a solid case for genocide can be made. Thus, as to the "scale and nature of the atrocities" as well as the "weapons employed and the extent of victims' injuries," the US killed and maimed huge swaths of the Vietnamese population with the most advanced technology at the time—certainly much more advanced and destructive than the guns, machetes, and garden tools used by the Rwandans. And through the use of chemical weapons used on a mass scale, US forces left Vietnamese poisoned for generations to come, with children still being born to this day with birth defects as a result. Such chemical weapons use was not present in the Rwandan conflict.

In addition, US forces targeted the Vietnamese people for death and dismemberment in a systematic way, which, as intended, left a huge proportion of the Vietnamese population dead, disabled, or displaced. And the intent to carry out this campaign of death is well documented by internal military records, most famously the Pentagon Papers, which revealed that military acts against the Vietnamese were motivated by racial hatred.[396]

Finally, another factor considered by the ICTR in convicting defendants such as Akayesu of genocide was the systematic sexual abuse of Tutsis (Pars. 189-212), which, by the way, Akayesu was not even accused of engaging in but merely knowing of or at times being present for. Again, such systematic sexual abuse was also carried out by US forces against the Vietnamese population. It is indeed well documented that the rape of Vietnamese girls and women, many times in the form of gang rape, was "Standard Operating Procedure" of US forces.[397] In fact, US soldiers who raped a Vietnamese girl or woman were considered "Double Veterans" as a result.[398]

Moreover, the US engaged in another genocidal act in Vietnam that is rarely told—the forced removal of children from their families. Thus, in what was called "Operation Babylift," the US flew 3,000 children it claimed to be orphans out of Vietnam to various Western countries where they were given to Western families for adoption.[399] Seventy-eight Vietnamese children died in the first flight of this operation, which crashed. Moreover, many families in Vietnam have claimed that these children were not indeed orphans, and many of these families and "orphans" are still trying to be reunited.[400]

This is a classic case of "forcibly transferring children of the [victim] group to another group" in violation of the Genocide Convention. This is also standard operating procedure for the West, and for the US in particular. Other such cases include the US forcibly removing 14,000 Cuban children from their families and homeland after the 1959 Cuban Revolution in what was known as "Operation Peter Pan";[401] the current forced removal of 700 Native children a year from their indigenous families in South Dakota in what some are challenging as a genocide[402]; and, of course, the Trump policy of removing thousands of immigrant children from their families, many of whom are now being quietly adopted by white parents.[403]

In short, whatever Akayesu's misdeeds, he was a small-time criminal when compared to so many Americans who participated in the ravaging of Vietnam. And yet there was never an International Criminal Tribunal for Vietnam empaneled. And very few Western humanitarians were calling for someone to intervene to protect the Vietnamese from their victimization by the US. Instead, we have the esteemed Samantha Power comparing those who carried out mass rape and murder of Vietnamese to Charlie Brown!

But again, as we learned from Human Rights Watch Executive Director, Kenneth Roth, the US, by definition, simply does not commit mass war crimes or genocide. It is only people of the undeveloped world who do such things. And, therefore, even those Americans who oversee what should be considered genocide under any fair legal system—such as Henry Kissinger who was one of the key intellectual authors of the US War on Vietnam, Cambodia, and Laos—can walk away not only scot-free, but also with a Nobel Prize in hand. What a wonderful world it is!

Before we leave the Vietnam war, it is important to ask one more important question—did the US, while losing militarily to the Vietnam liberation forces, actually obtain its original aims there? I would argue, as Noam Chomsky has, that the answer is yes.

As Noam Chomsky has opined, the main goal of the war was to keep Vietnam within the West's economic orbit. In Chomsky's words, the goal was "to create a dependent economy that adapts itself to the needs and capacities of the industrialized societies of the West (and Japan), under the rule of wealthy collaborators . . . ."[404]

And it takes little searching to discover that Vietnam, having been bombed to the Stone Age by the US, has been forced to come crawling back to the West and to become part of the current imperialist system of production in which the countries of the Global South produce cheap consumer goods for the West, which then receives nearly all the value for these products. Just go to your closet and check out, for example, how many of your Target- or Walmart-bought clothes, and especially T-shirts, are made in Vietnam. It certainly was not the goal of the Vietnam liberation movement—one that found its base in the peasantry (i.e., small farmers) of Vietnam—to provide sweatshop labor and goods for the West, but the US war guaranteed that this would be the result by intentionally destroying Vietnam's rural population and forcibly corralling it into urban centers.[405]

The result is that 75 percent of the total export economy of Vietnam—once a mostly agricultural society—comes from Export-Processing Zones (EPZs), which are defined by the World Bank as "an industrial estate, usually a fenced-in area of 10 to 300 hectares, that specializes in manufacturing for export. It offers firms free trade conditions and a liberal regulatory environment."[406] In layman's terms, these EPZs provide Western transnational corporations (TNCs) with union-free, mostly female, "ultra-flexible, low-waged employ[ees] in which all their [that is, the TNCs'] needs are laid out on a carpet and 'the burden of the cyclical nature of demand is placed on workers.'"[407]

As noted in *Imperialism in The Twenty-First Century*:

> Since their inception, EPZs have been the focus of intense controversy, and were singled out by scholars and activists . . . as the epitome of unbridled exploitation of low-wage labor by TNCs. In a survey for the ILO [International Labour Organization] published in 2007, Milberg concludes that "despite the presence of EPZs—for over 30 years in some cases—there are very few cases where EPZs have played an important role in accomplishing . . . direct developmental goals, and UNCTAD warned in 2004 that manufacturing EPZs were reproducing colonial forms of 'enclave-led growth' in which 'a relatively rich commodity-exporting sector, well connected to roads, ports, and supported by ancillary services, exist side by

side with large undeveloped hinterlands where the majority of the population live.'"[408]

A big reason countries of the Global South are attracted to EPZs, despite their utter failure to lead to real economic development of the host country, is that "employment creation in EPZs . . . [are] essential for absorbing excess labor." And, in the case of Vietnam, the US created such "excess labor" by destroying the land and livelihood of the peasantry and forcing them into the cities. The EPZs are a ready solution for absorbing these displaced peoples.

So again, the US, through mass destruction, ultimately achieved its aims in Vietnam—and we are consequently able to obtain the cheap crap we love so much as a result. This realization is critical to considering the issue of "humanitarian" intervention. If the US is willing and able to maintain economic hegemony and our beloved commodity culture by laying waste to whole nations, while doing so all the while in the name of defending freedom and democracy, this should lead honest observers to question the US's true war aims and whether the US is truly interested in humanitarian outcomes through its foreign interventions. Certainly, from a moral and legal point of view, going to war to defend imperial domination of other nations is not defensible and must be resisted.

Sadly, the Western "humanitarians" rarely question the war aims of the imperialist powers such as the US, and much to their discredit. Nor do they, for the most part, consider the question of economic rights and equality, despite the demands of such instruments as the ICESCR to do so. Indeed, our friend Kenneth Roth has openly defended the stance of human rights groups not to do so. Roth, unable to find any justification in law or morality for such a position, argues that it simply is not feasible for human rights groups to effectively police questions such as poverty, economic inequality, and economic exploitation because the ability of NGOs to improve such policies depends on their "ability to investigate, expose and shame" wrongdoers, and, Roth argues, one simply cannot shame people or governments into tackling such problems.[409]

Apparently, Roth has never heard of Charles Dickens, whose novels about 19th-century English workhouses, debtors' prisons, and child labor helped to propel reforms on such matters; or of Upton Sinclair, whose literary works led to reforms in food and workplace safety regulations; or of the successful antisweatshop movements that led such companies as Nike to make improvements in the treatment of their employees. All of these relied upon a form of investigating, exposing, and shaming to accomplish their ends.

Indeed, I would argue, we in the West are very well situated to use our purchasing power to change economic policies that lead to poverty, misery, and premature death throughout the world, but especially in the Global South. The divestment/disinvestment campaign against Apartheid South Africa, as well as the Boycott, Divestment, Sanctions (BDS) movement against Israel's brutal occupation of Palestine and the fledgling movement to divest from arms merchants, point the way toward such meaningful activism.

CONCLUSION

Introspection and Assistance— Not Intervention

THERE IS ANOTHER PART TO the quote of Jimmy Carter with which I open my book. He not only said, in a conversation with President Trump about China, that the US is "the most warlike nation in the history of the world." He also chided Trump, and really his predecessors as well, for focusing on continued military buildup while China was focused on, for example, building speed trains. He rhetorically asked Trump, "How many miles of high-speed railroad do we have in this country?"[410] Of course, the answer is none.

Indeed, where are our speed trains? And, for that matter, where is our Medicare for all, where is our desperately needed infrastructure investment we were promised by Trump, where is our education debt forgiveness? The answer is, as Carter was suggesting, that our hard-earned tax dollars have instead gone to investing in eternal war, if one can properly call that "investment." For the wages of such "investment" are only death and destruction. Meanwhile, China has used its resources to create, as we have used ours to destroy.

As an article in *Common Dreams* about this conversation explained:

> Since 1979, do you know how many times China has been at war with anybody?" Carter asked. "None, and we have stayed at war." . . .
>
> Carter then said the US has been at peace for only 16 of its 242 years as a nation. Counting wars, military attacks and military occupations, there have actually only been five years of peace in US history—1976, the last year of the Gerald Ford administration and 1977-80, the entirety of Carter's presidency. . . .
>
> China's peace dividend has allowed and enhanced its economic growth, Carter said. "How many miles of high-speed railroad do we have in this country?" he asked. China has around 18,000 miles (29,000 km) of high-speed rail lines while the US has "wasted, I think, $3 trillion" on military spending. According to a November 2018 study by Brown University's Watson Institute of International and Public Affairs, the US has spent $5.9 trillion waging war in Iraq, Syria, Afghanistan, Pakistan, and other nations since 2001.[411]

Sadly, few are willing to connect these issues of war spending and the lack of spending on programs we actually need. And those who do are vilified as not merely wrong-headed, but as indeed treasonous. The best example of this is the treatment of Tulsi Gabbard, congresswoman from Hawaii, and her candidacy for president. Tulsi is running essentially on an antiwar platform, calling for an end to aggressive war as well as intervention in other countries' internal affairs. In other words, she is calling for the US to follow international law—nothing more and nothing less.

In response, Ms. Gabbard has been accused of being a traitor. Hillary Clinton has gone so far as accusing Tulsi of being a puppet of Russia—apparently the worst thing you could say about someone in today's political crisis, and also the most absurd. For its part, the liberal *Politico*, relying in part on anonymous Democratic hacks, opined that Tulsi was threatening to destroy the Democratic Party with her "isolationist" views:[412]

The Hawaii congresswoman's presence on the debate stage is becoming a headache for the party as she uses the platform to appeal to isolationists, dissatisfied liberals, and even conservatives....

Gabbard met with Syrian President Bashar Assad in 2017 and has repeatedly attacked Clinton's foreign policy views, grating on Democrats who've broadly supported the center-left international platform of Democrats in recent decades.

"Assad is the butcher of Damascus. Assad is someone who violated all international norms in using chemical weapons against his people. How one thinks that a conversation with him is going to change the course of events in Syria is naive at best," fumed Sen. Robert Menendez (D-N.J.).

"She has views on foreign policy that are so outside the mainstream as to be a real liability to the Democratic Party," said another Democratic senator, who requested anonymity to candidly discuss the party's issue with Gabbard. "It is corrosive to have folks on that stage who represent views that are clearly not right."

There is much here worthy of analyzing. First of all, it is simply not true that Tulsi's antiwar platform is "outside the mainstream" of US public opinion, though it may indeed be outside the mainstream of the Democratic establishment. Thus, as the *Nation* magazine reported in 2018,[413] "the bipartisan Committee for a Responsible Foreign Policy—a bipartisan advocacy group calling for congressional oversight of America's lengthy list of military interventions abroad—released the results of a survey that show broad public support for Congress to reclaim its constitutional prerogatives in the exercise of foreign policy (see Article 1, Section 8 of the US Constitution) and for fewer US military interventions generally." Describing this survey, the *Nation* explained:

The headline findings show, among other things, that 86.4 percent of those surveyed feel the American military should be used only as a last resort, while 57 percent feel that US military aid to foreign countries is counterproductive. The latter sentiment "increases significantly" when involving countries like Saudi Arabia, with 63.9 percent saying military aid—including money and weapons—should not be provided to such countries.

The poll shows strong, indeed overwhelming, support, for Congress to reassert itself in the oversight of US military interventions, with 70.8 percent of those polled saying Congress should pass legislation that would restrain military action overseas in three specific ways:

- by requiring "clearly defined goals to authorize military engagement" (78.8 percent);
- by requiring Congress "to have both oversight and accountability regarding where troops are stationed" (77 percent);
- by requiring that "any donation of funds or equipment to a foreign country be matched by a pledge of that country to adhere to the rules of the Geneva Convention" (84.8 percent).

In other words, the American people of both major political parties want the US to follow both international law prohibitions against aggressive war as well as US Constitutional restraints on presidential war-making. It is not Tulsi Gabbard, then, who is "outside the mainstream," but the Democratic establishment (not so "center-left") that is.

Meanwhile, the trope of attacking Ms. Gabbard for meeting with Syrian President Bashar al-Assad as some type of trump card to destroy her credibility is without merit. First of all, the beloved President Obama not only met with, but indeed sold weapons to, the Saudi monarchy to carry out its deadly war upon Yemen—a war that will kill many more than have been killed in Syria. And yet no one questions Obama's bona fides. In addition, our "elder statesmen" like George W. Bush (apparently good friends with Michelle Obama and Ellen DeGeneres) and Henry Kissinger are not deemed suspect because of their use of chemical weapons (in Iraq and Vietnam, respectively) on a much larger scale than Assad has even been accused of.

Yet somehow Ms. Gabbard is disqualified because she merely met with another world leader. No one claims she sold him or anyone else weapons or that she herself ordered the attack, chemical or otherwise, on other nations. This alone makes her infinitely more blameless than Obama, Bush, and Kissinger. It also makes her more blameless than former Secretary of State Madeleine Albright, who oversaw and then shrugged off the killing-by-sanctions of 500,000 Iraqi children (the same total number of people killed *on all sides* of the conflict in Syria). But in our upside-down Orwellian world, Gabbard is a traitor and Obama and Kissinger are Nobel Peace Prize recipients, Bush is now a beloved grandpa who is fawned over for sharing candy with Michelle Obama or enjoying a ball game with Ellen DeGeneres, and Albright goes around the country showing off her button collection.

But again, it is not in fact Ms. Gabbard's meeting with Assad that makes her a traitor in the view of the Democratic elite; this is only a pretext. It is in fact her antiwar views, and her criticisms of people like Obama for waging war, that make her a traitor. And it is this vilification of antiwar spokespeople that allows the war machine to continue on in contravention of overwhelming US public opinion and unambiguous international law norms.

Moreover, the term "isolationist" to describe Tulsi and her supporters is also revealing. Thus, Tulsi and her antiwar supporters are not arguing that the US should withdraw from the world, as the term "isolationist" suggests; they simply don't want to interact with the world in a violent and destructive way. Claiming that advocates for peace like Tulsi are "isolationist" is like characterizing someone who does not go around raping others a "celibate."

And herein lies the problem—our rulers and their compliant press can only see US activity abroad in violent terms. Because the US, armed to the teeth, is a hammer, and every international issue appears to be a nail.

But it obviously doesn't have to be that way, and Jimmy Carter's lecture to Trump illustrates this. As he notes, China has been at peace since 1979 and has been busy ever since engaged in building, such as by laying high-speed train track. And they are laying this track not only in China, but throughout the world. They are building roads and hospitals too, as the US bombs such things in the name of progress.

Of course, the US could do as China does. It could decide to interact with the world in a constructive, creative way. It can make friends and secure peace and security by helping the poorer nations of the world with infrastructure, health, and food programs. And, it can use its resources at home on the very same types of programs. One of these roads leads to survival and life, and the other to death and extinction. As for myself, I choose life, and apparently most of the American electorate does, as well.

This brings us to another basic human right that is codified in numerous international law instruments—the right to life itself. For example, Article 3 of the Universal Declaration of Human Rights provides that "[e]veryone has the right to life, liberty and security of person." Similarly, Article 6(1) of the ICCPR provides that "[e]very human being has the inherent right to life. This right shall be protected by law. No one shall be arbitrarily deprived of his life." And, Article 4 of the ICCPR explicitly states that this right cannot be derogated from, even in times of national emergencies threatening the life of the nation. That is, it is inviolable.

This right to life may seem to be an obvious, fundamental right. But those who advocate for war and military intervention for any purpose, but certainly to advance human rights, are overlooking or simply disregarding this essential right. There simply is no basis in law or in morality of "liberating" someone by killing them. And yet, Western "humanitarian" interventionists seem to assume such a bizarre notion. Thus, we hear that the US somehow "liberated" Iraq or Afghanistan when in fact what really happened was that millions were simply "liberated" from their mortal coil. This is no liberation at all, of course, but that reality is often obscured in Orwellian platitudes.

In addition, people in this country have a right to life that the US government is obligated to protect. But this right to life of the US people is also being fatally undermined by our insatiable war machine.

For example, a recent study by the Institute for Policy Studies (IPS) showed how the US military budget is siphoning off valuable resources that could be used for such things as Medicare for All. As Lindsay Koshgarian, director of the National Priorities Project at the Institute for Policy Studies (IPS), explained:[414]

> Over 18 years, the United States has spent $4.9 trillion on wars, with only more intractable violence in the Middle East and beyond to show for it, ... That's nearly the $300 billion per year over the current system that is estimated to cover Medicare for All (though estimates vary).
>
> While we can't un-spend that $4.9 trillion, . . . imagine if we could make different choices for the next 20 years.

Koshgarian outlined a multitude of areas in which the US government could shift more than $300 billion per year, currently used for military spending, to pay for a government-run healthcare program. Closing just half of US military bases, for example, would immediately free up $90 billion.

The IPS study showed how military spending could be easily slashed to pay for Medicare for All without increasing taxes, as nearly every pundit claims is necessary. And again, there is huge popular support for such a move. Thus,

> progressive think tank Data for Progress released its own report showing that a majority of Americans support a "progressive foreign policy" far less focused on decades-long on-the-ground wars, establishing military bases around the world, drone strikes, and arms sales.
>
> "The public rejects the predominant, fear-based framing and policies; instead, they want to see a revamped, demilitarized

American foreign policy focused on international cooperation, human rights, and peacebuilding," wrote Data for Progress.

"Voters want to see US funding go to domestic needs such as healthcare, or to other national security tools like diplomacy, instead of to the Pentagon and more endless war," according to the report.

Polling more than 1,000 people with YouGov, Data for Progress found that 73 percent of Democratic primary voters ranked numerous issues—including economic challenges and the climate—as more important to them than national security and military funding.[415]

Again, the American people are much more in tune with the spirit of international law than their rulers, and it is because this law, borne of human experience, simply makes sense.

But instead, our rulers, having gotten their way for so long through fearmongering, have engineered our nation into one that is militarily strong but impoverished, both materially and spiritually. As just one example, the US even lags behind Cuba—a country it has blockaded for decades on ostensible human rights grounds—in health care and important health care outcomes. As an article in the *Atlantic* explains:

> After a visit to Havana in 2014, the director-general of the World Health Organization Margaret Chan called for other countries to follow Cuba's example in health care. Years before, the World Health Organization's ranking of countries with "the fairest mechanism for health-system finance" put Cuba first among Latin American and Caribbean countries (and far ahead of the United States).
>
> Cuba has long had a nearly identical life expectancy to the United States, despite widespread poverty. The humanitarian-physician Paul Farmer notes in his book *Pathologies of Power* that there's a saying in Cuba: "We live like poor people, but we die like rich people." Farmer also notes that the rate of infant mortality in Cuba has been lower than in the Boston neighborhood of his own prestigious hospital, Harvard's Brigham and Women's.

We in the West should learn from countries like Cuba—a country that the UN recently designated as the most sustainably developed country on earth[416]—on how to take care of our own people's health and well-being while at the same time assisting these other countries in their own efforts to maintain health and save lives. This would require, however, abandoning our blind and mistaken faith in our own moral superiority—a superiority we think gives us the right, despite well-established legal norms to the contrary, to drive countries like Cuba into the ground.

And meanwhile, as the West obsesses over trying to pick the speck from Cuba's eye, it ignores the plank in its own, including in a place that is rightfully Cuba's—Guantanamo Bay. Thus, the US for over a century has continued to occupy Guantanamo against the will of the Cuban people and, for the past nearly twenty years, has used it as a detention center and torture chamber. This, in fact, is the most appropriate symbol of what US intervention really means in practice.

Journalist Jessica Bran Murphy, whose father was killed on 9/11 but who writes about her disgust with what she saw on her visit to Guantanamo, sets the stage well in her description of the significance of Guantanamo:

> In *Taíno*, an indigenous language of the Caribbean islands, *Guantánamo* means "land between the rivers." It is the name of a province in southeast Cuba and its capital city. It is also the name of the oldest overseas US naval base, established in 1903. Nearly 100 years later, in January 2002, the base became the site of an infamous detention camp. The word has come to represent a generation of violence against Muslims, of fear-driven reactionary policies, of crimes against humanity in the name of national security, of exceptionalism, and of lawlessness.
>
> The word *Guantánamo* is now synonymous with terror, torture, and detention. A mere mention of the word elicits a near-ubiquitous shudder, or a groan. It evokes images of blindfolded, handcuffed

men in orange jumpsuits, people labeled "the worst of the worst," suicide bombers and radical Islamic fundamentalism, prison bars and military personnel, the American flag.[417]

In its most recent, 2014, report on US compliance with the Convention against Torture and Other Cruel, Inhuman or Degrading Treatment or Punishment—a Convention that the US is, *quelle surprise,* actually a party to—the Committee Against Torture condemned the US for the fact that it has continued

> to hold a number of individuals without charge at Guantanamo Bay detention facilities. Notwithstanding the State [US] party's position that these individuals have been captured and detained as "enemy belligerents" and that under the law of war is permitted "to hold them until the end of the hostilities", the Committee reiterates that indefinite detention constitutes per se a violation of the Convention. According to the figures provided by the delegation, to date, out of the 148 men still held at the facility, only thirty-three have been designated for potential prosecution, either in federal court or by military commissions—a system that fails to meet international fair trial standards. The Committee notes with concern that thirty-six others have been designated for "continued law of war detention." While noting that detainees held in Guantanamo have the constitutional privilege of the writ of habeas corpus, the Committee is concerned at reports that indicate that federal courts have rejected a significant number of habeas corpus petitions. While noting the explanations provided by the State party concerning the conditions of detention at Guantanamo, the Committee remains concerned about the secrecy surrounding conditions of confinement, especially in Camp 7 where high-value detainees are housed. It also notes the studies received on the cumulative effect that the conditions of detention and treatment in Guantanamo have had on the psychological health of detainees. There have been nine deaths in Guantanamo during the period

under review, including seven suicides. In this respect, another cause of concern is the repeated suicide attempts and recurrent mass hunger strike protests by detainees over indefinite detention and conditions of detention. In this connection, the Committee considers that force-feeding of prisoners on hunger strike constitutes ill-treatment in violation of the Convention. Furthermore, it notes that detainees' lawyers have argued in court that force feedings are allegedly administered in an unnecessarily brutal and painful manner (arts. 2, 11, 12, 13, 14, 15 and 16).[418]

As the ACLU concluded in May of 2018, "[w]ell over a decade has passed since the first prisoner arrived in Guantánamo Bay, making it the longest-standing war prison in US history. Almost 800 men have passed through Guantánamo's cells. Today, forty men remain. Fashioned as an 'island outside the law' where terrorism suspects could be detained without process and interrogated without restraint, Guantánamo has been a catastrophic failure on every front. It is long past time for this shameful episode in American history to be brought to a close."[419]

One of the emblematic cases of the absolutely unnecessary and cruel detention and treatment of individuals at Guantanamo is that of Adnan Latif, a Yemeni citizen who died at Guantanamo despite the fact that the US government, and particularly the Obama Administration, knew he was innocent. As the Center for Constitutional Rights lamented on September 11, 2012:

> Adnan Latif is the human face of indefinite detention at Guantánamo, a policy President Obama now owns. Mr. Latif, held without charge or trial, died a tragic and personal death—alone in a cell, thousands of miles from home, more than a decade after he was abducted and brought to Guantánamo Bay. Like other men, Mr. Latif had been on hunger strike for years to protest his innocence. His protests were in vain.
>
> Adnan Latif was indeed innocent of any wrongdoing that would

have justified his detention. President Obama's Justice Department knew he was innocent but appealed a district court order directing his release rather than send him home to Yemen. The president has imposed a moratorium on all transfers to Yemen, which is why more than half of the remaining detainees are Yemenis.

Adnan Latif was held indefinitely and ultimately for life because of his Yemeni citizenship, not his conduct.[420]

The tragic irony of all of this is almost too terrible to comprehend. The US, the self-proclaimed beacon of democracy and freedom, has been using a piece of land it brazenly stole from Cuba—a country it has been blockading for nearly sixty years based on alleged human rights concerns—to hold innocents in indefinite detention in violation of both US Constitutional and international law. And now, nearly all of those being held are from Yemen—a nation the US is helping Saudi Arabia destroy in what will most likely be a genocide dwarfing that of the Holocaust. To add to the irony, the Holocaustal war against Yemen began under the watchful eye of the great Western crusader against genocide, Samantha Power.

Meanwhile, the only way that the US ruling class has been able to continue its eternal wars is through outright lying to the American public. This was just underscored by an article in the *Washington Post* that detailed formerly declassified documents from a federal project looking into the failures of the Afghan war.[421] As these documents reveal, US officials have intentionally lied to the American public about the war in Afghanistan—just as they had about the war in Vietnam and the reasons for the 2003 invasion of Iraq and the 2011 regime-change operation in Libya—in order to continue fighting there for nearly two decades despite the US's outright incompetency and complete lack of understanding of the situation there. Thus, John Sopko, the head of the federal agency that conducted the interviews [which formed the basis of the declassified study], acknowledged to the *Post* that the documents show "the American people have constantly been lied to."

We are now much poorer as a country and countless lives have been lost on both sides of the conflict, and we now know with certainty that it has all been for naught.

First of all, the *Post* quotes one US official regarding the proposition that, contrary to the prevailing belief in "humanitarian" interventionism, the US does not go to war for such purposes.

> "We don't invade poor countries to make them rich," James Dobbins, a former senior US diplomat who served as a special envoy to Afghanistan under Bush and Obama, told government interviewers. "We don't invade authoritarian countries to make them democratic. We invade violent countries to make them peaceful and we clearly failed in Afghanistan."

Of course, the idea that we go to war for peace, as Dobbins claims, is straight out of Orwell's *1984* and should be shocking to anyone capable of rational thought. In addition, the claim that the US is trying to bring peace to Afghanistan ignores the obvious fact that it is the US that has broken the peace in Afghanistan to begin with—in 1979 and then again in 2001.

Meanwhile, as for the wastefulness and futility of this war, the *Post* explains that the US has spent around $1 trillion on this war, while knowing full well that it was futile:

> Since 2001, more than 775,000 US troops have deployed to Afghanistan, many repeatedly. Of those, 2,300 died there and 20,589 were wounded in action, according to Defense Department figures.
>
> With most speaking on the assumption that their remarks would not become public, US officials acknowledged that their warfighting strategies were fatally flawed and that Washington wasted enormous sums of money trying to remake Afghanistan into a modern nation.
>
> The interviews also highlight the US government's botched attempts to curtail runaway corruption, build a competent Afghan

army and police force, and put a dent in Afghanistan's thriving opium trade.

"What did we get for this $1 trillion effort? Was it worth $1 trillion?" Jeffrey Eggers, a retired Navy SEAL and White House staffer for Bush and Obama, told government interviewers. He added, "After the killing of Osama bin Laden, I said that Osama was probably laughing in his watery grave considering how much we have spent on Afghanistan."

And yet, despite all of the lies, all of the lost lives and treasure, we will continue to be told by officials and intellectuals who should know better that the US must remain vigilant and ready to invade the next nation in the name of human rights. Orwell is rolling in his grave at such a thought. Instead, those truly interested in human rights should remain vigilant and ready to prevent the next US war on some poor and unsuspecting nation. That is the greatest contribution a Western human rights advocate could possibly make.

APPENDIX A

CHARTER OF THE UNITED NATIONS

WE THE PEOPLES OF THE UNITED NATIONS DETERMINED
- to save succeeding generations from the scourge of war, which twice in our lifetime has brought untold sorrow to mankind, and
- to reaffirm faith in fundamental human rights, in the dignity and worth of the human person, in the equal rights of men and women and of nations large and small, and
- to establish conditions under which justice and respect for the obligations arising from treaties and other sources of international law can be maintained, and
- to promote social progress and better standards of life in larger freedom,

AND FOR THESE ENDS
- to practice tolerance and live together in peace with one another as good neighbors, and

- to unite our strength to maintain international peace and security, and
- to ensure, by the acceptance of principles and the institution of methods, that armed force shall not be used, save in the common interest, and
- to employ international machinery for the promotion of the economic and social advancement of all peoples,

HAVE RESOLVED TO COMBINE OUR EFFORTS TO ACCOMPLISH THESE AIMS

Accordingly, our respective Governments, through representatives assembled in the city of San Francisco, who have exhibited their full powers found to be in good and due form, have agreed to the present Charter of the United Nations and do hereby establish an international organization to be known as the United Nations.

CHAPTER I
PURPOSES AND PRINCIPLES

Article 1

The Purposes of the United Nations are:
1. To maintain international peace and security, and to that end: to take effective collective measures for the prevention and removal of threats to the peace, and for the suppression of acts of aggression or other breaches of the peace, and to bring about by peaceful means, and in conformity with the principles of justice and international law, adjustment or settlement of international disputes or situations which might lead to a breach of the peace;
2. To develop friendly relations among nations based on respect for the principle of equal rights and self-determination of peoples, and to take other appropriate measures to strengthen universal peace;

3. To achieve international co-operation in solving international problems of an economic, social, cultural, or humanitarian character, and in promoting and encouraging respect for human rights and for fundamental freedoms for all without distinction as to race, sex, language, or religion; and
4. To be a center for harmonizing the actions of nations in the attainment of these common ends.

Article 2

The Organization and its Members, in pursuit of the Purposes stated in Article 1, shall act in accordance with the following Principles.
1. The Organization is based on the principle of the sovereign equality of all its Members.
2. All Members, in order to ensure to all of them the rights and benefits resulting from membership, shall fulfill in good faith the obligations assumed by them in accordance with the present Charter.
3. All Members shall settle their international disputes by peaceful means in such a manner that international peace and security, and justice, are not endangered.
4. All Members shall refrain in their international relations from the threat or use of force against the territorial integrity or political independence of any state, or in any other manner inconsistent with the Purposes of the United Nations.
5. All Members shall give the United Nations every assistance in any action it takes in accordance with the present Charter, and shall refrain from giving assistance to any state against which the United Nations is taking preventive or enforcement action.
6. The Organization shall ensure that states which are not Members of the United Nations act in accordance with these Principles so far as may be necessary for the maintenance of international peace and security.

7. Nothing contained in the present Charter shall authorize the United Nations to intervene in matters which are essentially within the domestic jurisdiction of any state or shall require the Members to submit such matters to settlement under the present Charter; but this principle shall not prejudice the application of enforcement measures under Chapter VII.

CHAPTER II
MEMBERSHIP

Article 3
The original Members of the United Nations shall be the states which, having participated in the United Nations Conference on International Organization at San Francisco, or having previously signed the Declaration by United Nations of 1 January 1942, sign the present Charter and ratify it in accordance with Article 110.

Article 4
1. Membership in the United Nations is open to all other peace-loving states which accept the obligations contained in the present Charter and, in the judgment of the Organization, are able and willing to carry out these obligations.
2. The admission of any such state to membership in the United Nations will be effected by a decision of the General Assembly upon the recommendation of the Security Council.

Article 5
A Member of the United Nations against which preventive or enforcement action has been taken by the Security Council may be suspended from the exercise of the rights and privileges of membership by the General Assembly upon the recommendation of the Security Council.

The exercise of these rights and privileges may be restored by the Security Council.

Article 6
A Member of the United Nations which has persistently violated the Principles contained in the present Charter may be expelled from the Organization by the General Assembly upon the recommendation of the Security Council.

CHAPTER III
ORGANS

Article 7
1. There are established as principal organs of the United Nations: a General Assembly, a Security Council, an Economic and Social Council, a Trusteeship Council, an International Court of Justice and a Secretariat.
2. Such subsidiary organs as may be found necessary may be established in accordance with the present Charter.

Article 8
The United Nations shall place no restrictions on the eligibility of men and women to participate in any capacity and under conditions of equality in its principal and subsidiary organs.

CHAPTER IV
THE GENERAL ASSEMBLY
COMPOSITION

Article 9
1. The General Assembly shall consist of all the Members of the United Nations.

2. Each Member shall have not more than five representatives in the General Assembly.

FUNCTIONS and POWERS

Article 10
The General Assembly may discuss any questions or any matters within the scope of the present Charter or relating to the powers and functions of any organs provided for in the present Charter, and, except as provided in Article 12, may make recommendations to the Members of the United Nations or to the Security Council or to both on any such questions or matters.

Article 11
1. The General Assembly may consider the general principles of co-operation in the maintenance of international peace and security, including the principles governing disarmament and the regulation of armaments, and may make recommendations with regard to such principles to the Members or to the Security Council or to both.
2. The General Assembly may discuss any questions relating to the maintenance of international peace and security brought before it by any Member of the United Nations, or by the Security Council, or by a state which is not a Member of the United Nations in accordance with Article 35, paragraph 2, and, except as provided in Article 12, may make recommendations with regard to any such questions to the state or states concerned or to the Security Council or to both. Any such question on which action is necessary shall be referred to the Security Council by the General Assembly either before or after discussion.
3. The General Assembly may call the attention of the Security

Council to situations which are likely to endanger international peace and security.
4. The powers of the General Assembly set forth in this Article shall not limit the general scope of Article 10.

Article 12

1. While the Security Council is exercising in respect of any dispute or situation the functions assigned to it in the present Charter, the General Assembly shall not make any recommendation with regard to that dispute or situation unless the Security Council so requests.
2. The Secretary-General, with the consent of the Security Council, shall notify the General Assembly at each session of any matters relative to the maintenance of international peace and security which are being dealt with by the Security Council and shall similarly notify the General Assembly, or the Members of the United Nations if the General Assembly is not in session, immediately the Security Council ceases to deal with such matters.

Article 13

1. The General Assembly shall initiate studies and make recommendations for the purpose of:
   a. promoting international co-operation in the political field and encouraging the progressive development of international law and its codification;
   b. promoting international co-operation in the economic, social, cultural, educational, and health fields, and assisting in the realization of human rights and fundamental freedoms for all without distinction as to race, sex, language, or religion.
   c. The further responsibilities, functions and powers of the General Assembly with respect to matters

mentioned in paragraph 1 (b) above are set forth in Chapters IX and X.

Article 14

Subject to the provisions of Article 12, the General Assembly may recommend measures for the peaceful adjustment of any situation, regardless of origin, which it deems likely to impair the general welfare or friendly relations among nations, including situations resulting from a violation of the provisions of the present Charter setting forth the Purposes and Principles of the United Nations.

Article 15

1. The General Assembly shall receive and consider annual and special reports from the Security Council; these reports shall include an account of the measures that the Security Council has decided upon or taken to maintain international peace and security.
2. The General Assembly shall receive and consider reports from the other organs of the United Nations.

Article 16

The General Assembly shall perform such functions with respect to the international trusteeship system as are assigned to it under Chapters XII and XIII, including the approval of the trusteeship agreements for areas not designated as strategic.

Article 17

1. The General Assembly shall consider and approve the budget of the Organization.
2. The expenses of the Organization shall be borne by the Members as apportioned by the General Assembly.
3. The General Assembly shall consider and approve any financial and budgetary arrangements with specialized

agencies referred to in Article 57 and shall examine the administrative budgets of such specialized agencies with a view to making recommendations to the agencies concerned.

VOTING

Article 18
1. Each member of the General Assembly shall have one vote.
2. Decisions of the General Assembly on important questions shall be made by a two-thirds majority of the members present and voting. These questions shall include: recommendations with respect to the maintenance of international peace and security, the election of the non-permanent members of the Security Council, the election of the members of the Economic and Social Council, the election of members of the Trusteeship Council in accordance with paragraph 1 (c) of Article 86, the admission of new Members to the United Nations, the suspension of the rights and privileges of membership, the expulsion of Members, questions relating to the operation of the trusteeship system, and budgetary questions.
3. Decisions on other questions, including the determination of additional categories of questions to be decided by a two-thirds majority, shall be made by a majority of the members present and voting.

Article 19
A Member of the United Nations which is in arrears in the payment of its financial contributions to the Organization shall have no vote in the General Assembly if the amount of its arrears equals or exceeds the amount of the contributions due from it for the preceding two full years. The General Assembly may, nevertheless, permit such a Member

to vote if it is satisfied that the failure to pay is due to conditions beyond the control of the Member.

PROCEDURE

Article 20
The General Assembly shall meet in regular annual sessions and in such special sessions as occasion may require. Special sessions shall be convoked by the Secretary-General at the request of the Security Council or of a majority of the Members of the United Nations.

Article 21
The General Assembly shall adopt its own rules of procedure. It shall elect its President for each session.

Article 22
The General Assembly may establish such subsidiary organs as it deems necessary for the performance of its functions.

CHAPTER V
THE SECURITY COUNCIL
COMPOSITION

Article 23
1. The Security Council shall consist of fifteen Members of the United Nations. The Republic of China, France, the Union of Soviet Socialist Republics, the United Kingdom of Great Britain and Northern Ireland, and the United States of America shall be permanent members of the Security Council. The General Assembly shall elect ten other Members of the United Nations to be non-permanent members of the Security Council, due regard being specially paid, in the first instance to the contribution of Members of the United

Nations to the maintenance of international peace and security and to the other purposes of the Organization, and also to equitable geographical distribution.
2. The non-permanent members of the Security Council shall be elected for a term of two years. In the first election of the non-permanent members after the increase of the membership of the Security Council from eleven to fifteen, two of the four additional members shall be chosen for a term of one year. A retiring member shall not be eligible for immediate re-election.
3. Each member of the Security Council shall have one representative.

FUNCTIONS and POWERS

Article 24

1. In order to ensure prompt and effective action by the United Nations, its Members confer on the Security Council primary responsibility for the maintenance of international peace and security, and agree that in carrying out its duties under this responsibility the Security Council acts on their behalf.
2. In discharging these duties the Security Council shall act in accordance with the Purposes and Principles of the United Nations. The specific powers granted to the Security Council for the discharge of these duties are laid down in Chapters VI, VII, VIII, and XII.
3. The Security Council shall submit annual and, when necessary, special reports to the General Assembly for its consideration.

Article 25

The Members of the United Nations agree to accept and carry out the decisions of the Security Council in accordance with the present Charter.

Article 26

In order to promote the establishment and maintenance of international peace and security with the least diversion for armaments of the world's human and economic resources, the Security Council shall be responsible for formulating, with the assistance of the Military Staff Committee referred to in Article 47, plans to be submitted to the Members of the United Nations for the establishment of a system for the regulation of armaments.

VOTING

Article 27

1. Each member of the Security Council shall have one vote.
2. Decisions of the Security Council on procedural matters shall be made by an affirmative vote of nine members.
3. Decisions of the Security Council on all other matters shall be made by an affirmative vote of nine members including the concurring votes of the permanent members; provided that, in decisions under Chapter VI, and under paragraph 3 of Article 52, a party to a dispute shall abstain from voting.

PROCEDURE

Article 28

1. The Security Council shall be so organized as to be able to function continuously. Each member of the Security Council shall for this purpose be represented at all times at the seat of the Organization.
2. The Security Council shall hold periodic meetings at which each of its members may, if it so desires, be represented by a member of the government or by some other specially designated representative.
3. The Security Council may hold meetings at such places

other than the seat of the Organization as in its judgment will best facilitate its work.

Article 29
The Security Council may establish such subsidiary organs as it deems necessary for the performance of its functions.

Article 30
The Security Council shall adopt its own rules of procedure, including the method of selecting its President.

Article 31
Any Member of the United Nations which is not a member of the Security Council may participate, without vote, in the discussion of any question brought before the Security Council whenever the latter considers that the interests of that Member are specially affected.

Article 32
Any Member of the United Nations which is not a member of the Security Council or any state which is not a Member of the United Nations, if it is a party to a dispute under consideration by the Security Council, shall be invited to participate, without vote, in the discussion relating to the dispute. The Security Council shall lay down such conditions as it deems just for the participation of a state which is not a Member of the United Nations.

CHAPTER VI
PACIFIC SETTLEMENT OF DISPUTES

Article 33
1. The parties to any dispute, the continuance of which is likely to endanger the maintenance of international peace and security, shall, first of all, seek a solution by negotiation,

enquiry, mediation, conciliation, arbitration, judicial settlement, resort to regional agencies or arrangements, or other peaceful means of their own choice.
2. The Security Council shall, when it deems necessary, call upon the parties to settle their dispute by such means.

Article 34

The Security Council may investigate any dispute, or any situation which might lead to international friction or give rise to a dispute, in order to determine whether the continuance of the dispute or situation is likely to endanger the maintenance of international peace and security.

Article 35

1. Any Member of the United Nations may bring any dispute, or any situation of the nature referred to in Article 34, to the attention of the Security Council or of the General Assembly.
2. A state which is not a Member of the United Nations may bring to the attention of the Security Council or of the General Assembly any dispute to which it is a party if it accepts in advance, for the purposes of the dispute, the obligations of pacific settlement provided in the present Charter.
3. The proceedings of the General Assembly in respect of matters brought to its attention under this Article will be subject to the provisions of Articles 11 and 12.

Article 36

1. The Security Council may, at any stage of a dispute of the nature referred to in Article 33 or of a situation of like nature, recommend appropriate procedures or methods of adjustment.
2. The Security Council should take into consideration any

procedures for the settlement of the dispute which have already been adopted by the parties.
3. In making recommendations under this Article the Security Council should also take into consideration that legal disputes should as a general rule be referred by the parties to the International Court of Justice in accordance with the provisions of the Statute of the Court.

Article 37

1. Should the parties to a dispute of the nature referred to in Article 33 fail to settle it by the means indicated in that Article, they shall refer it to the Security Council.
2. If the Security Council deems that the continuance of the dispute is in fact likely to endanger the maintenance of international peace and security, it shall decide whether to take action under Article 36 or to recommend such terms of settlement as it may consider appropriate.

Article 38

Without prejudice to the provisions of Articles 33 to 37, the Security Council may, if all the parties to any dispute so request, make recommendations to the parties with a view to a pacific settlement of the dispute.

CHAPTER VII
ACTION WITH RESPECT TO THREATS TO THE PEACE, BREACHES OF THE PEACE, AND ACTS OF AGGRESSION

Article 39

The Security Council shall determine the existence of any threat to the peace, breach of the peace, or act of aggression and shall make recommendations, or decide what measures shall be taken in accordance with Articles 41 and 42, to maintain or restore international peace and security.

Article 40

In order to prevent an aggravation of the situation, the Security Council may, before making the recommendations or deciding upon the measures provided for in Article 39, call upon the parties concerned to comply with such provisional measures as it deems necessary or desirable. Such provisional measures shall be without prejudice to the rights, claims, or position of the parties concerned. The Security Council shall duly take account of failure to comply with such provisional measures.

Article 41

The Security Council may decide what measures not involving the use of armed force are to be employed to give effect to its decisions, and it may call upon the Members of the United Nations to apply such measures. These may include complete or partial interruption of economic relations and of rail, sea, air, postal, telegraphic, radio, and other means of communication, and the severance of diplomatic relations.

Article 42

Should the Security Council consider that measures provided for in Article 41 would be inadequate or have proved to be inadequate, it may take such action by air, sea, or land forces as may be necessary to maintain or restore international peace and security. Such action may include demonstrations, blockade, and other operations by air, sea, or land forces of Members of the United Nations.

Article 43

1. All Members of the United Nations, in order to contribute to the maintenance of international peace and security, undertake to make available to the Security Council, on its call and in accordance with a special agreement or agreements, armed forces, assistance, and facilities, including rights of passage, necessary for the purpose of maintaining international peace and security.

2. Such agreement or agreements shall govern the numbers and types of forces, their degree of readiness and general location, and the nature of the facilities and assistance to be provided.
3. The agreement or agreements shall be negotiated as soon as possible on the initiative of the Security Council. They shall be concluded between the Security Council and Members or between the Security Council and groups of Members and shall be subject to ratification by the signatory states in accordance with their respective constitutional processes.

Article 44

When the Security Council has decided to use force it shall, before calling upon a Member not represented on it to provide armed forces in fulfilment of the obligations assumed under Article 43, invite that Member, if the Member so desires, to participate in the decisions of the Security Council concerning the employment of contingents of that Member's armed forces.

Article 45

In order to enable the United Nations to take urgent military measures, Members shall hold immediately available national air-force contingents for combined international enforcement action. The strength and degree of readiness of these contingents and plans for their combined action shall be determined within the limits laid down in the special agreement or agreements referred to in Article 43, by the Security Council with the assistance of the Military Staff Committee.

Article 46

Plans for the application of armed force shall be made by the Security Council with the assistance of the Military Staff Committee.

Article 47

1. There shall be established a Military Staff Committee to

advise and assist the Security Council on all questions relating to the Security Council's military requirements for the maintenance of international peace and security, the employment and command of forces placed at its disposal, the regulation of armaments, and possible disarmament.
2. The Military Staff Committee shall consist of the Chiefs of Staff of the permanent members of the Security Council or their representatives. Any Member of the United Nations not permanently represented on the Committee shall be invited by the Committee to be associated with it when the efficient discharge of the Committee's responsibilities requires the participation of that Member in its work.
3. The Military Staff Committee shall be responsible under the Security Council for the strategic direction of any armed forces placed at the disposal of the Security Council. Questions relating to the command of such forces shall be worked out subsequently.
4. The Military Staff Committee, with the authorization of the Security Council and after consultation with appropriate regional agencies, may establish regional sub-committees.

Article 48

1. The action required to carry out the decisions of the Security Council for the maintenance of international peace and security shall be taken by all the Members of the United Nations or by some of them, as the Security Council may determine.
2. Such decisions shall be carried out by the Members of the United Nations directly and through their action in the appropriate international agencies of which they are members.

Article 49

The Members of the United Nations shall join in affording mutual assistance in carrying out the measures decided upon by the Security Council.

Article 50

If preventive or enforcement measures against any state are taken by the Security Council, any other state, whether a Member of the United Nations or not, which finds itself confronted with special economic problems arising from the carrying out of those measures shall have the right to consult the Security Council with regard to a solution of those problems.

Article 51

Nothing in the present Charter shall impair the inherent right of individual or collective self-defense if an armed attack occurs against a Member of the United Nations, until the Security Council has taken measures necessary to maintain international peace and security. Measures taken by Members in the exercise of this right of self-defense shall be immediately reported to the Security Council and shall not in any way affect the authority and responsibility of the Security Council under the present Charter to take at any time such action as it deems necessary in order to maintain or restore international peace and security.

CHAPTER VIII
REGIONAL ARRANGEMENTS

Article 52

1. Nothing in the present Charter precludes the existence of regional arrangements or agencies for dealing with such matters relating to the maintenance of international peace and security as are appropriate for regional action provided that such arrangements or agencies and their activities are consistent with the Purposes and Principles of the United Nations.

2. The Members of the United Nations entering into such arrangements or constituting such agencies shall make every effort to achieve pacific settlement of local disputes through such regional arrangements or by such regional agencies before referring them to the Security Council.
3. The Security Council shall encourage the development of pacific settlement of local disputes through such regional arrangements or by such regional agencies either on the initiative of the states concerned or by reference from the Security Council.
4. This Article in no way impairs the application of Articles 34 and 35.

Article 53

1. The Security Council shall, where appropriate, utilize such regional arrangements or agencies for enforcement action under its authority. But no enforcement action shall be taken under regional arrangements or by regional agencies without the authorization of the Security Council, with the exception of measures against any enemy state, as defined in paragraph 2 of this Article, provided for pursuant to Article 107 or in regional arrangements directed against renewal of aggressive policy on the part of any such state, until such time as the Organization may, on request of the Governments concerned, be charged with the responsibility for preventing further aggression by such a state.
2. The term enemy state as used in paragraph 1 of this Article applies to any state which during the Second World War has been an enemy of any signatory of the present Charter.

Article 54

The Security Council shall at all times be kept fully informed of activities undertaken or in contemplation under regional arrangements or by regional agencies for the maintenance of international peace and security.

CHAPTER IX
INTERNATIONAL ECONOMIC AND SOCIAL CO-OPERATION

Article 55
With a view to the creation of conditions of stability and well-being which are necessary for peaceful and friendly relations among nations based on respect for the principle of equal rights and self-determination of peoples, the United Nations shall promote:
  a. higher standards of living, full employment, and conditions of economic and social progress and development;
  b. solutions of international economic, social, health, and related problems; and international cultural and educational cooperation; and
  c. universal respect for, and observance of, human rights and fundamental freedoms for all without distinction as to race, sex, language, or religion.

Article 56
All Members pledge themselves to take joint and separate action in co-operation with the Organization for the achievement of the purposes set forth in Article 55.

Article 57
  1. The various specialized agencies, established by intergovernmental agreement and having wide international responsibilities, as defined in their basic instruments, in economic, social, cultural, educational, health, and related fields, shall be brought into relationship with the United Nations in accordance with the provisions of Article 63.
  2. Such agencies thus brought into relationship with the

United Nations are hereinafter referred to as specialized agencies.

Article 58

The Organization shall make recommendations for the co-ordination of the policies and activities of the specialized agencies.

Article 59

The Organization shall, where appropriate, initiate negotiations among the states concerned for the creation of any new specialized agencies required for the accomplishment of the purposes set forth in Article 55.

Article 60

Responsibility for the discharge of the functions of the Organization set forth in this Chapter shall be vested in the General Assembly and, under the authority of the General Assembly, in the Economic and Social Council, which shall have for this purpose the powers set forth in Chapter X.

CHAPTER X
THE ECONOMIC AND SOCIAL COUNCIL
COMPOSITION

Article 61

1. The Economic and Social Council shall consist of fifty-four Members of the United Nations elected by the General Assembly.
2. Subject to the provisions of paragraph 3, eighteen members of the Economic and Social Council shall be elected each year for a term of three years. A retiring member shall be eligible for immediate re-election.
3. At the first election after the increase in the membership of

the Economic and Social Council from twenty-seven to fifty-four members, in addition to the members elected in place of the nine members whose term of office expires at the end of that year, twenty-seven additional members shall be elected. Of these twenty-seven additional members, the term of office of nine members so elected shall expire at the end of one year, and of nine other members at the end of two years, in accordance with arrangements made by the General Assembly.
4. Each member of the Economic and Social Council shall have one representative.

FUNCTIONS and POWERS

Article 62

1. The Economic and Social Council may make or initiate studies and reports with respect to international economic, social, cultural, educational, health, and related matters and may make recommendations with respect to any such matters to the General Assembly to the Members of the United Nations, and to the specialized agencies concerned.
2. It may make recommendations for the purpose of promoting respect for, and observance of, human rights and fundamental freedoms for all.
3. It may prepare draft conventions for submission to the General Assembly, with respect to matters falling within its competence.
4. It may call, in accordance with the rules prescribed by the United Nations, international conferences on matters falling within its competence.

Article 63

1. The Economic and Social Council may enter into agreements with any of the agencies referred to in Article 57, defining

the terms on which the agency concerned shall be brought into relationship with the United Nations. Such agreements shall be subject to approval by the General Assembly.
2. It may co-ordinate the activities of the specialized agencies through consultation with and recommendations to such agencies and through recommendations to the General Assembly and to the Members of the United Nations.

Article 64

1. The Economic and Social Council may take appropriate steps to obtain regular reports from the specialized agencies. It may make arrangements with the Members of the United Nations and with the specialized agencies to obtain reports on the steps taken to give effect to its own recommendations and to recommendations on matters falling within its competence made by the General Assembly.
2. It may communicate its observations on these reports to the General Assembly.

Article 65

The Economic and Social Council may furnish information to the Security Council and shall assist the Security Council upon its request.

Article 66

1. The Economic and Social Council shall perform such functions as fall within its competence in connection with the carrying out of the recommendations of the General Assembly.
2. It may, with the approval of the General Assembly, perform services at the request of Members of the United Nations and at the request of specialized agencies.
3. It shall perform such other functions as are specified elsewhere in the present Charter or as may be assigned to it by the General Assembly.

VOTING

Article 67

1. Each member of the Economic and Social Council shall have one vote.
2. Decisions of the Economic and Social Council shall be made by a majority of the members present and voting.

PROCEDURE

Article 68
The Economic and Social Council shall set up commissions in economic and social fields and for the promotion of human rights, and such other commissions as may be required for the performance of its functions.

Article 69
The Economic and Social Council shall invite any Member of the United Nations to participate, without vote, in its deliberations on any matter of particular concern to that Member.

Article 70
The Economic and Social Council may make arrangements for representatives of the specialized agencies to participate, without vote, in its deliberations and in those of the commissions established by it, and for its representatives to participate in the deliberations of the specialized agencies.

Article 71
The Economic and Social Council may make suitable arrangements for consultation with non-governmental organizations which are concerned with matters within its competence. Such arrangements may be made with international organizations and, where appropriate, with

national organizations after consultation with the Member of the United Nations concerned.

Article 72
1. The Economic and Social Council shall adopt its own rules of procedure, including the method of selecting its President.
2. The Economic and Social Council shall meet as required in accordance with its rules, which shall include provision for the convening of meetings on the request of a majority of its members.

CHAPTER XI
DECLARATION REGARDING NON-SELF-GOVERNING TERRITORIES

Article 73
Members of the United Nations which have or assume responsibilities for the administration of territories whose peoples have not yet attained a full measure of self-government recognize the principle that the interests of the inhabitants of these territories are paramount, and accept as a sacred trust the obligation to promote to the utmost, within the system of international peace and security established by the present Charter, the well-being of the inhabitants of these territories, and, to this end:

    a. to ensure, with due respect for the culture of the peoples concerned, their political, economic, social, and educational advancement, their just treatment, and their protection against abuses;

    b. to develop self-government, to take due account of the political aspirations of the peoples, and to assist them in the progressive development of their free political institutions, according to the particular circumstances of each territory and its peoples and their varying stages of advancement;

    c. to further international peace and security;

d. to promote constructive measures of development, to encourage research, and to co-operate with one another and, when and where appropriate, with specialized international bodies with a view to the practical achievement of the social, economic, and scientific purposes set forth in this Article; and

e. to transmit regularly to the Secretary-General for information purposes, subject to such limitation as security and constitutional considerations may require, statistical and other information of a technical nature relating to economic, social, and educational conditions in the territories for which they are respectively responsible other than those territories to which Chapters XII and XIII apply.

Article 74

Members of the United Nations also agree that their policy in respect of the territories to which this Chapter applies, no less than in respect of their metropolitan areas, must be based on the general principle of good-neighborliness, due account being taken of the interests and well-being of the rest of the world, in social, economic, and commercial matters.

CHAPTER XII
INTERNATIONAL TRUSTEESHIP SYSTEM

Article 75

The United Nations shall establish under its authority an international trusteeship system for the administration and supervision of such territories as may be placed thereunder by subsequent individual agreements. These territories are hereinafter referred to as trust territories.

Article 76

The basic objectives of the trusteeship system, in accordance with the

Purposes of the United Nations laid down in Article 1 of the present Charter, shall be:
  a. to further international peace and security;
  b. to promote the political, economic, social, and educational advancement of the inhabitants of the trust territories, and their progressive development towards self-government or independence as may be appropriate to the particular circumstances of each territory and its peoples and the freely expressed wishes of the peoples concerned, and as may be provided by the terms of each trusteeship agreement;
  c. to encourage respect for human rights and for fundamental freedoms for all without distinction as to race, sex, language, or religion, and to encourage recognition of the interdependence of the peoples of the world; and
  d. to ensure equal treatment in social, economic, and commercial matters for all Members of the United Nations and their nationals, and also equal treatment for the latter in the administration of justice, without prejudice to the attainment of the foregoing objectives and subject to the provisions of Article 80.

Article 77

  1. The trusteeship system shall apply to such territories in the following categories as may be placed thereunder by means of trusteeship agreements:
     a. territories now held under mandate;
     b. territories which may be detached from enemy states as a result of the Second World War; and
     c. territories voluntarily placed under the system by states responsible for their administration.
  2. It will be a matter for subsequent agreement as to which territories in the foregoing categories will be brought under the trusteeship system and upon what terms.

Article 78

The trusteeship system shall not apply to territories which have become Members of the United Nations, relationship among which shall be based on respect for the principle of sovereign equality.

Article 79

The terms of trusteeship for each territory to be placed under the trusteeship system, including any alteration or amendment, shall be agreed upon by the states directly concerned, including the mandatory power in the case of territories held under mandate by a Member of the United Nations, and shall be approved as provided for in Articles 83 and 85.

Article 80

1. Except as may be agreed upon in individual trusteeship agreements, made under Articles 77, 79, and 81, placing each territory under the trusteeship system, and until such agreements have been concluded, nothing in this Chapter shall be construed in or of itself to alter in any manner the rights whatsoever of any states or any peoples or the terms of existing international instruments to which Members of the United Nations may respectively be parties.
2. Paragraph 1 of this Article shall not be interpreted as giving grounds for delay or postponement of the negotiation and conclusion of agreements for placing mandated and other territories under the trusteeship system as provided for in Article 77.

Article 81

The trusteeship agreement shall in each case include the terms under which the trust territory will be administered and designate the authority which will exercise the administration of the trust territory. Such authority, hereinafter called the administering authority, may be one or more states or the Organization itself.

Article 82

There may be designated, in any trusteeship agreement, a strategic area or areas which may include part or all of the trust territory to which the agreement applies, without prejudice to any special agreement or agreements made under Article 43.

Article 83

1. All functions of the United Nations relating to strategic areas, including the approval of the terms of the trusteeship agreements and of their alteration or amendment shall be exercised by the Security Council.
2. The basic objectives set forth in Article 76 shall be applicable to the people of each strategic area.
3. The Security Council shall, subject to the provisions of the trusteeship agreements and without prejudice to security considerations, avail itself of the assistance of the Trusteeship Council to perform those functions of the United Nations under the trusteeship system relating to political, economic, social, and educational matters in the strategic areas.

Article 84

It shall be the duty of the administering authority to ensure that the trust territory shall play its part in the maintenance of international peace and security. To this end the administering authority may make use of volunteer forces, facilities, and assistance from the trust territory in carrying out the obligations towards the Security Council undertaken in this regard by the administering authority, as well as for local defense and the maintenance of law and order within the trust territory.

Article 85

1. The functions of the United Nations with regard to trusteeship agreements for all areas not designated as strategic, including the approval of the terms of the

trusteeship agreements and of their alteration or amendment, shall be exercised by the General Assembly.
2. The Trusteeship Council, operating under the authority of the General Assembly shall assist the General Assembly in carrying out these functions.

CHAPTER XIII
THE TRUSTEESHIP COUNCIL
COMPOSITION

Article 86
1. The Trusteeship Council shall consist of the following Members of the United Nations:
    a. those Members administering trust territories;
    b. such of those Members mentioned by name in Article 23 as are not administering trust territories; and
    c. as many other Members elected for three-year terms by the General Assembly as may be necessary to ensure that the total number of members of the Trusteeship Council is equally divided between those Members of the United Nations which administer trust territories and those which do not.
2. Each member of the Trusteeship Council shall designate one specially qualified person to represent it therein.

FUNCTIONS and POWERS

Article 87
The General Assembly and, under its authority, the Trusteeship Council, in carrying out their functions, may:
    a. consider reports submitted by the administering authority;
    b. accept petitions and examine them in consultation with the administering authority;

c. provide for periodic visits to the respective trust territories at times agreed upon with the administering authority; and
   d. take these and other actions in conformity with the terms of the trusteeship agreements.

Article 88

The Trusteeship Council shall formulate a questionnaire on the political, economic, social, and educational advancement of the inhabitants of each trust territory, and the administering authority for each trust territory within the competence of the General Assembly shall make an annual report to the General Assembly upon the basis of such questionnaire.

VOTING

Article 89

1. Each member of the Trusteeship Council shall have one vote.
2. Decisions of the Trusteeship Council shall be made by a majority of the members present and voting.

PROCEDURE

Article 90

1. The Trusteeship Council shall adopt its own rules of procedure, including the method of selecting its President.
2. The Trusteeship Council shall meet as required in accordance with its rules, which shall include provision for the convening of meetings on the request of a majority of its members.

Article 91

The Trusteeship Council shall, when appropriate, avail itself of the assistance of the Economic and Social Council and of the specialized agencies in regard to matters with which they are respectively concerned.

Samantha Power and the banality of evil

Susan Rice and Benjamin Netanyahu. Israel's war crimes get a free pass from western "humanitarians"

The US War on Vietnam: A genocide the West will not acknowledge

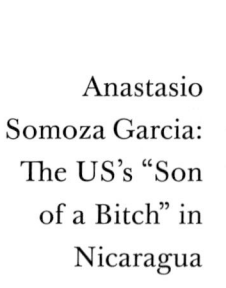

Anastasio Somoza Garcia: The US's "Son of a Bitch" in Nicaragua

Daniel Ortega: The Liberator of Nicaragua from US dictatorship
(Photo by jean-Louis Atlan/Sygma via Getty Images)

The US: Killing Iraqis in the name of freedom *(Photo by Scott Nelson/Getty Images)*

The not-so humanitarian destruction of Libya *(Photo by Scott Peterson/Getty Images)*

President Bill Clinton with Rwandan President Paul Kagame: The liberals' favorite genocidaires *(Photo by Lars Niki/Corbis via Getty Images)*

US uses chemical weapons in Iraq with little notice or concern *(Photo by Muhannad Fala'ah/ Getty Images)*

The Congo—the western genocide few will acknowledge *(Photo by Giles Clarke/Getty Images)*

Afghanistan remains worst country in the world for women after nearly two decades of US occupation

CHAPTER XIV
THE INTERNATIONAL COURT OF JUSTICE

Article 92

The International Court of Justice shall be the principal judicial organ of the United Nations. It shall function in accordance with the annexed Statute, which is based upon the Statute of the Permanent Court of International Justice and forms an integral part of the present Charter.

Article 93

1. All Members of the United Nations are ipso facto parties to the Statute of the International Court of Justice.
2. A state which is not a Member of the United Nations may become a party to the Statute of the International Court of Justice on conditions to be determined in each case by the General Assembly upon the recommendation of the Security Council.

Article 94

1. Each Member of the United Nations undertakes to comply with the decision of the International Court of Justice in any case to which it is a party.
2. If any party to a case fails to perform the obligations incumbent upon it under a judgment rendered by the Court, the other party may have recourse to the Security Council, which may, if it deems necessary, make recommendations or decide upon measures to be taken to give effect to the judgment.

Article 95

Nothing in the present Charter shall prevent Members of the United Nations from entrusting the solution of their differences to other tribunals by virtue of agreements already in existence or which may be concluded in the future.

Article 96

   a. The General Assembly or the Security Council may request the International Court of Justice to give an advisory opinion on any legal question.
   b. Other organs of the United Nations and specialized agencies, which may at any time be so authorized by the General Assembly, may also request advisory opinions of the Court on legal questions arising within the scope of their activities.

CHAPTER XV
THE SECRETARIAT

Article 97
The Secretariat shall comprise a Secretary-General and such staff as the Organization may require. The Secretary-General shall be appointed by the General Assembly upon the recommendation of the Security Council. He shall be the chief administrative officer of the Organization.

Article 98
The Secretary-General shall act in that capacity in all meetings of the General Assembly, of the Security Council, of the Economic and Social Council, and of the Trusteeship Council, and shall perform such other functions as are entrusted to him by these organs. The Secretary-General shall make an annual report to the General Assembly on the work of the Organization.

Article 99
The Secretary-General may bring to the attention of the Security Council any matter which in his opinion may threaten the maintenance of international peace and security.

Article 100
   1. In the performance of their duties the Secretary-General

and the staff shall not seek or receive instructions from any government or from any other authority external to the Organization. They shall refrain from any action which might reflect on their position as international officials responsible only to the Organization.
2. Each Member of the United Nations undertakes to respect the exclusively international character of the responsibilities of the Secretary-General and the staff and not to seek to influence them in the discharge of their responsibilities.

Article 101

1. The staff shall be appointed by the Secretary-General under regulations established by the General Assembly.
2. Appropriate staffs shall be permanently assigned to the Economic and Social Council, the Trusteeship Council, and, as required, to other organs of the United Nations. These staffs shall form a part of the Secretariat.
3. The paramount consideration in the employment of the staff and in the determination of the conditions of service shall be the necessity of securing the highest standards of efficiency, competence, and integrity. Due regard shall be paid to the importance of recruiting the staff on as wide a geographical basis as possible.

CHAPTER XVI
MISCELLANEOUS PROVISIONS

Article 102

1. Every treaty and every international agreement entered into by any Member of the United Nations after the present Charter comes into force shall as soon as possible be registered with the Secretariat and published by it.
2. No party to any such treaty or international agreement

which has not been registered in accordance with the provisions of paragraph 1 of this Article may invoke that treaty or agreement before any organ of the United Nations.

Article 103
In the event of a conflict between the obligations of the Members of the United Nations under the present Charter and their obligations under any other international agreement, their obligations under the present Charter shall prevail.

Article 104
The Organization shall enjoy in the territory of each of its Members such legal capacity as may be necessary for the exercise of its functions and the fulfilment of its purposes.

Article 105
1. The Organization shall enjoy in the territory of each of its Members such privileges and immunities as are necessary for the fulfilment of its purposes.
2. Representatives of the Members of the United Nations and officials of the Organization shall similarly enjoy such privileges and immunities as are necessary for the independent exercise of their functions in connection with the Organization.
3. The General Assembly may make recommendations with a view to determining the details of the application of paragraphs 1 and 2 of this Article or may propose conventions to the Members of the United Nations for this purpose.

CHAPTER XVII
TRANSITIONAL SECURITY ARRANGEMENTS

Article 106
Pending the coming into force of such special agreements referred to

in Article 43 as in the opinion of the Security Council enable it to begin the exercise of its responsibilities under Article 42, the parties to the Four-Nation Declaration, signed at Moscow, 30 October 1943, and France, shall, in accordance with the provisions of paragraph 5 of that Declaration, consult with one another and as occasion requires with other Members of the United Nations with a view to such joint action on behalf of the Organization as may be necessary for the purpose of maintaining international peace and security.

Article 107
Nothing in the present Charter shall invalidate or preclude action, in relation to any state which during the Second World War has been an enemy of any signatory to the present Charter, taken or authorized as a result of that war by the Governments having responsibility for such action.

CHAPTER XVIII
AMENDMENTS

Article 108
Amendments to the present Charter shall come into force for all Members of the United Nations when they have been adopted by a vote of two thirds of the members of the General Assembly and ratified in accordance with their respective constitutional processes by two thirds of the Members of the United Nations, including all the permanent members of the Security Council.

Article 109
1. A General Conference of the Members of the United Nations for the purpose of reviewing the present Charter may be held at a date and place to be fixed by a two-thirds vote of the members of the General Assembly and by a vote of any nine members of the Security Council. Each Member of the United Nations shall have one vote in the conference.

2. Any alteration of the present Charter recommended by a two-thirds vote of the conference shall take effect when ratified in accordance with their respective constitutional processes by two thirds of the Members of the United Nations including all the permanent members of the Security Council.
3. If such a conference has not been held before the tenth annual session of the General Assembly following the coming into force of the present Charter, the proposal to call such a conference shall be placed on the agenda of that session of the General Assembly, and the conference shall be held if so decided by a majority vote of the members of the General Assembly and by a vote of any seven members of the Security Council.

CHAPTER XIX
RATIFICATION AND SIGNATURE

Article 110
1. The present Charter shall be ratified by the signatory states in accordance with their respective constitutional processes.
2. The ratifications shall be deposited with the Government of the United States of America, which shall notify all the signatory states of each deposit as well as the Secretary-General of the Organization when he has been appointed.
3. The present Charter shall come into force upon the deposit of ratifications by the Republic of China, France, the Union of Soviet Socialist Republics, the United Kingdom of Great Britain and Northern Ireland, and the United States of America, and by a majority of the other signatory states. A protocol of the ratifications deposited shall thereupon be drawn up by the Government of the United States of

America which shall communicate copies thereof to all the signatory states.
4. The states signatory to the present Charter which ratify it after it has come into force will become original Members of the United Nations on the date of the deposit of their respective ratifications.

Article 111

The present Charter, of which the Chinese, French, Russian, English, and Spanish texts are equally authentic, shall remain deposited in the archives of the Government of the United States of America. Duly certified copies thereof shall be transmitted by that Government to the Governments of the other signatory states.

IN FAITH WHEREOF the representatives of the Governments of the United Nations have signed the present Charter. DONE at the city of San Francisco the twenty-sixth day of June, one thousand nine hundred and forty-five.

APPENDIX B

STATUTE OF THE INTERNATIONAL COURT OF JUSTICE

Article 1
The International Court of Justice established by the Charter of the United Nations as the principal judicial organ of the United Nations shall be constituted and shall function in accordance with the provisions of the present Statute.

CHAPTER I
ORGANIZATION OF THE COURT

Article 2
The Court shall be composed of a body of independent judges, elected regardless of their nationality from among persons of high moral character, who possess the qualifications required in their respective countries for appointment to the highest judicial offices, or are jurisconsults of recognized competence in international law.

Article 3

1. The Court shall consist of fifteen members, no two of whom may be nationals of the same state.
2. A person who for the purposes of membership in the Court could be regarded as a national of more than one state shall be deemed to be a national of the one in which he ordinarily exercises civil and political rights.

Article 4

1. The members of the Court shall be elected by the General Assembly and by the Security Council from a list of persons nominated by the national groups in the Permanent Court of Arbitration, in accordance with the following provisions.
2. In the case of Members of the United Nations not represented in the Permanent Court of Arbitration, candidates shall be nominated by national groups appointed for this purpose by their governments under the same conditions as those prescribed for members of the Permanent Court of Arbitration by Article 44 of the Convention of The Hague of 1907 for the pacific settlement of international disputes.
3. The conditions under which a state which is a party to the present Statute but is not a Member of the United Nations may participate in electing the members of the Court shall, in the absence of a special agreement, be laid down by the General Assembly upon recommendation of the Security Council.

Article 5

1. At least three months before the date of the election, the Secretary-General of the United Nations shall address a written request to the members of the Permanent Court of Arbitration belonging to the states which are parties to the present Statute, and to the members of the national groups

appointed under Article 4, paragraph 2, inviting them to undertake, within a given time, by national groups, the nomination of persons in a position to accept the duties of a member of the Court.
2. No group may nominate more than four persons, not more than two of whom shall be of their own nationality. In no case may the number of candidates nominated by a group be more than double the number of seats to be filled.

Article 6

Before making these nominations, each national group is recommended to consult its highest court of justice, its legal faculties and schools of law, and its national academies and national sections of international academies devoted to the study of law.

Article 7

1. The Secretary-General shall prepare a list in alphabetical order of all the persons thus nominated. Save as provided in Article 12, paragraph 2, these shall be the only persons eligible.
2. The Secretary-General shall submit this list to the General Assembly and to the Security Council.

Article 8

The General Assembly and the Security Council shall proceed independently of one another to elect the members of the Court.

Article 9

At every election, the electors shall bear in mind not only that the persons to be elected should individually possess the qualifications required, but also that in the body as a whole the representation of the main forms of civilization and of the principal legal systems of the world should be assured.

Article 10

1. Those candidates who obtain an absolute majority of votes in the General Assembly and in the Security Council shall be considered as elected.
2. Any vote of the Security Council, whether for the election of judges or for the appointment of members of the conference envisaged in Article 12, shall be taken without any distinction between permanent and non-permanent members of the Security Council.
3. In the event of more than one national of the same state obtaining an absolute majority of the votes both of the General Assembly and of the Security Council, the eldest of these only shall be considered as elected.

Article 11

If, after the first meeting held for the purpose of the election, one or more seats remain to be filled, a second and, if necessary, a third meeting shall take place.

Article 12

1. If, after the third meeting, one or more seats still remain unfilled, a joint conference consisting of six members, three appointed by the General Assembly and three by the Security Council, may be formed at any time at the request of either the General Assembly or the Security Council, for the purpose of choosing by the vote of an absolute majority one name for each seat still vacant, to submit to the General Assembly and the Security Council for their respective acceptance.
2. If the joint conference is unanimously agreed upon any person who fulfills the required conditions, he may be included in its list, even though he was not included in the list of nominations referred to in Article 7.

3. If the joint conference is satisfied that it will not be successful in procuring an election, those members of the Court who have already been elected shall, within a period to be fixed by the Security Council, proceed to fill the vacant seats by selection from among those candidates who have obtained votes either in the General Assembly or in the Security Council.
4. In the event of an equality of votes among the judges, the eldest judge shall have a casting vote.

Article 13

1. The members of the Court shall be elected for nine years and may be re-elected; provided, however, that of the judges elected at the first election, the terms of five judges shall expire at the end of three years and the terms of five more judges shall expire at the end of six years.
2. The judges whose terms are to expire at the end of the above-mentioned initial periods of three and six years shall be chosen by lot to be drawn by the Secretary-General immediately after the first election has been completed.
3. The members of the Court shall continue to discharge their duties until their places have been filled. Though replaced, they shall finish any cases which they may have begun.
4. In the case of the resignation of a member of the Court, the resignation shall be addressed to the President of the Court for transmission to the Secretary-General. This last notification makes the place vacant.

Article 14

Vacancies shall be filled by the same method as that laid down for the first election, subject to the following provision: the Secretary-General shall, within one month of the occurrence of the vacancy, proceed to issue the invitations provided for in Article 5, and the date of the election shall be fixed by the Security Council.

Article 15
A member of the Court elected to replace a member whose term of office has not expired shall hold office for the remainder of his predecessor's term.

Article 16
1. No member of the Court may exercise any political or administrative function, or engage in any other occupation of a professional nature.
2. Any doubt on this point shall be settled by the decision of the Court.

Article 17
1. No member of the Court may act as agent, counsel, or advocate in any case.
2. No member may participate in the decision of any case in which he has previously taken part as agent, counsel, or advocate for one of the parties, or as a member of a national or international court, or of a commission of enquiry, or in any other capacity.
3. Any doubt on this point shall be settled by the decision of the Court.

Article 18
1. No member of the Court can be dismissed unless, in the unanimous opinion of the other members, he has ceased to fulfill the required conditions.
2. Formal notification thereof shall be made to the Secretary-General by the Registrar.
3. This notification makes the place vacant.

Article 19

The members of the Court, when engaged on the business of the Court, shall enjoy diplomatic privileges and immunities.

Article 20

Every member of the Court shall, before taking up his duties, make a solemn declaration in open court that he will exercise his powers impartially and conscientiously.

Article 21

1. The Court shall elect its President and Vice-President for three years; they may be re-elected.
2. The Court shall appoint its Registrar and may provide for the appointment of such other officers as may be necessary.

Article 22

1. The seat of the Court shall be established at The Hague. This, however, shall not prevent the Court from sitting and exercising its functions elsewhere whenever the Court considers it desirable.
2. The President and the Registrar shall reside at the seat of the Court.

Article 23

1. The Court shall remain permanently in session, except during the judicial vacations, the dates and duration of which shall be fixed by the Court.
2. Members of the Court are entitled to periodic leave, the dates and duration of which shall be fixed by the Court, having in mind the distance between The Hague and the home of each judge.
3. Members of the Court shall be bound, unless they are on leave or prevented from attending by illness or other serious

reasons duly explained to the President, to hold themselves permanently at the disposal of the Court.

Article 24

1. If, for some special reason, a member of the Court considers that he should not take part in the decision of a particular case, he shall so inform the President.
2. If the President considers that for some special reason one of the members of the Court should not sit in a particular case, he shall give him notice accordingly.
3. If in any such case the member of the Court and the President disagree, the matter shall be settled by the decision of the Court.

Article 25

1. The full Court shall sit except when it is expressly provided otherwise in the present Statute.
2. Subject to the condition that the number of judges available to constitute the Court is not thereby reduced below eleven, the Rules of the Court may provide for allowing one or more judges, according to circumstances and in rotation, to be dispensed from sitting.
3. A quorum of nine judges shall suffice to constitute the Court.

Article 26

1. The Court may from time to time form one or more chambers, composed of three or more judges as the Court may determine, for dealing with particular categories of cases; for example, labour cases and cases relating to transit and communications.
2. The Court may at any time form a chamber for dealing with a particular case. The number of judges to constitute such a

chamber shall be determined by the Court with the approval of the parties.
3. Cases shall be heard and determined by the chambers provided for in this article if the parties so request.

Article 27

A judgment given by any of the chambers provided for in Articles 26 and 29 shall be considered as rendered by the Court.

Article 28

The chambers provided for in Articles 26 and 29 may, with the consent of the parties, sit and exercise their functions elsewhere than at The Hague.

Article 29

With a view to the speedy dispatch of business, the Court shall form annually a chamber composed of five judges which, at the request of the parties, may hear and determine cases by summary procedure. In addition, two judges shall be selected for the purpose of replacing judges who find it impossible to sit.

Article 30

1. The Court shall frame rules for carrying out its functions. In particular, it shall lay down rules of procedure.
2. The Rules of the Court may provide for assessors to sit with the Court or with any of its chambers, without the right to vote.

Article 31

1. Judges of the nationality of each of the parties shall retain their right to sit in the case before the Court.
2. If the Court includes upon the Bench a judge of the nationality of one of the parties, any other party may choose a person to sit as judge. Such person shall be chosen

preferably from among those persons who have been nominated as candidates as provided in Articles 4 and 5.

3. If the Court includes upon the Bench no judge of the nationality of the parties, each of these parties may proceed to choose a judge as provided in paragraph 2 of this Article.

4. The provisions of this Article shall apply to the case of Articles 26 and 29. In such cases, the President shall request one or, if necessary, two of the members of the Court forming the chamber to give place to the members of the Court of the nationality of the parties concerned, and, failing such, or if they are unable to be present, to the judges specially chosen by the parties.

5. Should there be several parties in the same interest, they shall, for the purpose of the preceding provisions, be reckoned as one party only. Any doubt upon this point shall be settled by the decision of the Court.

6. Judges chosen as laid down in paragraphs 2, 3, and 4 of this Article shall fulfill the conditions required by Articles 2, 17 (paragraph 2), 20, and 24 of the present Statute. They shall take part in the decision on terms of complete equality with their colleagues.

Article 32

1. Each member of the Court shall receive an annual salary.
2. The President shall receive a special annual allowance.
3. The Vice-President shall receive a special allowance for every day on which he acts as President.
4. The judges chosen under Article 31, other than members of the Court, shall receive compensation for each day on which they exercise their functions.
5. These salaries, allowances, and compensation shall be fixed by the General Assembly. They may not be decreased during the term of office.

6. The salary of the Registrar shall be fixed by the General Assembly on the proposal of the Court.
7. Regulations made by the General Assembly shall fix the conditions under which retirement pensions may be given to members of the Court and to the Registrar, and the conditions under which members of the Court and the Registrar shall have their travelling expenses refunded.
8. The above salaries, allowances, and compensation shall be free of all taxation.

Article 33
The expenses of the Court shall be borne by the United Nations in such a manner as shall be decided by the General Assembly.

CHAPTER II
COMPETENCE OF THE COURT

Article 34
1. Only states may be parties in cases before the Court.
2. The Court, subject to and in conformity with its Rules, may request of public international organizations information relevant to cases before it, and shall receive such information presented by such organizations on their own initiative.
3. Whenever the construction of the constituent instrument of a public international organization or of an international convention adopted thereunder is in question in a case before the Court, the Registrar shall so notify the public international organization concerned and shall communicate to it copies of all the written proceedings.

Article 35
1. The Court shall be open to the states parties to the present Statute.

2. The conditions under which the Court shall be open to other states shall, subject to the special provisions contained in treaties in force, be laid down by the Security Council, but in no case shall such conditions place the parties in a position of inequality before the Court.
3. When a state which is not a Member of the United Nations is a party to a case, the Court shall fix the amount which that party is to contribute towards the expenses of the Court. This provision shall not apply if such state is bearing a share of the expenses of the Court

Article 36

1. The jurisdiction of the Court comprises all cases which the parties refer to it and all matters specially provided for in the Charter of the United Nations or in treaties and conventions in force.
2. The states parties to the present Statute may at any time declare that they recognize as compulsory ipso facto and without special agreement, in relation to any other state accepting the same obligation, the jurisdiction of the Court in all legal disputes concerning:
   a. the interpretation of a treaty;
   b. any question of international law;
   c. the existence of any fact which, if established, would constitute a breach of an international obligation;
   d. the nature or extent of the reparation to be made for the breach of an international obligation.
3. The declarations referred to above may be made unconditionally or on condition of reciprocity on the part of several or certain states, or for a certain time.
4. Such declarations shall be deposited with the Secretary-General of the United Nations, who shall transmit copies

thereof to the parties to the Statute and to the Registrar of the Court.
5. Declarations made under Article 36 of the Statute of the Permanent Court of International Justice and which are still in force shall be deemed, as between the parties to the present Statute, to be acceptances of the compulsory jurisdiction of the International Court of Justice for the period which they still have to run and in accordance with their terms.
6. In the event of a dispute as to whether the Court has jurisdiction, the matter shall be settled by the decision of the Court.

Article 37

Whenever a treaty or convention in force provides for reference of a matter to a tribunal to have been instituted by the League of Nations, or to the Permanent Court of International Justice, the matter shall, as between the parties to the present Statute, be referred to the International Court of Justice.

Article 38

1. The Court, whose function is to decide in accordance with international law such disputes as are submitted to it, shall apply:
    a. international conventions, whether general or particular, establishing rules expressly recognized by the contesting states;
    b. international custom, as evidence of a general practice accepted as law;
    c. the general principles of law recognized by civilized nations;
    d. subject to the provisions of Article 59, judicial decisions and the teachings of the most highly qualified publicists of the various nations, as

subsidiary means for the determination of rules of law.
2. This provision shall not prejudice the power of the Court to decide a case *ex aequo et bono*, if the parties agree thereto.

CHAPTER III
PROCEDURE

Article 39
1. The official languages of the Court shall be French and English. If the parties agree that the case shall be conducted in French, the judgment shall be delivered in French. If the parties agree that the case shall be conducted in English, the judgment shall be delivered in English.
2. In the absence of an agreement as to which language shall be employed, each party may, in the pleadings, use the language which it prefers; the decision of the Court shall be given in French and English. In this case the Court shall at the same time determine which of the two texts shall be considered as authoritative.
3. The Court shall, at the request of any party, authorize a language other than French or English to be used by that party.

Article 40
1. Cases are brought before the Court, as the case may be, either by the notification of the special agreement or by a written application addressed to the Registrar. In either case the subject of the dispute and the parties shall be indicated.
2. The Registrar shall forthwith communicate the application to all concerned.
3. He shall also notify the Members of the United Nations through the Secretary-General, and also any other states entitled to appear before the Court.

Article 41

1. The Court shall have the power to indicate, if it considers that circumstances so require, any provisional measures which ought to be taken to preserve the respective rights of either party.
2. Pending the final decision, notice of the measures suggested shall forthwith be given to the parties and to the Security Council.

Article 42

1. The parties shall be represented by agents.
2. They may have the assistance of counsel or advocates before the Court.
3. The agents, counsel, and advocates of parties before the Court shall enjoy the privileges and immunities necessary to the independent exercise of their duties.

Article 43

1. The procedure shall consist of two parts: written and oral.
2. The written proceedings shall consist of the communication to the Court and to the parties of memorials, counter-memorials and, if necessary, replies; also all papers and documents in support.
3. These communications shall be made through the Registrar, in the order and within the time fixed by the Court.
4. A certified copy of every document produced by one party shall be communicated to the other party.
5. The oral proceedings shall consist of the hearing by the Court of witnesses, experts, agents, counsel, and advocates.

Article 44

1. For the service of all notices upon persons other than the agents, counsel, and advocates, the Court shall apply direct

to the government of the state upon whose territory the notice has to be served.

2. The same provision shall apply whenever steps are to be taken to procure evidence on the spot.

Article 45
The hearing shall be under the control of the President or, if he is unable to preside, of the Vice-President; if neither is able to preside, the senior judge present shall preside.

Article 46
The hearing in Court shall be public, unless the Court shall decide otherwise, or unless the parties demand that the public be not admitted.

Article 47
1. Minutes shall be made at each hearing and signed by the Registrar and the President.
2. These minutes alone shall be authentic.

Article 48
The Court shall make orders for the conduct of the case, shall decide the form and time in which each party must conclude its arguments, and make all arrangements connected with the taking of evidence.

Article 49
The Court may, even before the hearing begins, call upon the agents to produce any document or to supply any explanations. Formal note shall be taken of any refusal.

Article 50
The Court may, at any time, entrust any individual, body, bureau, commission, or other organization that it may select, with the task of carrying out an enquiry or giving an expert opinion.

Article 51

During the hearing any relevant questions are to be put to the witnesses and experts under the conditions laid down by the Court in the rules of procedure referred to in Article 30.

Article 52

After the Court has received the proofs and evidence within the time specified for the purpose, it may refuse to accept any further oral or written evidence that one party may desire to present unless the other side consents.

Article 53

1. Whenever one of the parties does not appear before the Court, or fails to defend its case, the other party may call upon the Court to decide in favor of its claim.
2. The Court must, before doing so, satisfy itself, not only that it has jurisdiction in accordance with Articles 36 and 37, but also that the claim is well founded in fact and law.

Article 54

1. When, subject to the control of the Court, the agents, counsel, and advocates have completed their presentation of the case, the President shall declare the hearing closed.
2. The Court shall withdraw to consider the judgment.
3. The deliberations of the Court shall take place in private and remain secret.

Article 55

1. All questions shall be decided by a majority of the judges present.
2. In the event of an equality of votes, the President or the judge who acts in his place shall have a casting vote.

Article 56

1. The judgment shall state the reasons on which it is based.
2. It shall contain the names of the judges who have taken part in the decision.

Article 57

If the judgment does not represent in whole or in part the unanimous opinion of the judges, any judge shall be entitled to deliver a separate opinion.

Article 58

The judgment shall be signed by the President and by the Registrar. It shall be read in open court, due notice having been given to the agents.

Article 59

The decision of the Court has no binding force except between the parties and in respect of that particular case.

Article 60

The judgment is final and without appeal. In the event of dispute as to the meaning or scope of the judgment, the Court shall construe it upon the request of any party.

Article 61

1. An application for revision of a judgment may be made only when it is based upon the discovery of some fact of such a nature as to be a decisive factor, which fact was, when the judgment was given, unknown to the Court and also to the party claiming revision, always provided that such ignorance was not due to negligence.
2. The proceedings for revision shall be opened by a judgment of the Court expressly recording the existence of the new fact, recognizing that it has such a character as to lay the

case open to revision, and declaring the application admissible on this ground.
3. The Court may require previous compliance with the terms of the judgment before it admits proceedings in revision.
4. The application for revision must be made at latest within six months of the discovery of the new fact.
5. No application for revision may be made after the lapse of ten years from the date of the judgment.

Article 62
1. Should a state consider that it has an interest of a legal nature which may be affected by the decision in the case, it may submit a request to the Court to be permitted to intervene.
2. It shall be for the Court to decide upon this request.

Article 63
1. Whenever the construction of a convention to which states other than those concerned in the case are parties is in question, the Registrar shall notify all such states forthwith.
2. Every state so notified has the right to intervene in the proceedings; but if it uses this right, the construction given by the judgment will be equally binding upon it.

Article 64
Unless otherwise decided by the Court, each party shall bear its own costs.

CHAPTER IV
ADVISORY OPINIONS

Article 65
1. The Court may give an advisory opinion on any legal

question at the request of whatever body may be authorized by or in accordance with the Charter of the United Nations to make such a request.
2. Questions upon which the advisory opinion of the Court is asked shall be laid before the Court by means of a written request containing an exact statement of the question upon which an opinion is required, and accompanied by all documents likely to throw light upon the question.

Article 66

1. The Registrar shall forthwith give notice of the request for an advisory opinion to all states entitled to appear before the Court.
2. The Registrar shall also, by means of a special and direct communication, notify any state entitled to appear before the Court or international organization considered by the Court, or, should it not be sitting, by the President, as likely to be able to furnish information on the question, that the Court will be prepared to receive, within a time-limit to be fixed by the President, written statements, or to hear, at a public sitting to be held for the purpose, oral statements relating to the question.
3. Should any such state entitled to appear before the Court have failed to receive the special communication referred to in paragraph 2 of this Article, such state may express a desire to submit a written statement or to be heard; and the Court will decide.
4. States and organizations having presented written or oral statements or both shall be permitted to comment on the statements made by other states or organizations in the form, to the extent, and within the time-limits which the Court, or, should it not be sitting, the President, shall decide in each particular case. Accordingly, the Registrar shall in

due time communicate any such written statements to states and organizations having submitted similar statements.

Article 67
The Court shall deliver its advisory opinions in open court, notice having been given to the Secretary-General and to the representatives of Members of the United Nations, of other states and of international organizations immediately concerned.

Article 68
In the exercise of its advisory functions the Court shall further be guided by the provisions of the present Statute which apply in contentious cases to the extent to which it recognizes them to be applicable.

CHAPTER V
AMENDMENT

Article 69
Amendments to the present Statute shall be effected by the same procedure as is provided by the Charter of the United Nations for amendments to that Charter, subject however to any provisions which the General Assembly upon recommendation of the Security Council may adopt concerning the participation of states which are parties to the present Statute but are not Members of the United Nations.

Article 70
The Court shall have power to propose such amendments to the present Statute as it may deem necessary, through written communications to the Secretary-General, for consideration in conformity with the provisions of Article 69.

Endnotes

1. Tick, Edward. *War and the Soul* (Wheaton, IL: Quest Books, 2005), 42; Hillman, James. *A Terrible Love of War* (New York: Penguin Press, 2004), 17–18, identifying "decisive wars, not counting thousands of indecisive ones."

2. Montagu, Ashley. *The Nature of Human Aggression* (Oxford: Oxford University Press, 1976), 43–53, 59–60; Montagu, Ashley, ed., *Learning Non-Aggression: The Experience of Non-Literate Societies* (Oxford: Oxford University Press, 1978); Guilaine, Jean, and Zammit, Jean. *The Origin of War: Violence in Prehistory*, trans. Melanie Hersey (2001; Malden, MA: Blackwell Publishing, 2005).

3. *Heart of Darkness*, written by Polish-born English novelist Joseph Conrad, was originally published in 1899 as a three-part series in U.K.'s *Blackwood's Magazine*. It is considered one of the most-read works of the last hundred years, largely an autobiographical description of Conrad's six-month journey in 1890 into the "Congo Free State," at the time being plundered by Belgium. In fact, the story could apply to almost any place in the world where European nations, later the United States, plundered peoples for profits and material privileges without acknowledging the terrible, ugly consequences. Francis Ford Coppola's 1979 movie *Apocalypse Now* translates *Heart of Darkness* to Viet Nam and Cambodia. Adam Hochschild's *King Leopold's Ghost* (New York: A Mariner Book, 1999) describes the diabolical exploitation of the Congo Free State by King Leopold II of Belgian between 1885 and 1908. Estimates of murdered Congolese in this period run as high as 13 million. Please don't read this

as if this is something that the United States or other European nations would not do, or have not done. Indeed, the US and Europe are founded on these practices, all under the cover of "civilization."

4   Veale, F.J.P. *Advance to Barbarism: How the Reversion to Barbarism in Warfare and War Trials Menaces Our Future* (Appleton, WI: C.C. Nelson, 1953), 8; *Wikipedia, List of Treaties*: http://en.wikipedia.org/wiki/List_of_treaties.

5   Ibid. xvi,138, 297.

6   Ibid.

7   Mumford, Lewis. *The Myth of the Machine: Technics and Human Development* (1966; New York: Harcourt, Brace & World, Inc., 1967), 186.

8   Blaut, J.M. *The Colonizer's Model of the World: Geographical Diffusionism and Eurocentric History* (New York: Guilford Press, 1993).

9   Enderwitz, Anne. *Modernist Melancholia: Freud, Conrad, and Ford* (UK: Palgrave Macmillan, 2015), 37.

10 I learned about the "megamachine" when exposed to the ideas of cultural historian Lewis Mumford, who started critiquing civilization in the early 1920s. Among his works are two complementary books: *The Myth of the Machine: The Pentagon of Power* (1964; New York: Harcourt Brace Jovanovich, Inc., 1970) and *The Myth of the Machine: Technics and Human Development* (New York: Harcourt, Brace & World, Inc., 1967). Mumford, born in 1895 in urban Flushing, New York, was a brilliant observer of the traumatic effects to humans and the Earth of so-called civilization, and his thinking on the long view remains extremely illuminating.

11 Mumford, *Myth of the Machine: Technics and Human Development*, 186.

12 Montagu, Ashley. *The Nature of Human Aggression* (Oxford: Oxford University Press, 1976), 43–53, 59–60; Montagu, Ashley, ed. *Learning Non-Aggression: The Experience of Non-Literate Societies* (Oxford: Oxford University Press, 1978); Guilaine, Jean, and Zammit, Jean. *The Origin of War: Violence in Prehistory*, trans. Melanie Hersey (2001; Malden, MA: Blackwell Publishing, 2005).

13 de la Boétie, Étienne. *The Politics of Obedience: The Discourse of Voluntary Servitude*, trans. Harry Kurz (ca. 1553; Montreal: Black Rose Books, 1997), 46, 58–60; Eisler, Riane. *The Chalice and the Blade* (San Francisco: Harper & Row, 1987, 45–58, 104–06.

14 Roszak, Theodore, Gomes, Mary E., and Kanner, Allen D., eds. *Ecopsychology: Restoring the Earth, Healing the Mind* (San Francisco: Sierra

Club Books, 1995), 41. Ecopsychology concludes that there can be no personal healing without healing the Earth, and that rediscovering our sacred relationship with it, i.e., our intimate Earthiness, is indispensable for personal and global healing and mutual respect.

15 See Willson, S. Brian. *Blood on the Tracks: The Life and Times of S. Brian Willson* (Oakland, CA: PM Press, 2011), 271; Weisman, Alan. *The World Without Us* (New York: St. Martin's Press, 2007), 224–29, describing the collapse of the Maya, one of the most advanced civilizations the world has ever known—lasting 1600 years, governing at least 50 independent states over a wide region, due, it is now speculated, to the kings becoming addicted to demands of greed, leading to overexploitation and malnourishment of the workers who fled to the mountains, leaving the kings to eventually starve; Harman, Chris. *A People's History of the World* (London: Verso, 2008), 35, citing 624n86.

16 Quinn, Daniel. *Beyond Civilization: Humanity's Next Great Adventure* (New York: Three Rivers Press, 1999), 91.

17 LeGuin, Ursula K. *Words Are My Matter: Writings About Life and Books, With a Journal of a Writer's Week* (Easthampton, MA: Small Beer Press, 2016), 115.

18 Childe, V. Gordon. *Man Makes Himself* (New York: New American Library, 1983; original, 1936), 180.

19 Hersh, Seymour M. "The Redirection." *The New Yorker*, June 19, 2017, http://www.newyorker.com/magazine/2007/03/05/the-redirection. As Hersh explains, "The U.S. has also taken part in clandestine operations aimed at Iran and its ally Syria. A by-product of these activities has been the bolstering of Sunni extremist groups that espouse a militant vision of Islam and are hostile to America and sympathetic to Al Qaeda."

20 See, October 9, 2019, Tweet of @realDonaldTrump https://twitter.com/realDonaldTrump/status/1181905659568283648.

21 Harris, Roger D. "An Unfaithful Servant of Imperialism: Why Trump Is Facing Impeachment." *MintPress News*, 11 Oct. 2019, www.mintpressnews.com/unfaithful-servant-imperialism-reason-trump-facing-impeachment/262275/.

22 Barsamian, David, et al. "Noam Chomsky Discusses Turkey with David Barsamian." *The Armenian Weekly*, 13 Mar. 2012, armenianweekly.com/2012/02/09/chomsky/.

23 Schwarz, Jon. "Eight Times the U.S. Has Betrayed the Kurds." *The*

Intercept, 7 Oct. 2019, theintercept.com/2019/10/07/kurds-syria-turkey-trump-betrayal/.

24 Dixon, Norm. "How Reagan Armed Saddam with Chemical Weapons." *CounterPunch.org*, 1 Apr. 2015, www.counterpunch.org/2004/06/17/how-reagan-armed-saddam-with-chemical-weapons/.

25 Ibid.

26 Power, Samantha. *"A Problem from Hell": America and the Age of Genocide.* (New York: Basic Books, 2013).

27 Oakford, Samuel. "As Saudis Block a Human Rights Inquiry in Yemen, America Stays Quiet." VICE News. October 02, 2015, https://news.vice.com/en_us/article/xw3yjn/as-saudis-block-a-human-rights-inquiry-in-yemen-the-us-stays-quiet. See also, Oakford, Samuel, Williams, Lance, Greenfield, Jeff, Wittes, Tamara Cofman, and Goldenberg, Ilan. "As the Saudis Covered Up Abuses in Yemen, America Stood By." *Politico*, July 30, 2016, https://www.politico.com/magazine/story/2016/07/saudi-arabia-yemen-russia-syria-foreign-policy-united-nations-blackmail-214124.

28 Lynch, Colum. "U.S. Support for Saudi Strikes in Yemen Raises War Crime Concerns." *Foreign Policy*, Oct. 15, 2015.

29 Ibid.

30 Ibid.

31 Revesz, Rachel. "Donald Trump signs $110 billion arms deal with the nation he accused of masterminding 9/11." *The Independent*, May 21, 2017.

32 Kane, Alex. "Here's Exactly Who's Profiting from the War on Yemen." *In These Times*, inthesetimes.com/features/us-saudi-arabia-yemen-war-arms-sales.html.

33 Ibid.

34 "Lockheed Martin CEO Marillyn Hewson Sends out Mass Email Attacking CODEPINK and Appealing to Congress Not to Stop the War in Yemen." *CODEPINK*, Sept. 26, 2018, www.codepink.org/marillyn_hewson_sends_out_mass_email_attacking_codepink.

35 "Yemen could be 'worst' humanitarian crisis in 50 years." Al Jazeera, Jan. 5, 2018, https://www.aljazeera.com/news/2018/01/yemen-worst-humanitarian-crisis-50-years-180105190332474.html.

36 OCHA summary of crisis in Yemen, http://www.unocha.org/yemen/about-ocha-yemen

37 Al Jazeera. "Yemen 'Could Lose Six Million Children' from Malnutrition." *Yemen News / Al Jazeera*, Al Jazeera, 23 Oct. 2019, www.aljazeera.com/news/2019/10/yemen-could-lose-million-children-malnutrition-191023134105371.html.

38 Nobles, Ryan. "Ex-Obama Administration Officials Push Democrats in Congress to Defund War in Yemen." *CNN*, Cable News Network, 15 Oct. 2019, www.cnn.com/2019/10/15/politics/democrats-congress-yemen-war/index.html.

39 "Susan Rice On Trump's Decision To Take U.S. Out Of Syria." NPR, 13 Oct. 2019, www.npr.org/2019/10/13/769946813/susan-rice-on-trump-s-decision-to-take-u-s-out-of-syria.

40 Rosen, Armin. "The Controversial Africa Policy of Susan Rice." *The Atlantic*, Atlantic Media Company, 30 Nov. 2012, www.theatlantic.com/international/archive/2012/11/the-controversial-africa-policy-of-susan-rice/265752/.

41 Bovard, James. "The Civil War and 150 Years of Forgotten US Military Atrocities." *CounterPunch.org*, 7 Oct. 2014, www.counterpunch.org/2014/10/07/the-civil-war-and-150-years-of-forgotten-us-military-atrocities/.

42 Milne, Seumas. "Now the Truth Emerges: How the US Fuelled the Rise of Isis in Syria and Iraq | Seumas Milne." *The Guardian*, Guardian News and Media, 3 June 2015, www.theguardian.com/commentisfree/2015/jun/03/us-isis-syria-iraq.

43 "Condemning Trump on Syria? It's 'Buffet Outrage.'" *Ray McGovern*, 17 Oct. 2019, raymcgovern.com/2019/10/17/condemning-trump-on-syria-its-buffet-outrage/.

44 Amnesty International, "Iraq: Suffering in Silence: Iraqi Refugees in Syria." May 12, 2008, https://www.amnesty.org/en/documents/MDE14/010/2008/en/.

45 Ibid.

46 Blumenthal, Max. "The US Has Backed 21 of the 28 'Crazy' Militias Leading Turkey's Brutal Invasion of Northern Syria." *The Grayzone*, 19 Oct. 2019, thegrayzone.com/2019/10/16/us-backed-crazy-militias-turkeys-invasion-syria/.

47 Germanos, Andrea. "US Forces May Have Committed War Crimes in Syria: UN Report." *Common Dreams*, 11 Sept. 2019, www.commondreams.org/news/2019/09/11/us-forces-may-have-committed-war-crimes-syria-un-report.

48 Orinocotribune. "Satellite Images: Russia Reveals US Oil Smuggling in Syria." *Orinoco Tribune*, 27 Oct. 2019, orinocotribune.com/satellite-images-russia-reveals-us-oil-smuggling-in-syria.

49 "Russia Releases Damning Evidence Of The U.S. Smuggling Syrian Oil." *Yahoo! Finance*, Yahoo!, 29 Oct. 2019, finance.yahoo.com/news/russia-releases-damning-evidence-u-173000250.html?soc_src=community.

50 Welna, David. "If U.S. Takes Syrian Oil, It May Violate International Laws Against Pillage." *Valley Public Radio*, www.kvpr.org/post/if-us-takes-syrian-oil-it-may-violate-international-laws-against-pillage.

51 Ibid.

52 Ibid.

53 Delevingne, Lawrence. "Trump Suggestion of Taking Syrian Oil Draws Rebukes." *Reuters*, Thomson Reuters, 28 Oct. 2019, www.reuters.com/article/us-mideast-crisis-baghdadi-oil/trump-suggestion-of-taking-syrian-oil-draws-rebukes-idUSKBN1X60RM.

54 Brennan, David. "Trump Is 'the Best American President,' Syria's Bashar Al-Assad Says: 'What Do We Want More than a Transparent Foe?'." *Newsweek*, Newsweek, 1 Nov. 2019, www.newsweek.com/donald-trump-best-american-president-syria-bashar-al-assad-want-transparent-foe-oil-foreign-policy-1469176.

55 Bricmont, Jean. *Humanitarian Imperialism: Using Human Rights to Sell War* (New York: Monthly Review Press, 2006), 30.

56 Norton, Ben. "US Troops Are Staying in Syria to 'Keep the Oil'—and Have Already Killed Hundreds over It." *The Grayzone*, 23 Oct. 2019, thegrayzone.com/2019/10/23/us-troops-staying-syria-oil/.

57 Bricmont, Jean, *Humanitarian Imperialism*.

58 Horne, Gerald. *White Supremacy Confronted, U.S. Imperialism and Anti-Communism vs. the Liberation of Southern Africa from Rhodes to Mandela* (New York: International Publishers 2019), p. 58, fn. 78.

59 Ibid.

60 Hochschild, Adam. *King Leopold's Ghost: A Story of Greed, Terror, and Heroism in Colonial Africa* (New York: Houghton Mifflin, 1999).

61 Ibid., p. 233.

62 Ibid., p. 42–43.

63 Ibid., p. 46.

64 Ibid., p. 120.
65 Ibid.
66 Ibid., p. 120–135.
67 Ibid., p. 81.
68 Ibid., p. 82.
69 Blackmon, Douglas A. *Slavery by Another Name, The Re-Enslavement of Black Americans from the Civil War to WWII* (New York: Doubleday Books, 2008).
70 Ibid., p. 7–8.
71 Hochschild, *King Leopold's Ghost*, p. 306.
72 Ibid.
73 Ibid.
74 Horne, Gerald, *White Supremacy*, p. 698.
75 Rubinstein, Alexander. "Amnesty International's Troubling Collaboration with UK & US Intelligence." *MintPress News*, 21 Jan. 2019, www.mintpressnews.com/amnesty-international-troubling-collaboration-with-uk-us-intelligence/253939/.
76 Eskola, Tuukka. Amnesty International and Apartheid 1965–1992, Human Rights for Everyone? Sept. 21, 2007, http://epublications.uef.fi/pub/URN_NBN_fi_joy-20080004/URN_NBN_fi_joy-20080004.pdf. Citing Bernstein, Dennis, 2002. "Interview with Francis Boyle: Amnesty on Jenin." Released in *CovertAction Quarterly*, issue 73, Covert Action Publications, Washington. Pages 9–12.
77 Horne, Gerald, *White Supremacy*, p. 698.
78 "The Secret History of How Cuba Helped End Apartheid in South Africa." *Democracy Now!*, www.democracynow.org/2013/12/11/the_secret_history_of_how_cuba.
79 "On Reagan's Legacy." *On Reagan's Legacy, Noam Chomsky Interviewed by Amy Goodman*, chomsky.info/20040607/.
80 Landay, Jonathan S. "In Ronald Reagan Era, Mandela Was Branded a Terrorist." *Mcclatchydc*, McClatchy Washington Bureau, 6 Dec. 2013, www.mcclatchydc.com/news/nation-world/world/article24760045.html.
81 Ibid.
82 "Nelson Mandela on How Cuba 'Destroyed the Myth of the Invincibility of the White Oppressor.'" *Democracy Now!*, www.democracynow.org/2013/12/11/nelson_mandela_on_how_cuba_destroyed.

83　Tamames, Jorge. "A War of Solidarity." *Jacobin Magazine*, April, 2018, https://www.jacobinmag.com/2018/04/cuba-angola-operacion-carlota-cuito-cuanavale-internationalism.

84　See Horne, Gerald, *White Supremacy*.

85　"The Secret History of How Cuba Helped End Apartheid in South Africa." *Democracy Now!*, www.democracynow.org/2013/12/11/the_secret_history_of_how_cuba.

86　Hochschild, Adam, *King Leopold's Ghost*. p. 13.

87　Frankel, Dr. Neil A. "Maps of Africa." *The Atlantic Slave Trade and Slavery in America*. Retrieved at: http://www.slaverysite.com/Body/maps.htm.

88　Hochschild, Adam, *King Leopold's Ghost*, p. 11.

89　Ibid. pp. 241–242.

90　Ibid. pp. 278–279.

91　Weissman, Stephen R. "Congo-Kinshasa: New Evidence Shows U.S. Role in Congo's Decision to Send Patrice Lumumba to His Death." *allAfrica*, August 1, 2010. Retrieved at: https://allafrica.com/stories/201008010004.html

92　Office of the Historian, "The Congo, Decolonization, and The Cold War, 1960-1965." US Department of State. Retrieved at: https://history.state.gov/milestones/1961-1968/congo-decolonization.

93　Nzongola-Ntalaja, Georges."Patrice Lumumba: the most important assassination of the 20th century, The US-sponsored plot to kill Patrice Lumumba, the hero of Congolese independence, took place 50 years ago today." *The Guardian*, Jan. 17, 2011. Retrieved at:https://www.theguardian.com/global-development/poverty-matters/2011/jan/17/patrice-lumumba-50th-anniversary-assassination.

94　Office of the Historian, Foreign Relations of the United States, 1964–1968, Volume XXIII, Congo, 1960–1968, US Department of State. Retrieved at: https://history.state.gov/historicaldocuments/frus1964-68v23/d1

95　Weissman, Stephen R, "Congo-Kinshasa."

96　Carney, Maurice. "Was Patrice Lumumba's assassination of the last century?" *TRTWORLD*, Aug. 6, 2018. Retreived at: https://www.trtworld.com/opinion/was-patrice-lumumba-s-assassination-the-most-important-of-the-last-century--19397.

97　Office of the Historian, Foreign Relations of The United States, 1964–1968, Volume XXIII, Congo, 1960–1968, US Department of State.

Retrieved at: https://history.state.gov/historicaldocuments/frus1964-68v23/d1.

98 Ibid.
99 Ibid.
100 Kalb, Madeleine G. "The CIA And Lumumba." *The New York Times Magazine*, Aug. 2, 1981, Retrieved at: https://www.nytimes.com/1981/08/02/magazine/the-cia-and-lumumba.html.
101 Office of the Historian, Foreign Relations of the United States, 1964–1968, Volume XXIII, Congo, 1960–1968, US Department of State. Retrieved at: https://history.state.gov/historicaldocuments/frus1964-68v23/d1.
102 Weissman, Stephen R., "Congo-Kinshasa."
103 Ibid.
104 Ibid.
105 Carney, Maurice, "Was Patrice Lumumba's Assassination."
106 Hochschild, "King Leopold's Ghost," p. 303.
107 Office of the Historian, "The Congo, Decolonization, and The Cold War, 1960-1965," US Department of State. Retrieved at: https://history.state.gov/milestones/1961-1968/congo-decolonization.
108 Rosen, Armin. "The Controversial Africa Policy of Susan Rice." *The Atlantic*, Atlantic Media Company, 30 Nov. 2012, www.theatlantic.com/international/archive/2012/11/the-controversial-africa-policy-of-susan-rice/265752/.
109 Kovalik, Daniel. "Genocide in Silence." *CounterPunch.org*, 1 Jan. 2016, www.counterpunch.org/2012/11/30/genocide-in-silence/.
110 Garrison, Ann. "Millions Die in Congo While the UN Keeps the Peace." *Black Agenda Report*, Dec. 4, 2019, https://www.blackagendareport.com/millions-die-congo-while-un-keeps-peace.
111 'Sickening' sex abuse alleged in CAR by UN peacekeepers." *Al Jazeera*, April 1, 2016, https://www.aljazeera.com/news/2016/03/sex-abuse-alleged-car-peacekeepers-160331183645566.html.
112 Shahtahmasebi, Darius, and Fiala, Emma. "UN Peacekeepers Fathered Hundreds of Babies With Girls in Haiti as Young as 11." *The Mind Unleashed*, 19 Dec. 2019, themindunleashed.com/2019/12/un-peacekeepers-fathered-hundreds-babies-girls-haiti.html.
113 Ibid.
114 United Nations. "Hillary Clinton Condemns Impunity in Eastern

Congo." *UNHCR*, www.unhcr.org/en-us/news/latest/2009/8/4a81af409/hillary-clinton-condemns-impunity-eastern-congo.html.

115 Kovalik, Daniel, "Genocide in Silence,"

116 "Behind the Numbers: Untold Suffering in the Congo." *Global Policy*, www.globalpolicy.org/component/content/article/181/33626.html.

117 Ibid.

118 Ibid.

119 Simon, Scott. "People Under Those Bombs." NPR, March 22, 2003, https://www.npr.org/news/specials/iraq2003/simon_essays.html.

120 Amnesty International. "Libya 2018," https://www.amnesty.org/en/countries/middle-east-and-north-africa/libya/report-libya/.

121 Ibid.

122 Elbagir, Nima, et al. "People for Sale: Where Lives Are Auctioned for $400." CNN, Cable News Network, 15 Nov. 2017, edition.cnn.com/2017/11/14/africa/libya-migrant-auctions/index.html.

123 Dowd, Maureen. "Fight of the Valkyries." *New York Times*, Mar. 23, 2011, www.nytimes.com/2011/03/23/opinion/23dowd.html.

124 Ibid.

125 Forte, Maximilian. *Slouching Towards Sirte: NATO's War on Libya and Africa*. (Montreal: Baraka Books, 2012).

126 Chengu, Garikai. "Libya: From Africa's Richest State Under Gaddafi, to Failed State After NATO Intervention." *Global Research*, 9 Mar. 2018, www.globalresearch.ca/libya-from-africas-richest-state-under-gaddafi-to-failed-state-after-nato-intervention/5408740.

127 Ibid.

128 Abedin, Huma. "Overnight Update From DCM in Tripoli." *Wikileaks*, February 21, 2011, https://wikileaks.org/clinton-emails/emailid/28720.

129 Mills, Cheryl, et al. "Not For Forwarding Outside USG: WFP–Libya Internal SIT REP As Of Mar 2," *Wikileaks*, March 2, 2011. https://wikileaks.org/clinton-emails/emailid/20861.

130 Blumenthal, Sidney. "Win This War." *Wikileaks*, "Clinton Emails," March 30, 2011, https://wikileaks.org/clinton-emails/emailid/6557.

131 Ibid.

132 Blumenthal, Sidney. "Lots of Intel; Possible Libyan Collapse." March 26, 2011, https://wikileaks.org/clinton-emails/emailid/6551.

133 Forte, Maximilian, "Slouching."

134 Horne, Gerard, "White Supremacy," p. 68.

135 Amnesty International. "Libya Organization Calls for Immediate Arms Embargo and Assets Freeze." March 27, 2011, https://www.amnestyusa.org/press-releases/libya-organization-calls-for-immediate-arms-embargo-and-assets-freeze/.

136 Seymour, Richard. "Libya's Spectacular Revolution Has Been Disgraced by Racism | Richard Seymour." *The Guardian*, Guardian News and Media, 30 Aug. 2011, www.theguardian.com/commentisfree/2011/aug/30/libya-spectacular-revolution-disgraced-racism.

137 Ibid.

138 Kafala, Tarik. "'Cleansed' Libyan Town Spills Its Terrible Secrets." *BBC News*, BBC, 12 Dec. 2011, www.bbc.com/news/magazine-16051349.

139 "US Blocks Russia's Draft Statement in UN on Peaceful Resolution of Bani Walid Violence." *RT International*, www.rt.com/news/us-russia-libya-statement-068/.

140 Amnesty International. "Libya 2018." https://www.amnesty.org/en/countries/middle-east-and-north-africa/libya/report-libya/.

141 Ibid.

142 "Wars and Conflict Likely to Worsen in 2016." *Australian Financial Review*, 7 Jan. 2016, www.afr.com/world/wars-and-conflict-is-likely-to-worsen-in-2016-20160106-gm05nx.

143 Wintour, Patrick. "UK Court Grants £1m Bail to Man Arrested over Sarkozy-Gaddafi Inquiry." *The Guardian*, Guardian News and Media, 10 Jan. 2018, www.theguardian.com/world/2018/jan/10/uk-court-grants-1m-bail-to-man-arrested-over-sarkozy-gaddafi-inquiry; see also Willsher, Kim. "Gaddafi 'Gave Nicolas Sarkozy €50m for 2007 Presidential Campaign'." *The Guardian*, Guardian News and Media, 15 Nov. 2016, www.theguardian.com/world/2016/nov/15/muammar-gaddafi-allegedly-gave-nicolas-sarkozy-50m-euros-2007-presidential-campaign.

144 Blumenthal, Sidney. "H: France's Client & Q's Gold." April 1, 2011, https://www.wikileaks.org/clinton-emails/emailid/6528.

145 Ibid.

146 Kington, Tom. "Italy Revives Gaddafi Deal to Reduce Migration." *World / The Times*, The Times, 9 July 2018, www.thetimes.co.uk/article/italy-revives-5bn-deal-with-libya-to-cut-migration-xx8p223w6.

147 Shane, Scott. "Western Companies See Prospects for Business in Libya."

New York Times, 29 Oct. 2011, www.nytimes.com/2011/10/29/world/africa/western-companies-see-libya-as-ripe-at-last-for-business.html.

148 Imaralu, Douglas. *Ventures Africa*. "Rebuilding Libya, GE Eyes Up to 10B in Revenue," May 31, 2012, http://venturesafrica.com/rebuilding-libya-ge-eyes-up-to-10bn-in-revenue/.

149 Browne, Ryan. "US Strikes Libya for First Time under Trump." *CNN*, Cable News Network, 24 Sept. 2017, edition.cnn.com/2017/09/24/politics/us-strikes-libya-trump/index.html.

150 Campbell, Matthew, and Chellel, Kit. "Hot Mess: How Goldman Sachs lost $1.2 Billion of Libya's Money." *Bloomberg*, September 29, 2016, https://www.bloomberg.com/features/2016-goldman-sachs-libya/.

151 "Billions Missing From Frozen Gaddafi Accounts in Belgium—reports." *RT News*, October 30, 2018, https://www.rt.com/business/442650-gaddafi-frozen-assets-investigation/.

152 Johnstone, Diane. "How Amnesty International Became the Servant of US Warmongering Foreign Policy." *MLToday*, 29 Aug. 2012, mltoday.com/how-amnesty-international-became-the-servant-of-us-warmongering-foreign-policy/.

153 Hobsbawm, Eric. *The Age of Extremes* (New York: Vintage Books, 1994), pp. 22–31.

154 Ibid., pp. 25–26.

155 Ibid., p. 23.

156 Ibid.

157 Ibid., pp. 23–24.

158 Graziano, MacKennan, and Mei, Lan. "The Crime of Aggression Under the Roe Statute and Implications for Corporate Responsibility." *Harvard International Law Journal*, 5 Nov. 2019, harvardilj.org/2017/04/the-crime-of-aggression-under-the-rome-statute-and-implications-for-corporate-accountability/.

159 Grossman, James. "Bigotry Stopped Americans from Intervening before the Holocaust. Not Much Has Changed." *Los Angeles Times*, Los Angeles Times, 29 Apr. 2018, www.latimes.com/opinion/op-ed/la-oe-grossman-holocaust-exhibit-20180429-htmlstory.html.

160 Brooks-Pollock, Tom. "Pope Francis: Why Didn't Allies Bomb Railway Routes Taking Prisoners." *The Independent*, Independent Digital News and Media, 22 June 2015, www.independent.co.uk/news/world/europe

/pope-francis-why-didnt-allies-bomb-railway-routes-taking-prisoners-to-auschwitz-10336001.html.

161 Kennan, George. "Memo PPS23." *Wikisource*. Feb. 4, 1948, https://en.wikisource.org/wiki/Memo_PPS23_by_George_Kennan.

162 "Use It and Lose It: The Outsize Effect of U.S. Consumption on the Environment." *Scientific American*, 14 Sept. 2012, www.scientificamerican.com/article/american-consumption-habits/.

163 Tharoor, Ishaan. "Don't Forget How the Soviet Union Saved the World from Hitler," Washington Post, May 8, 2015, https://www.washingtonpost.com/news/worldviews/wp/2015/05/08/dont-forget-how-the-soviet-union-saved-the-world-from-hitler/.

164 "Russia Helped 1,750,000 Jews to Escape Nazis, Says James N. Rosenberg," Jewish Telegraphic Agency, July 2, 1943. https://www.jta.org/1943/07/02/archive/russia-helped-1750000-jews-to-escape-nazis-says-james-n-rosenberg

165 Kramer, Ronald, Michalowski, Raymond, and Rothe, Dawn. "The Supreme International Crime: How the U.S. War in Iraq Threatens the Rule of Law." *Social Justice*, Vol. 32, No. 2 (100), The Many Faces of Violence (2005), pp. 52-81, https://www.jstor.org/stable/29768307.

166 Ibid.

167 See Text of the UN Charter in Appendix, supra.

168 McWhinney, Edward Q.C., Professor of International Law. "General Assembly Resolution 2131 (xx) of 21 December 1965 Declaration on the Inadmissibility of Intervention in the Domestic Affairs of States and the Protection of Their Independence and Sovereignty." http://legal.un.org/avl/pdf/ha/ga_2131-xx/ga_2131-xx_e.pdf.

169 Slatta, Richard W. "Time Line of US-Latin American Relations." https://faculty.chass.ncsu.edu/slatta/hi216/hi453time.htm.

170 Boyle, Francis A. *Destroying Libya & World Order: The Three-Decade US Campaign to Terminate the Qaddafi Revolution* (Atlanta: Clarity Press, 2013). 160–166.

171 Alston, Philip, and Goodman, Ryan. *International Human Rights, The Successor to International Human Rights in Context* (Oxford: Oxford University Press, 2012), 134.

172 Chomsky, Noam. "The Rule of Force in International Affairs." 80 *Yale Law Journal*, Issue 7, 1971, https://digitalcommons.law.yale.edu/cgi/viewcontent.cgi?article=6084&context=ylj.

173 UN Press Release. "Gaza 'Unliveable', UN Special Rapporteur for the Situation of Human Rights in the OPT Tells Third Committee." October 24, 2018, https://www.un.org/unispal/document/gaza-unliveable-un-special-rapporteur-for-the-situation-of-human-rights-in-the-opt-tells-third-committee-press-release-excerpts/.

174 AFP and TOI Staff. "UN Chief Proposes Military Force to Protect Palestinians from Israel." *The Times of Israel*, Aug. 18, 2018, https://www.timesofisrael.com/un-chief-proposes-military-force-to-protect-palestinians/

175 Cançado Trindade, Antônio Augusto, Former President of the Inter-American Court of Human Rights. *"Universal Declaration of Human Rights."* http://legal.un.org/avl/ha/udhr/udhr.html.

176 "Universal Declaration of Human Rights." https://www.ohchr.org/EN/UDHR/Pages/Language.aspx?LangID=eng.

177 "Final Act of the International Conference on Human Rights, Tehran, April 22 to May 23, 1968." http://legal.un.org/avl/pdf/ha/fatchr/Final_Act_of_TehranConf.pdf.

178 World Conference on Human Rights, Vienna, 14–25 June 1993. "Vienna Declaration and Programme of Action." https://www.un.org/ga/search/view_doc.asp?symbol=A/CONF.157/23.

179 Crawford, Neta C. "Pentagon Fuel Use, Climate Change, and the Costs of War." *Costs of War*, Watson Institute of International and Public Affairs, Brown University, https://watson.brown.edu/costsofwar/files/cow/imce/papers/2019/Pentagon%20Fuel%20Use%2C%20Climate%20-Change%20and%20the%20Costs%20of%20War%20Final.pdf.

180 Sachs, Jeffrey, and Weisbrot, Mark. "Economic Sanctions as Collective Punishment: The Case of Venezuela." *CEPR*, April, 2019, http://cepr.net/publications/reports/economic-sanctions-as-collective-punishment-the-case-of-venezuela.

181 Vaz, Ricardo. "Red Cross Chief: Venezuela Aid Being Politicized to 'Destabilize the Country'." *Telesur*, Dec. 4, 2019, https://venezuelanalysis.com/news/14738.

182 International Covenant on Civil and Political Rights. Adopted by the General Assembly of the United Nations, 19 of December 1966, https://treaties.un.org/doc/publication/unts/volume%20999/volume-999-i-14668-english.pdf.

183. Gosztola, Kevin. "Trump Applauds Bolivia's Military Coup As US Establishment Media Blame Morales For Turmoil." *Common Dreams*, 12 Nov. 2019, www.commondreams.org/views/2019/11/12/trump-applauds-bolivias-military-coup-us-establishment-media-blame-morales-turmoil.

184. Beeton, Dan. "No Evidence That Bolivian Election Results Were Affected by Irregularities or Fraud, Statistical Analysis Shows: Press Releases." *CEPR*, http://cepr.net/press-center/press-releases/no-evidence-that-bolivian-election-results-were-affected-by-irregularities-or-fraud-statistical-analysis-shows.

185. Johnson, Jake. "In Statement That 'Reads Like a Chilling Warning of More Coups to Come,' Trump Celebrates Military Coup in Bolivia." *Common Dreams*, 12 Nov. 2019, www.commondreams.org/news/2019/11/12/statement-reads-chilling-warning-more-coups-come-trump-celebrates-military-coup.

186. Gosztola, Kevin, "Trump Applauds."

187. Risen, James. "U.S. Identifies Vast Mineral Riches in Afghanistan." *New York Times*, 14 June 2010, www.nytimes.com/2010/06/14/world/asia/14minerals.html.

188. Kovarik, Jacquelyn. "Bolivia's Anti-Indigenous Backlash Is Growing." *The Nation*, 21 Nov. 2019, www.thenation.com/article/bolivia-morales-whipala/.

189. "Pepe Mujica Condemns OAS After Visiting Evo Morales." *Telesur*, Dec. 4, 2019, https://www.telesurenglish.net/news/Pepe-Mujica-Condemns-OAS-After-Visiting-Evo-Morales-20191204-0016.html.

190. Macleod, Alan. "How Human Rights Watch Whitewashed a Right-Wing Massacre in Bolivia." *MintPress News*, 20 Nov. 2019, www.mintpressnews.com/human-rights-watch-right-wing-massacre-bolivia/262887/.

191. "Studies Refute OAS Claims of Irregularities in Bolivian Elections." *Pressenza*, 15 Nov. 2019, www.pressenza.com/2019/11/studies-refute-oas-claims-of-irregularities-in-bolivian-elections/.

192. Macleod, Alan, "How Human Rights Watch."

193. Ibid.

194. International Covenant on Economic, Social and Cultural Rights, United Nations 1967, https://treaties.un.org/doc/Treaties/1976/01/19760103%2009-57%20PM/Ch_IV_03.pdf.

195. Alston, Philip, and Goodman, Ryan, *International Human Rights*, 139.

196 National Priorities Project. "US Military Spending v. the World." https://www.nationalpriorities.org/campaigns/us-military-spending-vs-world/.

197 UN Human Rights Council. "Report of the Special Rapporteur on extreme poverty and human rights on his mission to the United States of America." May 4, 2018, https://undocs.org/A/HRC/38/33/ADD.1.

198 Tsui, Anjali, *Pro Publica*. ""High Interest loan companies are using Utah's small claims courts to arrest borrowers and take their bail money." *Salt Lake Tribune*, December 4, 2019, https://www.sltrib.com/news/nation-world/2019/12/04/high-interest-loan/.

199 Wolfe, Anne, and Liu, Michelle. "'Something seems fishy': Bad bookkeeping and poor oversight plague a Mississippi inmate labor program." Mississippi Today, Jan. 9, 2020, https://mississippitoday.org/2020/01/09/restitution-accountability/.

200 Chapman, Isabelle. "Prison Inmates Are Fighting California's Fires, but Are Often Denied Firefighting Jobs after Their Release." *CNN*, 31 Oct. 2019, www.cnn.com/2019/10/31/us/prison-inmates-fight-california-fires-trnd/index.html.

201 Derysh, Igor. "Reports That Mike Bloomberg's Campaign 'Exploited' Women's Prison Labor Spark Outrage." *Salon*, Salon.com, 26 Dec. 2019, www.salon.com/2019/12/26/reports-that-mike-bloombergs-campaign-exploited-womens-prison-labor-spark-outrage/.

202 Ibid.

203 Hedges, Chris. America: *The Farewell Tour* (New York: Simon & Schuster 2019).

204 Kokotovic, Marlee, et al. "UN Study Claims US Has the Highest Rate of Children in Detention." *Nation of Change*, 19 Nov. 2019, www.nationofchange.org/2019/11/19/un-study-claims-us-has-the-highest-rate-of-children-in-detention/.

205 Ibid.

206 Alston, Philip, and Goodman, Ryan, *International Human Rights* 278.

207 Bricmont, Jean, *Humanitarian Imperialism*, 39–40.

208 Archibold, Randal C. "In Haiti's Cholera Fight, Cuba Takes Lead Role." *New York Times*, November 07, 2011. https://www.nytimes.com/2011/11/08/world/americas/in-haiti-cholera-fight-cuba-takes-lead-role.html.

209 "Cholera in Haiti, An End in Sight." United Nations, http://www.un.org/News/dh/Infocus/haiti/CholeraHaitiAnEndInSight.pdf.

210 Katz, Jonathan M. "U.N. Admits Role in Cholera Epidemic in Haiti." *New York Times*, 18 Aug. 2016, www.nytimes.com/2016/08/18/world/americas/united-nations-haiti-cholera.html.

211 Mendonça, Maria Luisa. "UN Troops in Haiti Accused of Continued Rights Abuses." *NACLA*, March 13, 2008, nacla.org/news/un-troops-haiti-accused-continued-rights-abuses.

212 Alston, Philip and Goodman, Ryan, *International Human Rights*, 697.

213 Ibid.

214 "Where the United States Stands on 10 International Human Rights Treaties." *The Leadership Conference Education Fund*, civilrights.org/edfund/resource/where-the-united-states-stands-on-10-international-human-rights-treaties/.

215 Rome Statute of the International Criminal Court, https://www.icc-cpi.int/resource-library/Documents/RS-Eng.pdf.

216 Graziano, MacKennan, and Mei, Lan. "The Crime of Aggression Under the Rome Statute and Implications for Corporate Accountability." *Harvard International Law Journal*, 5 Nov. 2019, https://harvardilj.org/2017/04/the-crime-of-aggression-under-the-rome-statute-and-implications-for-corporate-accountability/.

217 "Polls: US Is 'the Greatest Threat to Peace in the World Today'." *Strategic Culture Foundation*, www.strategic-culture.org/news/2017/08/07/polls-us-greatest-threat-to-peace-world-today/.

218 Roth, Kenneth. "The Court the US Doesn't Want." *The New York Review of Books*, Nov. 19, 1998, https://www.nybooks.com/articles/1998/11/19/the-court-the-us-doesnt-want/.

219 UN General Assembly. "Follow-up to the outcome of the Millennium Summit." Dec. 2, 2004, https://documents-dds-ny.un.org/doc/UNDOC/GEN/N04/602/31/PDF/N0460231.pdf?OpenElement.

220 Lamrani, Salim, Estrade, Paul, Smith, Wayne S., and Oberg, Larry. *The Economic War against Cuba a Historical and Legal Perspective on the US Blockade* (New York: Monthly Review Press, 2013).

221 "Cuba in the Cross-Hairs: A Near Half-Century of Terror," (excerpted from *Hegemony or Survival*). https://chomsky.info/hegemony02/.

222 Ibid.

223 Ibid.

224 Ibid.

225 Martin, Patrick. "25 Years Ago-The First US Attempt to Murder Gaddafi." *World Socialist Web Site*, 21 Oct. 2019, www.wsws.org/en/articles/2011/04/reag-a28.html.

226 Ibid.

227 Ibid.

228 Clark, Ramsey. *The Fire This Time: U.S. War Crimes in the Gulf* (New York: Thunder's Mouth Press, 1992), 38.

229 Ibid, 64.

230 Boyle, Francis A. "Amnesty International: Imperialist Tool." *Counter Currents*. Oct. 23, 2012, https://www.countercurrents.org/boyle231012.htm.

231 Bricmont, Jean, *Humanitarian Imperialism*, at 157–159.

232 Bery, Sunjeev, et al. "A Critic Gets It Wrong on Amnesty International and Libya." *Human Rights Now*, 2 Nov. 2012, blog.amnestyusa.org/middle-east/a-critic-gets-it-wrong-on-amnesty-international-and-libya/.

233 Ibid.

234 "Iraq: The Human Cost." *MIT Center for International Studies*, http://web.mit.edu/humancostiraq/.

235 Cockburn, Patrick. "Toxic Legacy of US Assault on Fallujah Worse Than Hiroshima." *Independent*, https://www.independent.co.uk/news/world/middle-east/toxic-legacy-of-us-assault-on-fallujah-worse-than-hiroshima-2034065.html.

236 Macleod, Alan. "Newsweek Journo Quits After Editors Kill Report on Syria Chemical Attack Scandal." *Mintpress*, Dec. 9, 2019, https://www.mintpressnews.com/newsweek-tareq-haddad-quits-syria-douma-opcw/263292/?utm.

237 Ibid.

238 Benjamin, Medea, and Davies, Nicolas J.S. "The Staggering Death Toll in Iraq." *Salon*, Salon.com, 19 Mar. 2018, www.salon.com/2018/03/19/the-staggering-death-toll-in-iraq_partner/.

239 de Zayas, Alfred, et al. "The US Tramples on International Law." *Indybay*, Nov. 1, 2019, www.indybay.org/newsitems/2019/11/01/18827768.php.

240 Kramer, Michalowski, and Rothe, "The Supreme International Crime."

241 Allo, Awol K. "The ICC's Problem Is Not Overt Racism, It Is Eurocentricism." *Al Jazeera*, Al Jazeera, 28 July 2018, www.aljazeera.com

/indepth/opinion/icc-problem-simple-racism-eurocentricism-180725111213623 .html.
242. Zavis, Alexandra, and Dixon, Robyn. "Q&A: Only Africans Have Been Tried at the Court for the Worst Crimes on Earth." *Los Angeles Times*, Los Angeles Times, 23 Oct. 2016, www.latimes.com/world/africa/la-fg-icc-africa -snap-story.html.
243. Ibid.
244. de Zayas, Alfred, et al., "The US Tramples."
245. Associated Press. "Trump Administration Revokes Visa of International Criminal Court Prosecutor." *Los Angeles Times*, Los Angeles Times, 5 Apr. 2019, www.latimes.com/world/la-fg-hague-icc-prosecutor-visa-revoked -trump-20190405-story.html.
246. Ibid.
247. Smith, David. "US Threatens to Arrest ICC Judges If They Pursue Americans for Afghan War Crimes." *France 24*, 11 Sept. 2018, www .france24.com/en/20180910-usa-trump-threatens-arrest-icc-judges -american-soldiers-afghan-war-crimes.
248. Toi Staff and Agencies. "Bolton Warns ICC Not to Go after Israel, Confirms Closure of PLO's DC Office." *The Times of Israel*, 10 Sept. 2018, www.timesofisrael.com/bolton-warns-icc-not-to-go-after-israel-confirms -close-of-plos-dc-office/.
249. "Locals in east Afghanistan complain of diseases caused by US 'mother of all bombs'." *Press TV*, Dec. 9, 2019, https://www.presstv.com /Detail/2019/12/09/613206/Afghanistan-US-mother-of-all-bombs -Nangarhar.
250. Ibid.
251. Berg, Stephanie van den. "ICC to Probe Alleged War Crimes in Palestinian Areas, Pending Jurisdiction." *Reuters*, Thomson Reuters, 21 Dec. 2019, www.reuters.com/article/us-icc-palestinians-israel/icc-to-probe -alleged-war-crimes-in-palestinian-areas-pending-jurisdiction-idUSKBN 1YO1S9.
252. UN General Assembly, 59th Session, "A more secure world: our shared responsibility Report of the High-level Panel on Threats, Challenges and Change." December 2, 2004, http://hrlibrary.umn.edu/instree/report .pdf.

253 Bricmont, Jean. *Humanitarian Imperialism*. Gleijeses, Piero. *Hope Shattered: The Guatemalan Revolution and the United States, 1944–1954* (Princeton: Princeton University Press, 1992), 330–332.

254 See Gleijeses, Piero, *Hope Shattered*.

255 Thomas, Evan. "You Can Own the World." *Washington Post*, Oct. 22, 1995, https://www.washingtonpost.com/archive/lifestyle/magazine/1995/10/22/you-can-own-the-world/c772e3f1-2634-4fb1-a223-b681d63a539d/.

256 Ibid.

257 Gleijeses, Piero, *Hope Shattrered*, 330–332.

258 Ibid.

259 Ibid.

260 Ibid.

261 Navarro, Mireya. "Guatemalan Army Waged 'Genocide', New Report Finds. *New York Times*, Feb. 26, 1999, https://www.nytimes.com/1999/02/26/world/guatemalan-army-waged-genocide-new-report-finds.html#.

262 Ibid.

263 "Who Is Elliott Abrams, US Special Envoy for Venezuela?" *Venezuela News/Al Jazeera*, 12 Feb. 2019, www.aljazeera.com/news/2019/02/elliott-abrams-special-envoy-venezuela-190212012146896.html.

264 Nevins, Joseph. "On Justifying Intervention." *The Nation*, May 20, 2012, https://www.thenation.com/article/archive/justifying-intervention/.

265 Ibid.

266 Thomas, Evan, *id*.

267 "The Ten Principles of Bandung." Updated April 23, 2005, http://www.chinadaily.com.cn/english/doc/2005-04/23/content_436882.htm.

268 Bricmont, Jean, *Humanitarian Imperialism*, 12.

269 McWhinney, Edward Q.C, "General Assembly Resolution."

270 Elich, Gregory. "Who Supported The Khmer Rouge?" *Counterpunch* (Oct. 16, 2014), retrieved at: http://www.counterpunch.org/2014/10/16/who-supported-the-khmer-rouge/.

271 Hobsbawm, Eric, *The Age of Extremes*, xv.

272 Chomsky, Noam and Herman, Edward S. *The Washington Connection* and *Third World Fascism* (The Political Economy of Human Rights–Volume I), Haymarket Books. (Chicago, 2014), 109–110.

273 World Peace Foundation. "Cambodia: U.S. bombing, civil war, & Khmer Rouge." *Mass Atrocity Endings*, Aug. 7, 2015, https://sites.tufts.edu/atrocityendings/2015/08/07/cambodia-u-s-bombing-civil-war-khmer-rouge/.

274 Ibid.

275 Ibid.

276 Herman, Edward S. and Peterson, David. *The Politics of Genocide*. Monthly Review Press (New York 2010), 18.

277 Ibid.

278 World Peace Foundation. "Cambodia: U.S. bombing, civil war, & Khmer Rouge."

279 Baehr, Peter. *Human Rights Universality in Practice*. (New York: Palgrave 2001), 99–100.

280 Ibid.

281 International Court of Justice, Case Concerning Military and Paramilitary Activities in and against Nicaragua (Nicaragua v. United States of America) Merits Judgment, June 27, 1986, https://www.icj-cij.org/files/case-related/70/070-19860627-JUD-01-00-EN.pdf.

282 Williams, Randall. *The Divided World* (Minneapolis: University of Minnesota Press, 2010), 84.

283 Chomsky, Noam. "Teaching Nicaragua a Lesson." Excerpted from What Uncle Sam Really Wants, 1992, https://chomsky.info/unclesam08/

284 Litkey, Charles, et al. "U.S. Waged 'Low-Intensity' Warfare in Nicaragua." December 1, 1989, http://www.brianwillson.com/u-s-waged-low-intensity-warfare-in-nicaragua/.

285 Harold Pinter 2005 Nobel Lecture, https://www.nobelprize.org/prizes/literature/2005/pinter/25621-harold-pinter-nobel-lecture-2005/. Excerpt reprinted with permission of the Nobel Prize Committee.

286 Williams, Ryan T. "Dangerous Precedent: America's Illegal War in Afghanistan." *University of Pennsylvania Journal of International Law*, Volume 33, Issue 2, Nov. 30, 2011, https://www.law.upenn.edu/journals/jil/articles/volume33/issue2/Williams33U.Pa.J.Int'lL.563(2011).pdf.

287 O'Connell, Ellen. "Responsibility to Peace: A Critique of R2P." *Journal of Intervention and State Building*, Volume 4, Issue 1, 2010, https://www.tandfonline.com/doi/abs/10.1080/17502970903541671.

288 Ibid.

289 UN Security Council, Press Release. "Security Council Condemns, 'In Strongest Terms', Terrorist Attacks on United States." Sept. 12, 2001, https://www.un.org/press/en/2001/SC7143.doc.htm.

290 Staff and Agencies. "Bush Rejects Taliban Offer to Hand Bin Laden Over." *The Guardian*, 14 Oct. 2001, www.theguardian.com/world/2001/oct/14/afghanistan.terrorism5.

291 Clewley, Robin. "How Osama Cracked FBI's Top 10." *Wired*, Condé Nast, 5 June 2017, www.wired.com/2001/09/how-osama-cracked-fbis-top-10/.

292 Williams, Ryan T., "Dangerous Precedent."

293 Borger, Julian, and Wintour, Patrick. "US gives evidence Iran supplied missiles that Yemen rebels fired at Saudi Arabia." *Guardian*, Dec. 14, 2017,https://www.theguardian.com/world/2017/dec/14/us-gives-evidence-iran-supplied-missiles-that-yemen-rebels-fired-at-saudi-arabia.

294 Ibid.

295 Lynch, Colum, and Gramer, Robbie. "Haley's 'Smoking Gun' on Iran Met With Skepticism at U.N." *Foreign Policy*, Dec. 14, 2017, https://foreignpolicy.com/2017/12/14/nikki-haley-yemen-houthi-rebels-iran-missiles-press-conference-pentagon-skepticism-united-nations-trump-nuclear-deal-diplomacy/.

296 Marciano, John. *The American War in Vietnam: Crime or Commemoration?* (New York: Monthly Review Press, 2016), 28.

297 Power, Samantha. *The Education of an Idealist*, Dey Street Books (New York 2019), 308.

298 Engelhardt, Tom. "Why Won't the Media Criticize US Interventionism?" *The Nation*, 2 July 2019, www.thenation.com/article/why-wont-the-media-criticize-us-interventionism/.

299 Blumenthal, Max. "Iraqi PM reveals Soleimani was on peace mission when assassinated, exploding Trump's lie of 'imminent attacks'." *Grayzone*, Jan. 6, 2019, https://thegrayzone.com/2020/01/06/soleimani-peace-mission-assassinated-trump-lie-imminent-attacks/.

300 See, e.g., Heller, Kevin Jon. "Why Preventive Self-Defense Violates The UN Charter." *OpinioJuris*, July 3, 2012. http://opiniojuris.org/2012/03/07/why-preventive-self-defense-violates-the-un-charter/.

301 Ibid.

302 Lee, Carol E., and Kube, Courtney. "Trump Authorized Soleimani Killing 7 Months Ago." *NBC News*, Jan. 13, 2020, https://www.nbcnews.com/politics/national-security/trump-authorized-soleimani-s-killing-7-months-ago-conditions-n1113271

303 deYoung, Karen. "Trump Says Its Doesn't Really Matter If Iranian General Posed an Imminent Threat." *Washington Post*, Jan. 13, 2020, https://www.washingtonpost.com/national-security/trump-says-it-doesnt-really-matter-if-iranian-general-posed-an-imminent-threat/2020/01/13/c9f7ea1c-362e-11ea-9541-9107303481a4_story.html.

304 "US Legal Experts say Soleimani Assassination Violated International Law." *PressTV*, Jan. 4, 2020, https://www.presstv.com/Detail/2020/01/04/615316/US-legal-experts-Iran-General-Qassem-Soleimani-violated-international-law.

305 Hedges, Chris. "War with Iran." *Truthdig*, Jan. 3, 2020, https://www.truthdig.com/articles/war-with-iran/.

306 Cecco, Leyland. "Iran Crash: Canadians feel like collateral damage of Trump's scattershot foreign policy." *The Guardian* Jan. 15, 2020, https://www.theguardian.com/world/2020/jan/14/canada-trump-foreign-policy-collateral-damage-iran-crash.

307 Conrad, Duncan. "US Arms Companies See Stocks Soar after Assassination of Solameini as Analysts Predict War with Iran." *Independent*, Jan. 4, 2020, https://www.independent.co.uk/news/world/americas/us-politics/soleimani-trump-iran-war-us-arms-company-stock-price-lockheed-martin-a9270426.html.

308 Shah, Anup. "United Nations World Summit 2005." *Global Issues*, Updated: September 18, 2005 http://www.globalissues.org/article/559/united-nations-world-summit-2005.

309 Ibid.

310 Ibid.

311 United Nations General Assembly, 2005 World Summit Outcome, Oct. 24, 2005, https://www.un.org/en/development/desa/population/migration/generalassembly/docs/globalcompact/A_RES_60_1.pdf.

312 O'Connell, Ellen, "Responsibility to Peace."

313 UN General Assembly, 59th Session, "A more secure world: our shared responsibility Report of the High-level Panel on Threats, Challenges and Change." December 2, 2004, http://hrlibrary.umn.edu/instree/report.pdf.

314 Herman, Edward S., and Peterson, David. *The Politics of Genocide*, 26.

315 Nimmo, Kurt. "There's a Special Place in Hell for Madeleine Albright." *Off Guardian*, March 28, 2016, https://off-guardian.org/2016/03/28/theres-a-special-place-in-hell-for-madeleine-albright/.

316 Talbot, Karen. "The Real Reasons for War in Yugoslavia: Backing up Globalization with Military Might," Social Justice Vol. 27, No. 4 (82), Neoliberalism, Militarism, and Armed Conflict (Winter 2000), 94–116.

317 Roberts, Adam. "NATO's 'Humanitarian War' Over Kosovo." *Survival*, vol. 41, no. 3, Autumn 1999, The International Institute of Strategic Studies. Retrieved at: http://www.columbia.edu/itc/sipa/S6800/courseworks/NATOhumanitarian.pdf.

318 Pourzal, Rostam. "Bombing for Peace, an Interview with Diana Johnstone." *MR Online*, Dec. 3, 2007, https://mronline.org/2007/12/03/bombing-for-peace-an-interview-with-diana-johnstone/.

319 Nimmo, Kurt. "There's a Special Place."

320 Szamuely, George. *Bombs for Peace: NATO's Humanitarian War on Yugoslavia*. (Amsterdam: Amsterdam University Press, 2013).

321 Hook, Brian. "Balancing Interests and Values," May 17, 2017, https://www.politico.com/f/?id=00000160-6c37-da3c-a371-ec3f13380001.

322 MacLeod, Alan. "With People in the Streets Worldwide, Media Focus Uniquely on Hong Kong." *FAIR*, 6 Dec. 2019, fair.org/home/with-people-in-the-streets-worldwide-media-focus-uniquely-on-hong-kong/.

323 Navarrate, Jose. "INDH Actualiza Reporte y Cifra En 352 Las Víctimas Con Heridas Oculares En Protestas." *La Tercera*, 7 Dec. 2019, www.latercera.com/nacional/noticia/indh-actualiza-reporte-cifra-352-las-victimas-heridas-oculares-protestas/930024/.

324 Auken, Bill Van. "Pompeo Vows Intervention against 'Riots' in Washington's 'Own Backyard.'" *Pompeo Vows Intervention against "Riots" in Washington's "Own Backyard."* World Socialist Web Site Wsws.org. Published by the International Committee of the Fourth International (ICFI), 5 Dec. 2019, www.wsws.org/en/articles/2019/12/05/pomp-d05.html.

325 Mackenzie, Lewis. "NATO's Libya 'hope' strategy is bombing." *The Globe and Mail* (Jun. 10, 2011). Retrieved at: http://www.theglobeandmail.com/opinion/natos-libya-hope-strategy-is-bombing/article598629/.

326 Ibid.

327 Roberts, Adam, "NATO's 'Humanitarian War'."

328 Ibid.

329 Bordelon, Brendan. "Gowdy: Sidney Blumenthal Sent Classified Info, Lobbied Clinton to Profit from Libya Intervention." *National Review*, 9 Oct. 2015, www.nationalreview.com/2015/10/sidney-blumenthal-hillary-clinton-emails-lobbying-libya-trey-gowdy/.

330 "NATO Dismisses Gaddafi Ceasefire Offer." *RTÉ*, 30 Apr. 2011, www.rte.ie/news/2011/0430/300460-libya/.

331 Blumenthal, Sidney. "UK Game Playing; New Rebel Strategists; Egypt Moves In. Sid." April 7, 2011, https://wikileaks.org/clinton-emails/emailid/12650.

332 Hedges, Chris. "Libya: Here We Go Again." *Truthdig*, 5 Sept. 2011, www.truthdig.com/articles/libya-here-we-go-again/.

333 Amnesty International. "A Fact Sheet on CEDAW: Treaty for the Rights of Women." https://www.amnestyusa.org/files/pdfs/cedaw_fact_sheet.pdf.

334 Baldez, Lisa. "U.S. Drops the Ball on Women's Rights." *CNN*, Cable News Network, 9 Mar. 2013, https://www.cnn.com/2013/03/08/opinion/baldez-womens-equality-treaty/index.html.

335 See Turse, Nick. *Kill Anything That Moves: The Real American War in Vietnam* (New York: Henry Holt & Company, 2013).

336 Morris, Madeleine. "By Force of Arms: Rape, War and Military Culture." *Duke Law Review*, Volume 45, Number 4 (February, 1996), fn. 5.

337 Ibid.

338 Ibid. 666–667.

339 Mesok, Elizabeth. "Sexual Violence and the US Military: Feminism, US Empire, and the Failure of Liberal Equality." *Feminist Studies*, Volume 42, No. 1 (2016). Retrieved at: https://www.jstor.org/stable/10.15767/feministstudies.42.1.41.

340 Vine, David. "Women's Labor, Sex Work and U.S. Military Bases Abroad." *Salon*, 8 Oct. 2017, www.salon.com/2017/10/08/womens-labor-sex-work-and-u-s-military-bases-abroad/.

341 Simon, Scott. "Opinion: As U.S. Seeks To Withdraw Troops, What About Afghanistan's Women?" *NPR*, 2 Feb. 2019, www.npr.org/2019/02/02/690857773/opinion-as-u-s-seeks-to-withdraw-troops-what-about-afghanistans-women.

342 Kolhatkar, Sonali. "The Impact of US Intervention on Afghan Women's

Rights." *Berkeley Women's Law Journal* (2002), https://scholarship.law.berkeley.edu/cgi/viewcontent.cgi?article=1176&context=bglj.

343 Maresca, John J., vice president of Unocal, in testimony before a U.S. House Committee, February 12, 1998, as cited in *Censored 2003, The Top 25 Censored Stories*, Peter Phillips & Project Censored (New York: Seven Stories Press, 2002), 150.

344 Rashid, Ahmed. "U.S.-Taliban Relations–Friend Turns Fiend," as quoted in *Censored 2003, The Top 25 Censored Stories*, Peter Phillips & Project Censored (New York: Seven Stories Press, 2002), 150

345 *Washington Post*, May 25, 2001, as quoted in *Censored 2003, The Top 25 Censored Stories*, Peter Phillips & Project Censored (New York: Seven Stories Press, 2002), 151.

346 Brisard, Charles, and Dasquie, Guillaume. "Bin Laden, The Forbidden Truth," as quoted in *Censored 2003, The Top 25 Censored Stories*, Peter Phillips & Project Censored (New York: Seven Stories Press, 2002), 152.

347 Bedi, Rahul. "India Joins Anti-Taliban Coalition." *Janes Defense Newsletter*, March 15, 2001, as quoted in *Censored 2003, The Top 25 Censored Stories*, Peter Phillips & Project Censored (New York: Seven Stories Press, 2002), 144.

348 Bohn, Lauren. "Why Afghanistan Is Still the Worst Place to Be a Woman." *Time*, Time, 8 Dec. 2018, time.com/5472411/afghanistan-women-justice-war/.

349 Goldstein, Joseph. "U.S. Soldiers Told to Ignore Sexual Abuse of Boys by Afghan Allies." *New York Times*, 20 Sept. 2015, https://www.nytimes.com/2015/09/21/world/asia/us-soldiers-told-to-ignore-afghan-allies-abuse-of-boys.html.

350 Kolhatkar, Sonali, "The Impact of US Invervention," 19.

351 Mesok, Elizabeth, "Sexual Violence."

352 Smith, Ashley. "Amnesty for Occupation?" *SocialistWorker.org*, Aug. 8, 2012, https://socialistworker.org/2012/08/08/amnesty-for-occupation.

353 Williams, David. "A Toy Company Will Make Little Green Army Women after Hearing from Vets and a 6-Year-Old Girl." *CNN*, 11 Sept. 2019, www.cnn.com/2019/09/11/us/woman-toy-soldiers-trnd/index.html.

354 Crossette, Barbara. "Taliban's Eradication of Poppies Is Convulsing Opium Market." *New York Times*, 13 June 2001, www.nytimes.com/2001

/06/13/world/taliban-s-eradication-of-poppies-is-convulsing-opium-market.html.

355 Hennigan, W.J. "U.S. Military Ends Anti-Drug Campaign in Afghanistan." *Time*, 21 Feb. 2019, time.com/5534783/iron-tempest-afghanistan-opium/.

356 Hadid, Diaa, and Ghani, Khwaga. "Women and Children Are the Emerging Face of Drug Addiction in Afghanistan." *NPR*, 29 Oct. 2019, www.npr.org/sections/goatsandsoda/2019/10/29/771374889/women-and-children-are-the-emerging-face-of-drug-addiction-in-afghanistan.

357 International Observatory for Human Rights. "A Tribute to Hevrin Khalaf: 'the loudest voice that fought for women's rights in Syria'." Oct. 27, 2019, https://observatoryihr.org/priority_posts/a-tribute-to-hevrin-khalaf-the-loudest-voice-that-fought-for-womens-rights-in-syria/.

358 Sanger, David E., et al. "Trump Ends Covert Aid to Syrian Rebels Trying to Topple Assad." *New York Times*, 20 July 2017, www.nytimes.com/2017/07/19/world/middleeast/cia-arming-syrian-rebels.html.

359 Hersh, Seymour M. "The Red Line and The Rat Line," *London Review of Books*, April 17, 2014, https://www.lrb.co.uk/v36/n08/seymour-m-hersh/the-red-line-and-the-rat-line.

360 "Libyan Fighters Join 'Free Syrian Army' Forces." *Al Bawaba*, www.albawaba.com/news/libyan-fighters-join-free-syrian-army-forces-403268.

361 Convention on the Prevention and Punishment of the Crime of Genocide, https://www.un.org/en/genocideprevention/genocide-convention.shtml.

362 Ibid.

363 Power, Samantha. *The Education of an Idealist*, 306.

364 Ho Chi Minh letter to US Secretary of State, October 18, 1945, http://www.historyisaweapon.com/defcon2/hochiminh/.

365 Butterfield, Fox. "Pentagon Papers: Eisenhower Decisions Undercut the Geneva Accords, Study Says," *New York Times* (July 5, 1971), https://www.nytimes.com/1971/07/05/archives/pentagon-papers-eisenhower-decisions-undercut-the-geneva-accords.html.

366 Ibid.

367 Ibid.

368 Chomsky & Herman, *The Washington Connection*, 345-346

369 Turse, Nick, *Kill Anything*, 2–3.

370 Ibid., 1.

371 Ibid., 60.

372 Ibid., 208–212.

373 Chomsky & Herman, *The Washington Connection*, 355.

374 Turse, *Kill Anything*, 28.

375 Ibid., 50.

376 International Criminal Tribunal for Rwanda. Case of Prosecutor v. Jean-Paul Akayesu, Decision of the Appeals Chamber, June 1, 2001, https://unictr.irmct.org/sites/unictr.org/files/case-documents/ictr-96-4/appeals-chamber-judgements/en/010601.pdf.

377 Sullivan, Tony. "A history of Rwanda and Burundi: 1894–1990," *libcom.org*, Sept. 8, 2006, https://libcom.org/history/1894-1990-a-history-of-rwanda-and-burundi.

378 Ibid.

379 Ibid.

380 Ibid. (citing by Frank Smyth, *The Australian*, Oct. 6, 1994).

381 "The 1972 and 1993 Burundi Genocides." *atrocitieswatch.org*, http://atrocitieswatch.org/the-1972-and-1993-burundi-genocides/.

382 Smith, John. *Imperialism in the Twenty-First Century, Globalization, Super-Exploitation and Capitalism's Final Crisis* (New York: Monthly Review Press, 2016), 33.

383 Ibid., 32.

384 Herman, Edward, and Peterson, David. *The Politics of Genocide*, 53–56.

385 Ibid.

386 Ibid., 53.

387 Power, Samantha. "Bystanders to Genocide." *The Atlantic*, 8 Sept. 2019, www.theatlantic.com/magazine/archive/2001/09/bystanders-to-genocide/304571/.

388 Herman & Peterson, *The Politics of Genocide*, 57–58.

389 Ibid., 57

390 Reid, Timothy B. "It's Time for a Reckoning for Kagame and His Western Cheerleaders." *The M&G Online*, April 23, 2019, https://mg.co.za/article/2019-04-23-00-its-time-for-a-reckoning-for-kagame-and-his-estern-cheerleaders.

391 Kovalik, Daniel. "Hotel Rwanda Revisited: an Interview with Paul Rusesabagina." *CounterPunch.org*, 26 July 2015, www.counterpunch.org/2013/01/11/hotel-rwanda-revisited-an-interview-with-paul-rusesabagina/.

392 Turse, *Kill Anything*, 42–45.

393 Ibid., 73.

394 Ibid., 192–195.

395 Sterio, Milena. "The Karadžić Genocide Conviction: Inferences, Intent, and the Necessity to Redefine Genocide," *Emory International Law Review*, Volume 31, Issue 2 (2017), 280–281.

396 Turse, Nick, *Kill Anything*, 240–241.

397 Ibid., 167.

398 Ibid., 170.

399 Parry, Hannah. "Incredible Pictures of Planes Packed with 'Orphaned' Babies Fleeing War-Torn Vietnam for Adoption by U.S. Families in Controversial Operation Babylift." *Daily Mail Online*, Associated Newspapers, 22 Sept. 2016, www.dailymail.co.uk/news/article-3801399/Incredible-pictures-planes-packed-orphaned-babies-fleeing-war-torn-Vietnam-adoption U-S-families-controversial-Operation-Babylift.html.

400 Ibid.

401 Ojito, Mirta. "Cubans Face Past as Stranded Youths in U.S." *New York Times*, 12 Jan. 1998, www.nytimes.com/1998/01/12/us/cubans-face-past-as-stranded-youths-in-us.html.

402 Bender, Albert. "South Dakota Commits Shocking Genocide against Native Americans." *People's World*, 3 June 2013, www.peoplesworld.org/article/south-dakota-commits-shocking-genocide-against-native-americans/.

403 Rodrigo, Chris Mills. "Migrant Children May be Adopted After Parents Are Deported." *The Hill*, Oct. 9, 2018, https://thehill.com/policy/international/americas/410653-ap-migrant-children-may-be-adopted-after-parents-are-deported.

404 Chomsky, Noam, *The Rule of Force in International Law*.

405 Ibid.

406 Smith, John. *Imperialism in the Twenty-First Century: Globalization, Super-Exploitation and Capitalism's Final Crisis* (New York: Monthly Review Press, 2016), 54–56.

407 Ibid.

408 Ibid.

409 Alston, Philip, and Goodman, Ryan, *International Human Rights*, 295–296.
410 Wilkins, Brett. "Jimmy Carter: US 'Most Warlike Nation in History of the World'." *Common Dreams*, 18 Apr. 2019, www.commondreams.org/views/2019/04/18/jimmy-carter-us-most-warlike-nation-history-world.
411 Ibid.
412 Everett, Burgess, and Levine, Marianne. "Democratic Establishment Reaches Boiling Point with Tulsi Gabbard." *Politico*, 22 Nov. 2019, www.politico.com/amp/news/2019/11/21/tulsi-gabbard-dems-072672.
413 Carden, James. "A New Poll Shows the Public Is Overwhelmingly Opposed to Endless US Military Interventions." *The Nation*, 9 Jan. 2018, www.thenation.com/article/new-poll-shows-public-overwhelmingly-opposed-to-endless-us-military-interventions/.
414 Conley, Julia. "Researchers Detail How Slashing Pentagon Budget Could Pay for Medicare for All While Creating Progressive Foreign Policy Americans Want." *Common Dreams*, 17 Oct. 2019, www.commondreams.org/news/2019/10/17/researchers-detail-how-slashing-pentagon-budget-could-pay-medicare-all-while.
415 Ibid.
416 Trinder, Matt. "Cuba Found to Be the Most Sustainably Developed Country in the World, New Research Finds." *Morning Star*, 29 Nov. 2019, morningstaronline.co.uk/article/w/cuba-found-to-be-the-most-sustainably-developed-country-in-the-world-new-research-finds.
417 Murphy, Jessica Bram. "My Father Was Killed on 9/11 When I Was Five, but What I Experienced at Guantánamo Bay Did Not Feel Like Justice." *Common Dreams,* April 10, 2019, https://www.commondreams.org/views/2019/04/10/my-father-was-killed-911-when-i-was-five-what-i-experienced-guantanamo-bay-did-not.
418 Committee Against Torture. "Conclusions on the Third to Fifth Periodic Reports of the United States of America." November, 2014, https://tbinternet.ohchr.org/Treaties/CAT/Shared%20Documents/USA/INT_CAT_COC_USA_18893_E.pdf.
419 ACLU. "Guantanamo by the Numbers." May, 2018, https://www.aclu.org/issues/national-security/detention/guantanamo-numbers.
420 Center for Constitutional Rights. "Adnan Latif—the Face of Indefinite Detention—Dies at Guantánamo." *Common Dreams*, 11 Sept. 2012, www

.commondreams.org/newswire/2012/09/11/adnan-latif-face-indefinite-detention-dies-guantanamo.

421 Whitlock, Craig. "Confidential Documents Reveal U.S. Officials Failed to Tell the Truth about the War in Afghanistan." *The Washington Post*, 9 Dec. 2019, www.washingtonpost.com/graphics/2019/investigations/afghanistan-papers/afghanistan-war-confidential-documents/.

Index

A

Afghanistan, *xiv, xxii, xxxii*, 29, 31, 59, 63, 95-96, 128-132; 162, 167-176, 208, 212, 218-220, 297, 301, 303; 307-308, 312
    and Mujahadeen, *xxxii*, 169-172;
    and Taliban, 128-129, 169-175, 303, 307-308;
    women's rights in, 167-176;
Al Qaeda, *xxxii*, 128-129, 133, 285
Amnesty International, *xxxii, xxxiv*, 6-9, 21, 24-26, 29, 33-34, 87-88, 94, 163, 169, 287, 289, 292-294, 299, 306;
    and Apartheid, 6-9;
    and Libya, 21, 24-26, 29, 33-34
Anticolonial, 7-8, 11, 57, 61, 97-99, 102, 105-106, 113
Apartheid, 6-11, 98, 206, 289
Arbenz, Jacobo, 99-100, 102
Article 51 of UN Charter, 49, 125-132, 134, 145, 146, 239, 277

B

Bolton, John, 96, 138
Boyle, Francis A., 7, 49-50, 87, 289, 295, 299
Bricmont, Jean, *v, xxxvi*, 1, 74, 97, 106, 123, 155, 285-286, 296-298
Burundi, 94, 195, 309
Bush, George W., *xxxii*, 95, 128, 138

C

Cambodia, 110-112, 144, 203, 283, 302
Carter, Jimmy, *xi, xxxii*, 114, 208, 211, 311
Castro, Fidel, 82
CEDAW (Convention on the Elimination of All Forms of Discrimination Against Women), 163-164, 168, 174, 306
Chomsky, Noam, *v, xxiii, xxxiv*, 8, 51, 83, 111, 189-190, 203, 285, 289, 292, 295, 299, 302, 309-310

CIA (Central Intelligence Agency), *iv*, *xiii*, *xvi*, *xviii-xx*, *xxxiii-xxxiv*, 2, 4-5, 8-17, 20-21, 25-26, 31-32, 37-39, 45-48, 52-67, 72-77, 80-87, 91-92, 95-108, 111, 115, 118, 120-124, 128, 132-136, 140, 144, 146, 148, 151, 158-160, 163-178, 181-184, 187-190, 194, 196, 198, 202, 204, 206, 214, 216, 218-262, 267-274, 280, 287, 290-312

Clinton, Bill, 19, 20, 79, 150, 197

Clinton, Hillary, 19, 21, 22-23, 29, 33, 158-161, 177-178, 198, 208, 291

Cold War, *xxiii*, 14, 102, 152

Congo (also, DRC), *xxix*, *xxxiv*, 2-6, 11, 12-20, 33, 99, 283, 290-291

Contras, *xxxi*, 66, 109, 113-115, 119, 121-124, 154

Crime of Aggression, *vii*, 78-81, 294, 299

Crimes Against Humanity, 28, 38, 78, 81, 93, 141-142

Cuba, 7-11, 47-48, 60, 73-75, 82-84, 99, 202, 214-215, 218, 289-290, 298-299, 310-311

D

de Zayas, Alfred, 91, 95, 239, 300

E

El Salvador, 101, 116, 127

F

Feminism, 21-22, 306

G

Gaddafi, Muammar, *v*, 22-34, 84, 159-160, 178, 292-294, 299, 306

Gaddafi, Saif, 22

Geneva Conventions, 23,-24, 60, 86, 134, 158

Genocide, *vii*, *xxiv*, *xxv*, 24, 39, 42, 58, 78, 93, 100-101, 109-111, 117, 139, 141-144, 147, 180-186, 193-203, 218, 283, 286, 291, 301-302; 305, 308-310

and Cambodia, 110-112
and Burundi, 195
and Guatemala, 100-101
and Kosovo, 149-157
and Rwanda, 193-201
and Serbia, 149-157
and Vietnam, 185-193, 200-205
and Yugoslavia, 182-183
see also, Holocaust, *infra*.

Genocide Convention, *vii*, 180-186, 194, 202, 361
text of, 181

Germany, *xv*, *xxiv*, 37-42, 51-53, 63, 80, 151, 167-168, 182, 194

Guatemala, 48, 99-101, 297, 301
1954 coup as greatest blow to UN, 99-101

Gulf of Tonkin, 131

H

Herman, Edward S., *v*, 92, 111, 184-185, 189-190, 197, 302, 305, 309
Hobsbawm, Eric, 35-36, 110, 294, 302
Holocaust, *xxviii*, 37, 39, 52, 180, 185, 218, 294
Human Rights Council (of UN), 66-67, 72-77, 297
Human Rights Watch, 64, 77, 79, 87, 94, 203, 297

I

ICC (International Criminal Court), *vii*, 61, 65, 75, 78-79, 82, 85, 87, 93-96, 138, 212, 299-301
ICCPR (International Covenant on Civil and Political Rights), 61, 65, 75, 212
ICESCR (International Covenant on Economic, Social and Cultural Rights), 65, 75, 205
ICJ (International Court of Justice), 51, 109, 302
  and Nicaragua case, 113-127
  Text of ICJ Statute, Appendix B
Imperialism, *xxii*, 80, 123, 166, 196, 204, 285, 288, 298-302, 309-310
Iran, *xiv*, *xxiii-xxiv*, *xxxi*, 24, 46, 60, 80, 99, 129-130, 133-136, 153, 163, 285, 303-304

Iraq, *xxii-xxiv*, *xxviii*, *xxxi-xxxiv*, 7, 29, 31-32, 59, 80, 82, 85-95, 131-135, 161, 165-167, 185, 208, 210-212, 218, 287, 292, 295, 300, 304
ISIS, *xxi*, *xxv*, *xxx-xxxiii*, 24, 26, 29, 124, 134, 143, 208, 286-288, 309, 311
Israel, 6, 8, 11, 52-53, 75, 95-96, 100, 206, 295, 301

J

Johnstone, Diana, *v*, 34, 150, 294, 305

K

Kagame, Paul, 197-199
King, Martin Luther, *xi*, 174
King Leopold, *vii*, 1, 2, 4, 6, 12, 17, 33, 283, 288-291
Kissinger, Henry, 102, 203, 210
Kosovo, 149-152, 155-157, 305
Kurds, *xxi-xxiv*, *xxix*, *xxxii-xxxiii*, 285

L

Libya, *v*, 7, 20-34, 80, 82, 84, 88, 119, 131- 132, 155, 158-162, 178-179, 186, 218, 292-295, 306, 308
Lumumba, Patrice, 14, 16, 99, 290-291

M

Mujahadeen, *xxxii*, 169-172
Mandela, Nelson, 6, 9-10, 289

N

Nazis, 37, 39, 42, 150, 182, 187, 295
Nicaragua, *v*, *vii*, 48, 60, 63, 109-127, 302-303
NPR (National Public Radio), *xxix*, 20, 33, 37, 83, 88, 91, 121, 168, 175-176, 287, 292, 307, 308
Nuremberg, *vii*, *xv*, *xxxv*, 35-39, 51, 150

O

Obama, Barack, *xiv*, *xxv-xxvi*, *xxviii*, *xxxii*, *xxxiv*, 19, 22-23, 26, 84, 102, 177-178, 190, 210-211, 217-220, 287

P

Palestine, 98, 206
Palestinians, 52-53, 295, 301
Pol Pot, 110-111, 144
Power, Samantha, *vii*, *xxvi*, 1, 21, 33, 101, 110, 131, 141, 158, 161, 177-179, 185, 193-194, 197, 203, 218

R

R2P (Responsibility to Protect), 92-93, 137, 141-144, 148, 152, 157- 158, 162, 194, 303
Reagan, Ronald, 8, 9, 84, 113, 289
Regime Change, *xiii*, 13, 21, 60, 101

Rice, Susan, *xxviii*, 26, 33, 102, 158, 178, 287-291
Right of Self-Defense, *vii*, 49, 125-126, 239
Roth, Kenneth, 64, 79, 80-96, 110, 141, 203, 205-206, 299
Rusesabagina, Paul, 198
Rwanda, *xxiv*, 17, 193-201, 309-310

S

Serbia, 39, 149, 152, 155-157
Simon, Scott, 20, 168, 292, 307
South Africa, 2, 6-11, 16, 18, 24, 98, 109, 206
Syria, *xxi*, *xxviii-xxxv*, 29, 58-59, 67, 89-90, 119, 132, 135, 176-179, 208-211, 285-288, 300, 308
Soviet Union, 8, 17, 41-42, 83, 106, 294

T

Taliban, 128-129, 169-175, 303, 307-308
Trump, Donald J., *xiv*, *xxi-xxix*, *xxxiii-xxxv*, 46,62, 95-96, 133-138, 177, 203, 207, 210-211, 285-288, 293, 296-297, 301, 303, 304, 308
Twain, Mark, 12

U

UDHR (Universal Declaration of Human Rights), 54-57, 60, 72, 212, 296
UN (United Nations), *passim*

UN Charter, 11, 43-51, 58, 66,
    88, 91, 105-110, 116-117,
    125, 129- 130, 136, 142-146,
    149, 163, 192, 295, 304
    Text of, Appendix A
USSR, 7, 9, 10, 37, 42, 106

V

Venezuela, 46, 60-63, 74, 84, 98,
    101, 160, 296, 301, 302
Vietnam, *xxix*, *xxxiv*, 93, 98-99,
    110-111, 130- 131, 164-165,
    185-193, 200-205, 210, 218,
    303, 306, 310

W

War Crimes, *xv*, *xxv-xxvi*, 37-38,
    78-87, 93-96, 134, 139-142,
    167, 193, 203, 287, 300-301

Weapons of Mass Destruction,
    91, 133
Willson, Brian S., 130, 285, 303
    Forward by, *xiii-xix*
WWI (World War I), *xxii*, *xxvii*,
    4, 12, 18, 39, 41-43, 53, 128,
    148, 165, 180, 182, 187, 289
WWII (World War II), *xxii*,
    xxvii, 4, 18, 39, 41-42, 53,
    128, 148, 165, 180, 182, 187,
    289

Y

Yemen, *xiv*, *xxiv-xxviii*, *xxxiv*,
    93, 129-130, 132, 136, 210,
    217-218, 286-287, 303
Yugoslavia, 109, 148-162, 182-
    183, 305